GET

SC

☆ ☆ ☆ ☆ ☆ ☆ ☆ ☆

ASTEN YOUR SEAT BELTS FOR HIGH
VENTURE with the best secret agent in the
Middle East—and the greatest master of the close
escape since James Bond. Part Sir Galahad, part
Indiana Jones, part Lawrence of Arabia, the Scorpion
is all that stands between the free world and World
War III.

"*Scorpion* is a supercharged thriller about Soviet
menace and Arab fanaticism in the volatile Middle
East. It has everything: a Congressman's beautiful
daughter sold into white slavery . . . a sexually
perverted Saudi prince with fanatic global ambitions
. . . an aging British spy with a penchant for Arab
youths . . . a Bedouin blood feud . . . explosive
nonstop action . . . heart-stopping heroics . . .
splendidly sinister villainy. And Andrew Kaplan, who
interweaves these elements in an intricate and
ingenious plot, proves as nimble in delineating
character and evoking exotic locales as he is in
sustaining razor-edged excitement."

—*Mystery News*

"A FAST-PACED, SUPERCHARGED DEBUT
THRILLER."

—*Kirkus Reviews*

more . . .

"PURE DYNAMITE . . . espionage laced with high-voltage Middle East adventure."
—*Washington Times*

"AN EXCITING THRILLER WITH NONSTOP ACTION. . . . The book truly reads like 'James Bond in Arabia' and, once started, is hard to put down."
—*Tulsa Daily World*

"TERRORISM, DOUBLE-CROSSES AND A BLOOD FEUD. . . . The plot has more twists than a tornado, including a totally unexpected finale."
—*The Drood Review*

"KAPLAN HAS A FINE KNACK FOR TELLING A STORY. He writes in a breathless, Saturday-movie-serial style, a cliffhanger ending every chapter, and only the most hardened cynic will fail to keep turning to the next adventures."
—*Louisville Times*

SCORPION

ANDREW KAPLAN

WARNER BOOKS

A Warner Communications Company

WARNER BOOKS EDITION

This Warner Books Edition is published by arrangement with Macmillan Publishing Company, 866 Third Avenue, New York, N.Y. 10022

Cover design by Stanislaw Fernandez

Warner Books, Inc.
666 Fifth Avenue
New York, N.Y. 10103

W A Warner Communications Company

Printed in the United States of America

First Warner Books Printing: July, 1987

10 9 8 7 6 5 4 3 2 1

For Annie with love

The center of the aspirations of the Soviet Union lies south of Batum and Baku in the general direction of the Persian Gulf.

—SOVIET FOREIGN MINISTER V.M. MOLOTOV in conversation with the German ambassador, 1940.

PROLOGUE

The old man was dying at last. This time the doctors were certain. He wouldn't survive the night. With a grim nod, Fyedorenko had settled down to wait outside the bedroom door, while the doctors gathered around the living corpse like ancient priests, rattling their tubes and oscilloscopes and oxygen tanks like gourds to celebrate the rite of death. Fyedorenko lit an English cigarette and inhaled deeply, trying to control his impatience. If his lifelong friend wasn't dead by morning, he was tempted to strangle the old bastard himself.

For months they had desperately propped the old man up like a scarecrow, allowing him out for rare public appearances under carefully orchestrated conditions, while the western press speculated over the rise and fall of his blood pressure as though it were the Dow Jones average. Periodically, someone would report that he had died, sending the currency markets into wild gyrations and diplomats scurrying like midnight mice into hurried conferences. Then they would have to trot the scarecrow out in one of those carefully-staged, public pantomimes to squelch the rumors. They had to keep him alive then, because they desperately needed the time. But now everything was ready and the sooner he died, the better. If the old man lingered much longer, Fyedorenko feared that his enemies in the Politburo might learn about his preparations and act first. Every minute that the old man lingered on increased his jeopardy. The Central Committee was thick with the old man's appointees and there were plenty of those who still believed in the old man's policies of coexistence with the West. Well, they would change their line when the time came and, once things settled down, they would be purged, one by one. If only the old man would die now!

1

Yet, his hand did not tremble as he held the cigarette, and his face might have been carved from marble as he calmly waited for the doctors' verdict. After all, Fyedorenko was not given to any outward display of emotion. If he had been, he would have disappeared long ago, like so many others. His coarse peasant's face had long since acquired the bland and amiable expression of the polished diplomat. He was known for it. Once Bulgarov, who loved to drink and tell dirty jokes, had jeered at his impassivity.

"You're a damned bookkeeper. Do you have blood in your veins or what? You wouldn't have lasted five minutes with those young hotheads who stormed the Winter Palace with us that cold morning," Bulgarov had said, sloshing the vodka from his glass as he gestured with it towards Fyedorenko.

"Fyedorenko has no emotions, didn't you know?" the old man had remarked archly. "He is like a statue. *Da*, and like a statue he will survive us all," the old man muttered and his gaze suddenly pierced Fyedorenko, turning his heart to ice.

But that had been long ago, before Bulgarov had been sent to that labor camp in the Urals where they didn't bother to put up a fence, because no one could make it across the snow without freezing to death anyway. The old man had been right about him. He had survived them all, even the old man.

But the old man had grown soft in his dotage. "Since nuclear war is unthinkable, our only alternative is *coexistence* with the West," he used to say. When the Old Guard purists objected, the old man had responded, "We will nibble away at the West, bit by bit. The fat capitalist capon is more easily devoured by an army of mice than a single gulp of the bear."

Fyedorenko had something else entirely in mind.

If only the old man would die now, Fyedorenko thought, and found himself clenching his fists. He guiltily looked around the salon. The room was located in the old Arsenal building in the Kremlin and was a part of the apartment the old man had taken when he had suffered his first heart attack. It was decorated in the massive marble style filled with the overstuffed furniture favored by senior Party officials. Now it seemed still and empty, so early in the morning. The only sound was the quiet ticking of the old Regency clock, covered with the gilt of the period. Once it had belonged to Alexandra, the last Tsarina. Fyedorenko carefully wiped his damp palms on his trousers. Imagine if any of the others waiting in the ante-chamber outside had seen it, he mused wryly. Comrade Fye-dorenko clenching his fists! Unheard of! They would be gossiping about it for days. It was the waiting, making him nervous.

He stood up and walked over to the window, his reflection blurred by the double-glazed glass. The reflection in the win-dow showed a paunchy middle-aged man in the gray suit that is the uniform of the eastern European bureaucrat. With his small dark eyes and jowly cheeks he looked like an intelligent bulldog. But those dark eyes showed nothing. They could have been made of glass.

He leaned closer to the window, his breath frosting its surface. Outside the inky blackness of night was broken only by a single lamp in the Alexandrovsky Gardens down below. Thick wet snowflakes fell through the feeble yellow lamplight, the wind swarming them like moths around the light. A black winter's night, the wind howling around the cupolas of the Kremlin like . . . what was Mayakovsky's line? ". . . as though the gargoyles of Notre Dame were howling." Snowflakes wove a shroud of icy lace across the window. "Ice flowers," his mother had called it, when he was still a boy and snow was something to play in.

He stared at his reflection. It looked like a ghost against the darkness of the winter night. Perhaps the earth itself would be a ghost when this was all over. He remembered how the frozen bodies were stacked like cordwood in the snow during the Great Patriotic War and an unaccustomed shudder trickled down his spine like a bead of sweat. Perhaps they were making a mistake. There was still time to call it off, he thought, knowing he wouldn't.

He remembered when Svetlov first outlined the operation

3

to him. They sat in front of the fireplace in Fyedorenko's country *dacha* near Zhukovka, southwest of Moscow. Outside, birds chirped in the birch trees, as the dappled sunlight glittered off the icicles hanging from the branches. For a long moment, Fyedorenko didn't say anything. They listened to the music of a pine log burning in the fireplace. The operation was characteristic of Svetlov, brilliant and ruthless. Svetlov played chess the same way. Although Fyedorenko was the best player at the Moscow Metropolitan Chess Club, Svetlov was the one man who could beat him consistently.

"Suppose something goes wrong," Fyedorenko said at last.

"It makes no difference. All options lead to checkmate," Svetlov said.

Fyedorenko peered curiously at Svetlov.

"It could mean nuclear war," he said.

"Better sooner than later," Svetlov smiled complacently.

Svetlov had an almost pathological hatred of the West, Fyedorenko remembered. Svetlov's father, mother and twin brother had been wiped out by a shell from a British warship, covering the evacuation of Denikin's army from Novorossisk during the last days of the Cossack revolt. An infant still in diapers, Svetlov had been staying with his grandmother at the time and she had raised him on the story.

But they had to act soon, Fyedorenko thought with sudden urgency. Anything so drastic was bound to terrify the fat sheep of the Old Guard who waited in the antechamber, like pigs at the trough. He turned away from the window and began to walk towards the bedroom, when the door opened and the two doctors came out, fatigue and a sort of lugubrious solemnity painted on their faces. They faced each other across the room, all of them swollen with a sense of their parts in this tableau. It was a historical moment and they all knew it.

"Well then—" Fyedorenko said, just to get it started.

"I regret to inform you of the death of the party secretary, Comrade—" the taller of the doctors began.

"All over is it?" Fyedorenko prompted.

4

"It is a great loss to all of us," the other doctor pronounced solemnly.

"Of course, of course," Fyedorenko said and thanked them as he guided them to the door. "Ask the others to give me a moment alone with him. We were so close you see." His voice broke.

The doctors looked at each other in astonishment. Imagine how everyone would react when they heard of how broken up the famous stone-faced Fyedorenko was over the death of his mentor. They nodded understandingly as they stepped from the salon into the crowded antechamber to make the announcement. As they did so, the quiet murmur of conversation abruptly stopped.

Fyedorenko went into the bedroom and closed the door behind him. He could see the body still connected by tubes and wires to the ineffectual tools of this world. The electrocardiograph was still on, a single blip racing across the screen, endlessly repeating itself.

He glanced at the old man's face, but it had already begun to acquire the waxy expression common to all corpses which proclaimed so clearly that whatever was human no longer inhabited that shriveled old body with its shrewd homely features. Fyedorenko wasted no time looking at the face of the man he had followed for over forty years. He had more important things to do.

He crossed over to the phone on the night stand and dialed Svetlov's private number. He knew Svetlov would be awake and was not surprised when the receiver was picked up before the first ring was completed. Out of habit, Fyedorenko glanced at his watch. It was 3:15 a.m. He took a slight breath, because once he spoke, there was no stopping, no going back, no matter what.

"It has begun," he said.

You should never beat a woman, not even with a flower.
        —The Prophet Mohammed

Paris

IT WAS AN OLD nightmare, as terrifyingly familiar as the darkness of sleep itself. She was running for her life down the dark empty streets of the Latin Quarter, the sound of her footsteps echoing in the silent night. The streetlights reflected wetly on the pavement, still damp from the afternoon rain. The cafés and shops were closed and shuttered as firmly as the eyelids on a corpse. There was no help anywhere. As in a dream, there was that nameless terror of the shadowy man relentlessly pursuing her. Dreamlike too was that horrible feeling that flight was useless. Sooner or later he would catch her and kill her. Except that it wasn't a dream.

At the corner of the rue de Seine, Kelly paused to catch her breath in the shadow of a kiosk plastered with posters advertising the Théâtre Odéon. Her breath came in great, heaving sobs and she wondered whether if she screamed it would bring lighted windows and help, or whether it would just make it easier for him to find her. Her chest heaved and she tried to scream, but nothing came out. Her throat was blocked by a burning lump, as though she had swallowed hot wax. She sucked in desperate gasps of night air and tried to think of what to do, but nothing came. The air tasted of the night and fear. It smelled like wet clothes.

A wave of nausea rippled through her and she was sick again. When she stopped heaving, she found herself on all fours, moaning softly like an animal. She gagged at the smell and from somewhere came the irrelevant thought that her dress and stockings were ruined. Imagine worrying about that now, she thought wildly. A hysterical laugh began to bubble out of her and then she froze at the soft purr of the Mercedes, its lights out, as it slowly prowled next to the curb. Her beautiful eyes went flat with terror, like a rabbit caught by a car's headlights, and there was nothing but the fear.

Then the Mercedes stopped and she heard the sound of the car door opening and then being carefully closed. The sounds of his footsteps came closer and she pressed her face against the hard embrace of the kiosk, curling her body into a tight ball, wishing she could shrivel away and disappear in the shadows. The footsteps stopped nearby and she could hear his breathing as he stood there, listening. Without realizing it, she was making soft whimpering sounds, like a whipped puppy. He came closer and his teeth glowed in his dark face as though they were phosphorescent. A ray of streetlight glowed with a pearly sheen from the metal as he motioned with the gun for her to get up. She shook her head, her long blond hair rippling with the movement.

"Please," she whimpered.

He grabbed her hair and harshly pulled her to her feet. His smile had more in common with an animal baring its teeth than a human expression. He twisted her face to his and put the muzzle to her temple, gripping her hair as if he wanted to pull it out by the roots. They stood there like lovers, close enough to kiss.

"Let's not have any more of this nonsense, *chérie*," he whispered.

She nodded dumbly and walked stiffly beside him to the Mercedes. He shoved her in from the driver's side and told her to cross her wrists behind her. Then he tied her hands and started the car. The cords were too tight and it was very painful. She could feel the knots digging into her skin and told him so.

"*Ça m'est égal,*" he shrugged with icy indifference, but there was a harsh note in his voice and a gleam in his eye that might have been hatred, or perhaps just the greenish reflection of the dash lights. He was enjoying her pain, she thought, and began to feel queasy again. It reminded her of the ferocious resentment she had once heard in her father's voice after a quarrel with her mother. The ice cubes in his highball tinkled like wind chimes as he stared at her, damning her for the irrevocable crime of being female. That was when he first got into politics. Her parents had quarreled a lot in those days.

"A woman's main purpose in life is showing men how noble women are compared to the male beast," her father had said, that bitter edge in his voice.

She thought he meant that he didn't love her.

They sped down the Porte Maillot and headed out towards the périphérique, the autoroute almost empty in the three o'clock darkness. Every once in a while, he glanced over at her, a thin curious kind of smile on his handsome face. But there was nothing sexual in the smile and she shuddered. She kept thinking that he was certainly going to a lot of trouble if all he wanted to do was to rape her and then the bitter taste of bile was at the back of her throat, because she didn't think that he would be satisfied with just raping her. Tears stung her eyes and she tried to think over the pounding in her temples. Perhaps if she seduced him, let him think that he could have her now and any time he wanted, he would let her live. If she could just survive tonight, she'd make it somehow, she told herself.

"You don't have to do this, you know," she said, surprised at how calm, even seductive her voice sounded. Inside, she was quivering like a leaf in a high wind. "I'm terribly attracted to you. I'll do things for you no woman ever has," she whispered.

He looked at her with contempt, as if she were the sleaziest whore in Pigalle. She recoiled, her face flushed with embarrassment. Again, for some bizarre reason it reminded her of her father and the time she had worn make-up for the first time on a date. When she had walked into the living room, he had called her "a cheap slut" in front of Brad and sent her back upstairs to wash it all off. She ran up the stairs, humiliated, knowing it would be all over the school the next day.

11

That night, when Brad parked the car, she let him take her panties off for the first time. And when he put his hand between her thighs, all she could think of was not sex, but how much she hated her father.

"You don't have to force me. I want to," she whispered, her eyes dry and calculating. His lip curled with disgust.

"Shut up," Gerard snapped, his eyes gleaming in the dashboard light.

The taste of bile burned the back of her throat and she thought she was going to throw up again. Her stomach heaved and she begged him to please pull over for a minute.

"So you can run away again, *pas encore*," he growled.

"I'm sick, can't you see?"

"Tant pis," he shrugged and it came with a rush that he was really going to kill her. She was going to be one of those articles in the paper, the details of her body described in humiliating detail, something people glance at for a moment over their morning coffee and mutter some pious platitude about the crime rate before going on to the crossword.

She glanced down at the door and thought about jumping, but the car was going too fast and it was locked anyway. There was absolutely nothing she could do and she felt like crying, except that it seemed silly because she couldn't believe it was happening. That sense of unreality, as if it was all a bad dream, had returned. It couldn't be happening to her. None of it was real, except for the cool vibrating surface of the car window as she rested her head against it. Soon she would wake up and tell Lori about this horrible dream she'd had. It would be all right, this was happening to her dream self, not her. Except that she had fallen down a macabre rabbit hole, flying through the tunnel of light carved by the car's headlights, and she wasn't even sure who she was any more.

She glanced at the car window. The vague dark shapes of fields and houses slid silently through the reflection of her face in the glass. He had turned off the périphérique to the A-6 Autoroute Sud towards Lyons. Wake up Kelly, she urgently told herself, but there was only the pain in her hands and the pain told her with a horrible certainty that it wasn't a dream.

She had spent her life living in a fool's paradise, she told herself bitterly. One moment everything was just as it had always been and suddenly, it was as if she had taken a single step off a curb and the gutter had turned out to be a dark and bottomless pit. It was all the more shocking because the day had begun so well . . .

It had been one of those rare sunny days in Paris when the city seems to shimmer with light, when the flowers in the Tuileries sparkle with color and when even the taxi drivers manage a smile now and then. She and Lori wanted to take advantage of the light and spent the morning snapping photos of the barges and flower stalls along the pea-green Seine from the Ile St. Louis. In the afternoon it had rained on and off. Strands of drops hung like pearls from the café awnings, each of them a tiny miniature of the street. In Paris, the summer rain is warm and teasing, like a brief flirtation.

They went shopping for an umbrella at the Galeries Lafayette near the Opéra. It was still raining when they came out and they stopped off for a *kir* at the nearby Café de la Paix to wait it out. She remembered how they laughed when an American woman at a nearby table had slipped the Dubonnet ashtray into her purse, self-righteously assuring her husband that "they expect you to take it."

When the contact came, it wasn't at all what she'd expected. They met Randy, a long-haired American in jeans searching for the ghosts of '68 at the café. He was with Jean-Paul, a good-looking would-be actor. They went to the Bois and passed around some joints and wound up at Ondine's. The crowded chrome-plated club on the rue de Ponthieu was one of the places that everyone went to, if only to say they'd been there. Later, they all climbed into Jean-Paul's battered

13

Renault and went to a party on a private barge moored near the Pont d'Iena.

The party was packed with people shouting in a dozen languages and soon the barge began to glide down the river. There was a stereo blasting in the salon and couples danced, while women wearing originals from the rue Sainte Honoré shrieked as they greeted each other, as though they hadn't seen each other in twenty years. The air reeked of perfume and the unique smell of Paris, that unmistakable melange of garlic, Gauloise smoke and *café au lait*. Lori and Randy disappeared and Jean-Paul was taken in tow by Angela, an attractive blonde, in her forties at least, Kelly thought cattily, who had once appeared in a Truffaut film.

Kelly wished someone would ask her to dance, but the men seemed afraid to approach her, somehow intimidated by her classic blond beauty. She wondered if she would always feel that way. Once, when she was a teenager, her father had said, "Beauty can be as much of a burden as ugliness, kiddo." In school, the boys who had always been so brash, would fall silent and nudge each other when she went by. As she passed, she could feel their hot eyes on her body. She remembered how Brad would always stammer, "You're so beautiful" in the car, before they began their nightly tussle.

"Beauty is only skin deep," she had snapped, when she finally realized that all he was after was to brag that he had screwed the prettiest girl in the school.

"Who wants more . . . a cannibal?" he had retorted with a silly grin, and he couldn't understand why she had began to cry.

She stepped outside the salon and found a spot not occupied by the embracing couples. Beauty didn't merely snare those attracted to it, it trapped its owners forever, she thought.

She stood at the rail, holding a glass of wine and watching reflections of the city lights shattered like glass on the surface of the Seine. The light breeze of the boat's passage ruffled her hair and she could hear the sounds of the stereo in the salon, thumping its way through an old Beatles tune. She was still annoyed because of the way Jean-Paul was acting. He was dancing with Angela, his slim tan body tightly pressed against hers, and he was murmuring something that made Angela's eyes burn as though with fever. Just an hour before, at the club, he had told Kelly that she was brilliant, truly *"éclatante"* and now he was probably telling Angela the same thing. He couldn't be the one, she thought. The boat was approaching the Pont de la Tournelle and ahead she could see the spotlighted towers of Notre Dame, bathed in white light. She remembered thinking that it was so beautiful and somehow sad too and her eyes began to water.

"Vous êtes triste, mademoiselle?" a modulated masculine voice said and she turned and saw him standing there. He was tall and dark, with soft brown eyes in a handsome triangular face. He was wearing an expensive blue suit, obviously cut by a London tailor who knew what he was doing. His dark curly hair was cut short and neat and she felt her heart flutter like a bird ruffling its feathers.

"What was that?" she stammered in English and her glance involuntarily shot over at Jean-Paul and Angela.

"He is handsome, yes, but he is also a fool," he said with a wry smile, following her glance.

"What makes you say that?" she asked.

"Mon chèr papa used to say that the true fool smiles even as he exchanges gold for brass," he replied in a musically accented English. He told her his name was Gerard. They stood at the rail, chatting about nothing and watching the city lights as the barge slid silently down the river.

It wasn't until later, after he had brought her the champagne, that she had begun to feel sick. She had thrown up twice in the *toilette* by the time the barge tied up near the Pont Neuf. Suddenly she straightened, as the realization hit her. He had drugged her! It was the champagne! He had planned it all along, she realized miserably. At the time she thought he was being generous, offering to drive her back to the hotel in his gleaming white Mercedes. Lori had offered to come back with her, but she hadn't wanted to spoil it for Lori, who was clearly taken with Randy and it seemed silly not to go with Gerard. Besides, she was too miserable to argue. She had felt so awful that she hadn't really paid attention to where they were going until, instead of turning up the rue de Chateaubriand to the hotel, he entered the whirl of lights around the Etoile. When they recrossed the Seine to the Left Bank, she knew something was terribly wrong.

The first time she told Gerard he was going the wrong way, he simply ignored her. His profile stared fixedly at the windshield. She repeated herself, raising her voice and he viciously slapped her face with the back of his hand. Something exploded inside her and she clawed at him, yelling for him to let her out. He hit her again and showed her the gun and her world blew apart like a house of feathers in a strong breeze, just like that.

Her mind raced. She knew she had to get away before he took her out of the center of town. There must be some people still awake she thought desperately. She told him she was going to be sick again and he carefully pulled over. Given the way she felt, it was hardly a lie. Fortunately, the door wasn't locked then and she opened it and bent over as if to throw up. But instead, she rolled head over heels the way she used to in high-school gym and was momentarily blocked from his view by the wing. She desperately scrambled on all fours around a parked car and began to run, her spine tensed for the impact of a bullet. She ran wildly, terrified that she might slip because of her high heels. When she rounded the corner into the shadows of the rue de Seine, she briefly thought she might make it. But she never really had a chance, she realized dully.

They turned off the autoroute near Fontainebleau and drove

down a country road overhung with dark and ancient trees. It felt as if they were entering a primordial forest. Every so often Gerard glanced over at her, his eyes dark and calculating. Mercifully, her hands had gone numb, but she felt a terrible urge to urinate. She squeezed her legs together to hold it in, like a child. Then he pulled into a dark driveway and left the car to open an old metal gate. She briefly thought of running again, but how and where? She was helpless.

He drove the car past the gate, then went and locked it. She felt a warm flush between her thighs and wondered if she had wet herself. Then he drove up to a dark house, with a single light in one of the windows. He hauled her out of the Mercedes and unlocked the front door. There was a murmur of voices coming from what appeared to be the living room. Then a small dark-skinned man peered from the doorway. Kelly was about to beg him to help her, when she realized that he didn't seem in the least surprised to see her.

"*Tout va bien?*" the man said to Gerard, in a harsh voice that grated like fingernails on metal.

"*Pas des problems,*" Gerard replied. No, no problems. She had been easy as pie, she thought miserably. Gerard led her down a dimly lit stairway to a tiny room lit by the harsh glare of a naked bulb and walled with whitewashed stone. Except for a narrow bed and a dirty sink, the room was bare as a nun's cell. Gerard clicked open a long stiletto blade. It glittered like ice.

"Please . . . don't kill me . . . oh, please," she gasped.

"Kill you," Gerard frowned. "Pas de tout. You're worth more to me than that, *ma petite.*"

He cut the knots tying her wrists and stepped away, as she rubbed them gratefully, the pain flooding into her fingers.

"Here, clean up," he said, tossing a towel at her.

"Thank you," she said, her eyes blurred with tears. She took her time washing, trying to find some sense of normality in the everyday actions. He took her chin in his hand and turned her face to his. He looked so handsome, even approving.

"*Bien,*" he murmured and she felt a strange gratitude. Perhaps he wouldn't kill her after all, she thought.

"Take off your clothes," he ordered.

"Yes, anything," she whispered, and began to unbutton her dress with clumsy fingers. When she had stripped down to her bra and panties, she looked expectantly at him, but he just stood there. Confused, she hesitantly unhooked her bra and then, after a moment, stepped out of her panties.

"Do you want me to lay down?" she asked, motioning at the bed. If there was a bulge in his pants, she couldn't see it.

"Just stand there," he snapped irritably.

Then she heard the heavy steps of men coming down the wooden stairs. Four men in suits entered the room and studied her as if she were in a cage at the zoo. One looked like a fat, graying French businessman with dark, beady eyes and a moustache which he twitched like a rodent. The other three were dark-skinned. Algerians or Arabs, she guessed. One of the Arabs, a scrawny man with a scar on his cheek and long hairs growing out of his nose, came up to her and fondled her breasts. He breathed heavily in her face and she thought she was going to pass out. His breath was foul, as if he fed on carrion. A tear edged its way out of the corner of her eye. Then another Arab gestured for her to bend over. She closed her eyes and felt his harsh fingers probing. She felt their hands all over her, moving her this way and that, as though she was a giant plastic doll. She let them do what they wanted, thinking Kelly's not here. Kelly's far away with her Daddy and her Mommy who are still married and they still love their little girl.

Then the hands were gone and when she opened her eyes, they had gathered in a circle and were babbling furiously in French. She felt her legs were about to collapse under her and somehow made it to the edge of the bed and sat down. Every once in a while, one of the men would glance over at her. She looked pleadingly at Gerard, but his eyes were cold and calculating; they followed the conversation back and forth as though it were a tennis ball.

They were arguing and although her French wasn't good enough to understand all the words, she had the strange impression that they were bidding for her. It was almost as if it was an auction and she was the prize, she thought and then shook her head, because that seemed more bizarre than anything else that had happened tonight. It just couldn't be, she thought.

When she looked up, they had stopped talking and were all looking expectantly at her. One of the Arabs gave Gerard a thick roll of money and Gerard smiled crookedly at her. Then he was gone. A tall, thin Arab said something and the others laughed harshly. It sounded like dogs barking.

"Why not?" the ugly Arab with the bad breath said suddenly in English and she knew that he wanted her to understand. "Nobody expects a western woman to be virgin," and the men laughed again. Kelly looked down at her naked breasts, watching drops of water trickle down, not even aware that she was crying. Kelly's not here. Kelly's gone away, the voice inside her kept saying.

She felt their hot breath as they gathered around her like a wolf pack closing in for the kill. The fat gray-haired Frenchman came closer and grunted something. Teardrops spattered on her breasts, weaving tiny streams on her skin. Then Kelly looked up defiantly, her eyes large and luminous. Once, a handsome young district attorney she had dated briefly had told her that her eyes should be registered as a lethal weapon. But they didn't seem to have any effect on these men. The fat Frenchman harshly pushed her back on the bed.

One by one, the men in the room began to undress.

Pakistan

THE SAFE HOUSE was a small copper and brass shop in the Misgaran Bazaar. Over the doorway hung a corrugated metal awning which made it indistinguishable from the other shops and stalls crowded along the Street of the Storytellers. Near the front of the shop, a brass coffee pot with its lid open sat on the upside-down copper kettle. It was the signal that it was clear to approach, but still he held back. The Russians had put a price on his head and Peshawar was thick with men who would stick a knife in someone's back for a dollar and give you back change.

The street shimmered in the afternoon heat, as throngs of Pakistanis and turbanned Pathan tribesmen and women veiled in white from head to foot haggled in the bazaar. The air was ripe with the smells of animals and herbs, meat roasting over charcoal braziers and sweetish scents of *khat* and hashish smoke, that unmistakable scent of the Orient which whispers of ancient sins. Motor scooters weaved through the crowd, buzzing like giant insects in the gas haze.

Near the corner, a blind storyteller sat under a canvas awning, calling to passers-by in Urdu and Pushtu. From an unseen loudspeaker near the mosque came the tinny wail of a Pakistani love song. In the distance, sunlight turned the parapets of Bala Hisar to gold, like a fairy-tale castle. The huge brick fortress towered over the city as it had since the time of the Moguls, the sun casting its shadow far across the sea of rooftops. Soon it would be time for dusk prayers.

"In the name of Allah, the Compassionate, the Merciful," the blind storyteller said and began to tell the story of how the great Afridi leader, the Fakir of Ipi, had annihilated a British regiment in the shadow of the holy mountain, Shahur Tangi. A small crowd of old men and wide-eyed boys clustered around the storyteller. Near the edge of the crowd, a Pathan in a dark brown robe casually gazed over at the copper shop, rapidly quartering the street in a single glance. The Pathan was taller than most tribesmen, his body wiry and desert-hardened. He sat listening to the storyteller, with the deadly stillness of a beast of prey. With his dark stubbly beard and skin burned mahogany by the sun, only the most careful observer would have spotted him as a westerner by his features and cold gray eyes. Yet he was noticed.

A dark-skinned Mahsud, still in his teens, couldn't resist stealing a shy glance at the foreigner, although he knew that no one was to speak of him. The *moujahadeen* of the Khyber said that he was a great warrior. Others said that he was an escaped murderer. Wherever he went, he was followed by whispers. No one even knew his name. Among the tribes he was known only by his code name. They called him "the Scorpion."

The storyteller spoke of how the tribesmen had shot down the British biplanes with their breech-loading rifles and there was a murmur from the crowd. Did not the *moujahadeen* do the same to the godless Russians? Were they not men like their fathers? Then he told of how the great Fakir, who could not be defeated in battle, was finally slain by treachery. The crowd grumbled threateningly. The soul of the infidel was black with sin.

"It is said that the British cut out his heart. It was placed in a gold box lined with silk and sent to a museum in London city. The heart weighed ten pounds. Who can doubt it?" declared the storyteller.

A *tonga* piled high with oranges and pulled by a water buffalo rumbled slowly down the dusty street. They always reminded the Scorpion of the carts in Vietnam. The memory reeked with the smells of *nuoc mam* and cordite and as always, he immediately pushed it away. He stood up and moved towards the shop, using the cart for cover. For a moment, the storyteller's glance caught his, the sightless eyes covered with a milk-white glaze, like the eyes of a statue. They made him uneasy, as though the old man could see him. It's nothing, he's blind, the Scorpion told himself as he moved with a fluid ground-eating stride alongside the *tonga*.

When the young Mahsud glanced over again, the Scorpion had simply disappeared.

The shop was cool after the blazing heat of the street. It was empty, except for a fat, sweating Pakistani in a white robe, who rose like a *jinn* from behind a large copper urn. The merchant bowed his head and touched his hand to his heart.

"Sahib Khattak?" the Scorpion asked.

"You honor my shop, Sahib," the man said and bowed again.

"Have you the copper lamp I ordered? The one with a tiger's face?"

"There are no tigers in Peshawar, Sahib," Khattak said, glancing anxiously at the bright street outside, looking for eyes that looked back.

"There are tigers that smile in Islamabad," the Scorpion replied, completing the sequence.

Khattak went to the front of the shop and noisily pulled the metal shutter across the doorway, sealing them in the suddenly dim light, as in a tomb. When he turned back to the Scorpion, he held a .45 automatic in his hand.

"Did anyone see you come here?" Khattak asked nervously, his sweat-slick face shining like the man in the moon.

"Only the storyteller without eyes."

"I am to search your person," Khattak said, coming closer. The .45 was cocked.

"Do you know who I am?"

"Does anyone know who anyone is in Peshawar?" Khattak said, his eyes darting about like fish in a tank. The Scorpion smiled.

"I am called 'the Scorpion,' " he said.

Khattak paled. The gun began to shake in his hand. He

nervously stuffed it back inside his robe and bowed, his hand over his heart.

"A thousand pardons, Sahib. The one you seek is waiting," he said and with a series of anxious bows, he led the Scorpion through a beaded curtain to a small airless room in the back, where Bob Harris was sitting like a sultan on a leather hassock. Harris was grinning as though it was all a glorious adventure. Iced lime drinks for both of them were already set up on a large copper tray.

"Oh Christ," the Scorpion muttered and shook his head. With another bow, Khattak eased his huge bulk past the curtain, leaving them alone. Harris winked and gestured for him to sit down, but the Scorpion just stood there.

"What was all that James Bond bullshit with Khattak?"

"Oh that," Harris shrugged. "He's not a contact. This is just a one-time deal. Besides, don't worry about it. We've bigger fish to fry."

"Worry is what keeps people like me alive," the Scorpion said quietly.

"Of course. Sorry," Harris said, with an understanding grin. He had a smile for every occasion, like Hallmark cards, the Scorpion thought. He sat down on a hassock, positioning himself so he could watch the doorway and Harris at the same time.

Harris was tall and fair, his boyish face alive with the mischievous charm of an urchin who has gone to all the better prep schools. In his spanking-new safari jacket and pith helmet, Harris looked as if he had just stepped out of the window of Abercrombie & Fitch. The Scorpion scratched his five-day growth of beard and tried to remember the last time he'd had a hot bath. Harris always managed to make him feel that way, like the character in the commercial who uses the wrong kind of deodorant soap.

But seeing Harris, he knew that whatever it was had to be top drawer. Harris was the DCI's protégé, so he wouldn't have been sent out unless someone very high up was interested. Harris handed him a glass of iced lime juice and he sipped at it, hoping it would help to dissolve the knot he felt at the pit of his stomach. The last time he had seen Harris was in Abu Dhabi, when Harris had roped him into Operation Eagle Claw, the Blue Light Brigade's abortive attempt to rescue the American hostages in Iran. "A Pentagon Blue Plate special," Harris had called the operation. He had tried to squirm out of it, but Harris had hooked him and he had been lucky to get out of Teheran in one piece, just two steps ahead of the Revolutionary Guards. The brass had handled the fiasco in the usual way, by handing out posthumous medals, and Harris had wound up with a promotion. That was Harris all right, the Scorpion mused. Throw him into a manure pile and he'd come out sniffing a rose.

"There's a little job we'd like you to do for us," Harris said in his best briefing-room manner. The only things missing were the wall maps and pointer.

"Another Blue Plate Special?" the Scorpion couldn't resist asking. Harris gave him his patented "Come on, don't be that way" smile, a lop-sided grin that had toppled more women into bed than champagne.

"No, you'll like this one. Money-back guarantee," Harris said.

"If it's as good as the last one, I can hardly wait."

Harris pulled out a handkerchief and dabbed at his face. The heat was starting to get to him. He looked around at the cramped storeroom with distaste, then sighed to show he was ever the good soldier and stuffed the handkerchief back in his pocket.

"Why don't you get Khattak to set up a fan?" the Scorpion grinned. He was beginning to enjoy watching Harris squirm.

"No electricity, besides there isn't time. As soon as you get cleaned up and out of your Gunga Din outfit"—looking at the Scorpion as if he had just stepped out of a cesspool—"you have to be on a plane out of here."

"I still have business here," the Scorpion said. He'd spent

months trying to set up the gun deal with the Afghani rebels and now he had the queasy feeling that the Company was about to pick up its marbles and tell him that they didn't want to play any more.

"We'd be appreciative if you'd handle this little matter for us first. Very," Harris said, making a steeple with his fingers. It reminded the Scorpion of the Thai *wai* greeting and the night a thousand years ago when Alex and he had met Harris for the first time. It was at the Derby King on Patpong Road, the CIA's favorite watering hole in Bangkok. That was the night Harris had told them about a quick little op in Phitsanulok province. Alex had never come back from that one, and later they learned that the Pathet Lao had impaled him on a bamboo stake.

"How much is appreciation going for these days?" the Scorpion asked.

"I had a feeling you were going to use dirty words." Harris reached into his pocket and pulled out a color photo and tossed it over to him. It showed a beautiful young woman posing on a park bench which might have been in the Luxembourg Gardens. If people came out of files, hers would have been labeled "All-American Girl—Pretty." She wore a green silk blouse, designer jeans and a smile that said she could have a love affair with the camera any time she wanted. Her shoulder-length blond hair was tousled in the way that took a top-notch hairdresser half a day to achieve. Her eyes were a disturbing violet with silver specks, sparkling with intelligence. They'd have made the ugliest girl special, and if it weren't for a touch of wistfulness in them, she could have been posing for a magazine cover. She was the grown-up version of the head cheerleader whom everyone had a crush on in high school. She was a dream girl, the kind who attracts tragedy the way honey attracts flies.

"I hope you'll be very happy together," the Scorpion said.

"She turned up missing in Paris five weeks ago. We want you to find her."

"Have you tried the French lost and found?" the Scorpion said and put the photo on the tray. He was annoyed. This wasn't his kind of job and Harris knew it.

"The rue des Saussaies put us on to it. I don't know if they'd appreciate that description," Harris said drily.

"How did the Sûreté and the Company suddenly get involved? I mean, she's cute, but nobody's that pretty."

"Her daddy is Congressman Max Ormont, the oil millionaire. He's a member of the Republican National Committee." Harris winked.

"How do you know she didn't run off for a dirty weekend on the Côte d'Azur?"

"She was snatched," Harris said with finality.

"Political?"

Harris shook his head. "It looks like white slavery."

The Scorpion whistled silently to himself. Now he knew why Harris needed him. Arabia was his personal briarpatch and that's where the biggest market was for white females. But it was also a dead end, because the one sure way to get Arabs to kill you was to go around trying to sniff out their womenfolk.

"How good is the data, Bob?" the Scorpion asked.

Harris looked insulted and turned his profile to the Scorpion to show how bravely he could suffer. In a way, a pique was justifiable, the Scorpion mused. In theory, any data passed from a senior case officer to a field agent was supposed to be sacrosanct. They might—and usually did—withold a lot, but what they gave you was supposed to be good. Except that he had known men to die in the gap between theory and practice. When Harris looked back at him, a hard glint had come into his eyes.

"Don't worry about the data. This is straight from the Sûreté and we independently confirmed. It's got the Good Housekeeping Seal of Approval."

"Oh sure, Grade A. Just like Warsaw," the Scorpion shrugged.

Harris winced at that one. He had been in Warsaw when the Company had paid thirty thousand dollars for the latest Soviet military plan on Poland; except that the report turned out to be a rewrite of an article in *Le Figaro*. Then he leaned forward and the Scorpion saw that the flush in his face was anger, not embarrassment. His naked fury surprised the Scorpion. Harris was a born actor. Normally, he held his real emotions like a miser, carefully doling them out like coins.

"Do you want the guns, or don't you?" Harris said through gritted teeth.

The Scorpion nodded. As Sergeant Walker used to say in his easy Georgia drawl, "They got you by the short and curlies, boy. Y'all can't complain about the price when it's the only store in town." Harris leaned back and smiled, back in control again. That was the way he liked it.

The two men sipped their drinks. Dimly, they could hear the distant cry from the mosque loudspeaker calling the faithful to prayer. The Scorpion glanced down again at the photo on the table. If she had been sold as a white slave in Arabia, she'd either wind up in a brothel or the desert. Either way, she probably wouldn't live out the year. There was a tilt of independence in her chin. Slavery would be a kind of death in life for her, he thought. Harris noticed him looking at the photo and pushed it a little closer to him. There was something dirty about the way he did it, as though Harris were bribing him with the girl's beauty.

"Pretty, isn't she?" Harris said.

Pretty wasn't the word, the Scorpion thought. With that exquisite face and that sexy young body, she must have started a thousand daydreams every time she walked down the street.

"What happened to her?" he said at last. Harris almost sighed with relief and he mopped his brow again with the wet handkerchief. He raised his glass in a silent toast to himself. He'd come a long way to hook this fish.

"Once upon a time there were two American girls in Paris," Harris began.

"Jesus, Bob. Don't give me the whole *Ring* cycle. Just jump to the part where they meet the traveling salesman."

Harris straightened up, annoyed at the lack of respect for his briefing style. Then he took a long swallow of lime juice and tried the sincere smile that had taken him so far up the ladder.

"Okay," Harris began again. "The Congressman's Pride and Joy is Kelly Ormont. Two months ago, she and a girlfriend, Lori, packed their traveler's checks and Kaopectate and took off for Europe. They were at a ritzy party on a private barge on the Seine when Kelly became ill after a little too much champagne. A handsome Frenchman named Gerard offered to take her back to the hotel. Lori saw her get into a white Mercedes with him. That was the last time she ever saw Kelly.

"The next day she went to Kelly's room and found that she hadn't come in. She stewed for a while, trying to figure out what to do and finally took it to the American embassy, who sent her to the Quai des Orfèvres. For two days, the Froggies gave her the usual bureaucratic runaround until she told them about the congressman. Then they figured it might be political and they might actually have to do something about it," he said, pursing his lips with the bureaucrat's distaste for someone else's bureaucracy. "They turned it over to the Sûreté and eventually it got to Interpol, who sent out a Blue. By then the congressman was steaming and he called the Oval Office. That's when we got involved."

"That's a lot of high-priced talent for what sounds like a police matter," the Scorpion said, scratching his stubbled beard.

Harris sighed and sipped his drink. Dark sweat stains were beginning to grow under his arms.

"The congressman is an important man," Harris said pointedly.

"What did the Sûreté come up with?"

"Nobody at the party knew this Gerard character."

"Naturally," the Scorpion shrugged.

"The Mercedes was stolen, of course. It was found a few days later in St. Germain en Laye. No signs of a struggle. The Sûreté checked with the Duane and sure enough, the girl and two men boarded an Air France flight to Rome the night of the party. By then the trail wasn't exactly red-hot, but they did come up with something. According to some unconfirmed reports from the SDECE, someone known as Gerard Aupin was rumored to be supplying choice white females out of Paris and Marseilles to the Middle East. He was supposed to be quite a lady-killer."

"Literally, it seems," the Scorpion remarked. Harris nodded.

"According to the Air France passenger list, the name of one of the two men with Kelly Ormont was Gerard Dupin."

The two men looked at each other. The one-letter name change was the easiest kind of a passport fix. The Scorpion picked up the girl's photo and studied it again. It was an action that was to become obsessive with him in the days to come. He felt the faint stirrings of something that he couldn't put a name to, almost as if something was coming to life inside him. Not curiosity or attraction. Not a quest, with a sword in an anvil at the end of it. Something else. A kind of second chance. He thought of Tuyet and the child and that last night on the Saigon River, the night the world ended for all of them. He shook his head to clear away the memory, but there was no escaping the past for any of them. He remembered once, a long time ago, Sheikh Zaid teaching him to hunt with the falcon. Although the bird was trained and tethered, it began to wildly flap its powerful wings the moment its hood was removed. Zaid released the falcon and they watched it soar to a pinpoint in the empty blue sky of the desert.

"You see, little *dhimmi*," Zaid had said. "Even the falcon born in a cage never forgets the sky."

"What did the Italians come up with?" the Scorpion asked.

"A girl answering Kelly's description boarded a flight to Bahrain, under the name Lucy Morton. The Alitalia flight hostess remembered her because she was so pretty and because she slept during the entire flight."

"Drugs?"

"Who knows?" Harris said, raising his eyebrows.

"Was this Gerard with her?"

Harris shrugged. From somewhere the sweet smell of hashish came floating on the hot dead air.

"What about the girl?"

Harris shrugged again and smiled uneasily. This was his "Don't blame me, I just got here" smile.

"According to the authorities at Muharraq Airport, she never got off the plane. She just vanished into thin air. That's all we know."

For a long moment the two men just looked at each other. From outside they could hear the muffled rumble of a car with a bad exhaust roaring like a squadron of bombers as it passed the shop, the sound slowly fading away. Harris slapped irritably at a fly that settled on his neck.

"You like all this don't you?" Harris said oddly, with a vague hand gesture that somehow took in the entire Middle East.

"I like the desert."

Harris nodded, looking at him with the kind of polite condescension reserved for madmen, as if the Scorpion had said that his hobby was talking to little green men in flying saucers. The Scorpion looked down again, knowing that Harris would never understand what he was talking about. He studied the girl's face in the photo. Was there some sadness there, some premonition of her fate, he wondered.

"What have you got from the stations in Manama and Riyadh?" he asked at last.

Harris shifted uncomfortably. This was the sticky part and the Scorpion heard mental alarm bells ringing as Harris mopped his face.

"Things are a little dicey in Arabia right now," Harris said finally, with the uneasy smile of a corporate vice-president telling the TV camera that there was no proof that tobacco caused cancer. The Scorpion had never seen Harris look so uncomfortable and that really worried him. It was beginning to sound like the worst kind of mission. The one where they collect your dogtags even before you leave.

In fact, now that he thought about it, Harris was a bird of ill omen, a raven in a Brooks Brothers suit. Saying things were dicey in Arabia made Harris sound like a scout admitting to Custer that there might be a few Indians waiting at the Little Big Horn.

"What the hell does that mean, Bob?"

"We can't use the stations in Arabia. This has to be completely unofficial. Besides, it wouldn't do any good. You can't just ask an Arab if somebody's got a new toy for his harem. You should know that better than anyone."

The Scorpion's eyes turned cold and gray as the sea and he stood up, trying to control his temper.

"Look, is this a straight 'Search and Retrieve' or has something been fucked up?" he demanded angrily.

Harris looked up sharply, his face flushed. "Nothing is fucked up and nothing better get fucked up," he said. The two men glared at each other, their mutual dislike finally out in the open.

"The contact has to be somebody I know," the Scorpion said finally.

"Braithwaite is on it."

The Scorpion nodded. That sounded a little better. They'd obviously done some advance planning with him in mind for a change.

"What about communications?"

"Use Macready. He's in Doha," Harris said, unable to keep the distaste out of his voice.

The Scorpion's mind raced. They had to be desperate if they were willing to use Macready. Mentally, he raised the price.

"I want a quarter mill in U.S. dollars or Swiss francs. Usual terms."

"You always did have an exaggerated idea of what you were worth," Harris said.

The Scorpion shrugged. He knew they wouldn't have turned to an independent like him if they'd had a better alternative.

Harris nodded reluctantly. He didn't bargain and that worried the Scorpion even more, because it meant they knew it was going to be trouble and they'd probably never have to pay off. Harris stood up and carefully straightened his safari jacket.

"Well, what do you think?" Harris asked finally.

"What do you think I think? She could be anywhere from Baghdad to Casablanca by now. Arabia alone is half the size of the U.S. and even the king doesn't know what his borders are or what the population is. A pretty white woman is worth about seventy thousand bucks on the hoof and you can't even ask anyone 'How's your wife?' without getting your throat cut. And even if I found her, anyone rich enough to buy her is powerful enough to keep her and all we can offer is more money, which he probably needs like a hole in the head. And I can't use Company resources or go near the embassy. What do you think I think? Anyone who figures we can find her, much less get her back, probably thinks a ticket on the Irish Sweepstakes is a conservative investment."

"What shall I tell the congressman?" Harris asked quietly.

"Tell him to call 'Dial-a-Prayer,' " the Scorpion retorted.

Harris sighed, like a high-school coach with a primadonna player.

"Find the girl, Scorpion," he said seriously. "Just find the girl."

"Is there a back way out of here?" the Scorpion asked.

Harris nodded and glanced at the curtained doorway.

"One more thing. You were our second choice on this. We pulled Chambers out of Istanbul last week. They found his body on the beach near Manama. Both his arms and legs had been cut off," he added, his face bland and emotionless. All the CIA types were like that, the Scorpion mused. Always trying to show how cool and efficient they were.

"You son of a bitch," the Scorpion whispered. He'd liked Chambers, who'd had a bigger repertoire of corny jokes than Bob Hope.

Harris grinned maliciously. He reminded the Scorpion of the Cheshire Cat. Then he shrugged, hands in pockets, like good old Jimmy Stewart, faithfully doing his job. "I just thought you ought to know, if you know what I mean."

The Scorpion knew what he meant.

Bahrain

THE GIANT *houbara* stabbed its beak at the sandy ground as though pecking, then raised its head back up and lowered it again and again. The giant zebra-striped image of the bird had been painted as a decoration on an oil pump. Actually, it was as much a piece of nostalgia as a New England weather vane. The bird itself, a wild migratory chicken that could outrun a Saluki dog on the ground, no longer existed in Arabia. It had been hunted to extinction by the Gulf Arabs. Now, Arabian falconers had to travel to Morocco and Pakistan to maintain the traditions of the hunt.

The bird was but one of a bobbing zoo of brightly painted bustards and horses and giraffes that decorated the small oil field outside Manama. Against the glowing horizon, the silhouette of the BAPCO refinery looked like the gantry of Cape Canaveral. Electric lights strung along the oil derricks twinkled like Christmas decorations in the tangerine twilight. What with all the alien shapes and the strange-colored sky, he might

33

have been in a space port on another planet. As the taxi turned from the Muharraq Causeway into traffic-jammed Government Road, the Scorpion could see beyond the oil field to the gold and turquoise waters of the Persian Gulf, called the Arabian Gulf in this part of the world. Beyond the molten surface of the sea lay the dark shadow of the Arabian mainland.

The *sheshbesh* players had already settled in the green oasis of a traffic circle. Insects swirled thick as rain around the sodium arc lights, as the players banged their counters in the greenish glare, oblivious to the hurricane of evening traffic swirling around them.

The humid Gulf heat draped itself around him like a steaming wet cloak. The whiny quarter-tones of an Egyptian love song blared from the taxi's radio, the driver's head bobbing like an oil pump in time to the music.

The taxi itself was painted in an arabesque of colors, like a psychedelic dream gone wild, so that it was impossible to say what model it had been originally. The seats were red velvet; gold tassels hung over the windows and the flush interior resembled a *fin de siècle* brothel. The singer on the radio moaned that she yearned for him in the long empty nights and the Scorpion grinned. It was good to hear Arabic again. It was almost like coming home.

The driver said something, but he missed it in the blare of the radio and the cars, the drivers pounding on their horns as if it was a contest to see who could make the most noise.

"You want the *fondok* Gulf Hotel, *asayid*?" the driver repeated, turning his head and barely missing sideswiping a pink and white Cadillac aggressively driven by a young Bahraini with a peach-fuzz moustache.

"*Aiwa, min fadlak,*" the Scorpion said.

"You speak good Arabic, *asayid.* For a *Giaour,*" the driver added, using the contemptuous term for an infidel foreigner, but there was no offense in the words. All foreigners were infidels.

"*Shokran*," the Scorpion thanked him, "but I think you are also a foreigner in Bahrain."

"I am Palestinian, from Akko, near Haifa," the driver said, slapping his chest proudly. "I am here only temporarily," he declared.

"How long have you been in Bahrain?"

"Fifteen years, *asayid.*"

Along Government Road, new concrete buildings had been thrown up almost overnight. They gleamed white as tombstones in the sodium-bright streetlights, block after block. Once, Bahrain had been a crowded *souk* of squat mud houses, the Scorpion mused. Now, crowded with skyscrapers and smart shops, it looked like downtown Anywhere. The driver was wrong, he decided. They were all exiles: the driver who wanted a homeland which wasn't there, the Arabs hunting the extinct *houbara*, and him. There was no going home for any of them.

"I think I go home pretty soon now," the driver said.

"*Inshallah,*" God willing, the Scorpion replied.

The taxi swerved suddenly through a gap in traffic and turned into the driveway of the Gulf Hotel. As the porter took his bag inside, the Scorpion paid the driver, who glanced at him curiously. Then the driver smiled.

"*Inshallah, asayid,*" he said and with a blast of his horn pulled away, fitting the taxi between two creeping trucks, like a piece in a moving jigsaw puzzle. The Scorpion watched the traffic flow by. There were no tails, but he couldn't shake the feeling of being watched.

By the time he checked in, changed shirts and had grown accustomed to the asthmatic wheeze of the air-conditioner, night had fallen over the island. He took the elevator down to the long dark bar, where Braithwaite was already holding court.

Everyone in the Arabian Gulf knows the Gulf Hotel bar. It's an air-conditioned *souk* where everyone is either buying or selling, or usually both, where deals are made and broken in minutes over outrageously priced cocktails and where contracts worth millions are traded on the flimsy hope of a whispered "connection." The bar was dense with tobacco smoke and murmurs of "agencies" and "consultants' fee" in a dozen languages. A TV over the bar showed Sheikh al-Khatifa, resplendent in a gold-trimmed *thaub*, officially welcoming the airport arrival of Prince Abdul Sa'ad, the Saudi Deputy Defense Minister, on a state visit. No one paid any attention to the TV. As in the rest of the Arab world, all news here was carefully censored. Real information was passed by word of mouth in the *souks*.

Near the middle of the bar two slim BOAC stewardesses sipped tall rainbow-colored drinks through straws and tried to ignore the perspiring Levantine businessman who kept offering to buy them drinks, leering as he put them through their paces in the X-rated movie of his mind.

"Eileen's miserable," the stewardess with long blond hair noted.

"I thought she was marrying Biff the Stiff," the short-haired brunette replied.

"She was, then he went off to the Bahamas with his secretary."

"It could have been worse. She might have married him," the blonde said.

"Perhaps you nice ladies would like cocktails. I have big expense account," the Levantine said, flashing a thick roll of *riyals*.

"Get stuffed, tubby," the brunette snapped. The Levantine grinned widely enough for them to assay the gold in his teeth. He pulled out his wallet and flashed an accordion of credit cards.

"I flew in with Fast Freddy. He told me all about it," the blonde said.

"You know why they call him 'Fast Freddy?' " the brunette said with a mischievous smile. The blonde shook her head and the brunette whispered something that had the two of them cackling like the hags in *Macbeth*.

"God!" the brunette exclaimed, sucking on her straw like a teeny-bopper.

"Yes, Moslems are very religious peoples," the Levantine breathlessly put in.

The brunette glared at the Levantine crowding close to her. "Do you mind?" she snapped. He moved back a fraction of an inch, his face beaming with good will.

"All the good men are taken," the blonde said glumly.

"The bastards!" the brunette said and with a sigh told the Levantine she was drinking Singapore Slings, as the Scorpion walked by. They didn't bother to glance at him. Apparently, the market in men had turned distinctly bearish. He elbowed his way to the bar and ordered a whisky and soda.

"I'm getting the hell outa this here place tomorrow," grumbled a big red-faced American in a tartan sports jacket to his left, in a drawl that reached back to East Texas. "I been in so many damn offices and paid so much 'baksheesh,' " I plumb forgot who got what. And I'm still waitin' on the lousy contract."

"You need a local agent," an expensively dressed Arab said with oily sympathy. He was probably a Palestinian, the New Jews of the Middle East, the Scorpion mused.

"Shee-yit, boy. That's what I need here, shee-yit," the Texan said, and ordered another bourbon and branch.

"Things are different here, my friend," the Palestinian put in. He had smooth skin and a thin moustache which made him look like the toy groom on a wedding cake. He was right, the Scorpion thought. A local agent knew who to pay baksheesh to and how much to skim off the top. Sometimes, they were even worth it.

"I ain't your friend, pard," the American said indistinctly to his drink.

The Palestinian's smile never wavered, but it grew brittle.

"The minister whose approval you seek is the nephew of my half-brother Achmet. That is a very sound basis for friendship," the Palestinian said, his smile broadening, and the

Scorpion knew the Palestinian had just mentally raised the price.

"I might be interested," the American muttered casually.

When it comes to business, the Americans are children compared to Arabs, the Scorpion thought and nodded at Braithwaite, who had motioned for him to come over. Braithwaite was sitting with a Bahraini in a white *thaub* and *kaffiyeh*, who sipped coffee and calmly fingered his prayer beads.

"Well, if it isn't Mr.—" Braithwaite called.

"Shaw," the Scorpion said quickly, supplying the name on the passport Harris had given him. In all the world, Braithwaite was the only man outside the Company who knew his real name and the last thing the Scorpion wanted was to hear it pronounced in a public place.

"Ah yes, Shaw," Braithwaite smiled wickedly, his red alcoholic's face breaking into a spider's web of seams and wrinkles.

Braithwaite was tall and thin, his dark eyes beginning to blear with age, yet still retaining a keen, if sardonic, intelligence. He was wearing a loud yellow sportshirt from God knows where, open at the neck to reveal a scrawny gray tuft of chest hair, like a half-plucked chicken breast. He looked like one of those windy old farts who inhabit retirement homes and golf-club bars, but in fact, he was the last of the old British Arabists. His reminiscences were filled with names like C. M. Doughty, Wilfred Thesiger, T. E. Lawrence, John Glubb Pasha and Philby. "Old St. John Philby, not that young snake, Kim," Braithwaite would stipulate. Once, when the Scorpion was still a boy living with the Mutayr, he had gone with Youssef on his first camel trek in the Nefud desert. They had become lost trying to find Wadi er Rumna and it was Braithwaite who rode out from Buraida and found them down to the last drops in their water bags.

"Sit down lad, sit down. It's been . . . ages . . . simply ages since we d-d-dipped a beak, eh?" Braithwaite said.

"It's been a while," the Scorpion admitted. Braithwaite

hadn't changed. The old stutter was still there. As for the Bahraini, he had the smell of cop about him, as unmistakable as the scent of aftershave lotion, and the Scorpion was instantly on guard.

"Sorry . . . Shaw, this is Jassim al-Amir," Braithwaite said.

"*Salaam aleikem*," al-Amir murmured with a nod.

"*Aleikem es-Salaam*," the Scorpion replied.

"Heard you were over in Vietnam," Braithwaite said.

"Ancient history," the Scorpion replied.

"How was it?" al-Amir asked, his eyes bright with curiosity. Say what you will, there was something about a war in an exotic place that fascinated men who had to get it second hand, the Scorpion mused.

"It just was," the Scorpion shrugged. What was there to say?

"Not like the old d-d-days in the *Ikhwan*, eh?" Braithwaite said, rubbing his hands as he prepared to launch into one of those long reminiscences of tribal warfare that would end with the story of how he had convinced King Abd al Aziz to allow SOCAL into Arabia and never saw a penny of it.

Looking at the red alcoholic's face, the Scorpion wondered if Braithwaite was beginning to live entirely in the past.

"That was a long time ago," he said.

"You are a soldier, *asayid* Shaw?" al-Amir inquired politely. He had trouble with a capital "O" for "Official" written all over him, and the Scorpion felt uncomfortable at his frank interest.

"Was, past tense," he replied, taking sanctuary in his drink.

"Nasty b-business," Braithwaite said, apropos of nothing.

"How about yourself? What do you do?" the Scorpion asked the Arab.

"I'm a policeman," al-Amir said modestly, spreading his fingers as though to refuse food.

"Nonsense, Jassim is too modest. He's Chief of Police, the local *bimbashi* as it were," Braithwaite said, his eyes narrowing as if warning the Scorpion off.

The Scorpion acknowledged Jassim with a raised eyebrow, his senses completely alert. This was no casual meeting. It was a setup. He remembered Koenig, his instructor at the Farm in Virginia, telling them, "There are no coincidences in this business. None. The moment you smell something that even looks like a coincidence, you've been blown. Then the only question is, who are they working for . . . Them or us?" It really came down to a question of trust. Once Sheikh Zaid had told him, "If you don't know the thing, you must know the man."

Still, Braithwaite had always worn a white hat, the Scorpion told himself. But it was no longer just a question of the girl. Women simply didn't matter that much in the Middle East. What had Harris dropped him into this time, he wondered. If he had owned any life insurance, now was the time to start inspecting the policy.

"How is it you speak Arabic so well, *asayid* Shaw?" al-Amir probed.

"My father was an oilman. He brought me out to Dharan when I was still a boy."

"Those were the days," Braithwaite muttered nostalgically.

Braithwaite was taking his own sweet time getting to it, the Scorpion thought. What was the old man afraid of?

"Were they?" the Scorpion said sharply.

"Have a b-bit of the old single malt, *habibi*," Braithwaite said, gesturing at the bottle of Glenlivet on the table.

The Scorpion uneasily poured himself a stiff one. All this hail-fellow-well-met was making him nervous. What comes next? he wondered. The Good Conduct Medal and an engraved invitation to Buckingham Palace?

"Prince Abdul Sa'ad's back in town," Braithwaite remarked mildly, glancing over at the TV. "He's been over quite a bit, lately."

"The prince is an important man," al-Amir remarked enigmatically. He rubbed his cheek and the Scorpion noticed a thin white trace of a scar there. He'd been making a mistake if he took the smooth, mild-mannered Bahraini for a cream puff, he told himself.

"Maybe the bank forgot to stamp his deposit slip," the Scorpion said and the two men chuckled. While the gleaming row of banks on Government Road had become the money center of the Middle East ever since Beirut had fallen apart, Prince Abdul Sa'ad could have one of his retainers do all the banking he needed by telephone from Riyadh.

"I knew him as a b-b-boy . . . selfish little b-bugger," Braithwaite remarked. The Scorpion looked at him curiously. It was a serious charge. A true Bedu would rather die than be labeled "selfish." Everything belongs to Allah. To be selfish about possessions was to deny God what was rightfully his. Arabs judged a man not by what he kept, but by what he gave away.

"They say he likes western women . . . very much western women," al-Amir said, wrinkling his nose with distaste. It was probably incomprehensible to al-Amir, who like most Arabs undoubtedly liked his women fleshy, functional and obedient.

"So do I," the Scorpion grinned.

"Too skinny," al-Amir sniffed. "They think they are men in disguise."

"That's how we like them," the Scorpion smiled.

"You're a *Ciaour*. For you there is no hope," al-Amir grinned back. It was like old home week, the Scorpion thought. Next they'd be discussing the World Cup finals.

"Blondes," Braithwaite put in, his eyes beginning to dull with the whisky.

"What was that?" the Scorpion replied, putting down his drink. His eyes had gone icy gray, like winter frost. They were finally getting down to it.

"They say he's p-partial to long-haired blondes, *habibi*," Braithwaite said, nervously glancing at al-Amir for support. The Scorpion's eyes were cold as stainless steel as he glanced at the two men. No wonder Harris had warned him away from the station in Riyadh and told him to report through poor

George Macready in Doha. He had known George in Nam and he supposed that they had posted Macready to a shithole like Qatar for the unpardonable sin of opposing Company policy in Southeast Asia and being proven right. He had thought at the time that Harris was doing it to protect his cover from a leaky embassy, but that wasn't it at all. They were telling him that the snatch reached into the Saudi royal family itself. Of course they were running scared. It was political, after all. Nobody would want to touch it. As for the girl, nobody gave a shit about her . . . except maybe him, he thought.

"Sheikh al-Khatifa is curious about Prince Abdul Sa'ad's recent visits," al-Amir said, playing nervously with his prayer beads.

"Why doesn't he just ask him?" the Scorpion said and the three men laughed loudly enough to attract attention from the next table where an Iraqi businessman had been bragging about the new Japanese TV he had bought for his son's Pontiac Firebird, and shooting his cuffs so that no one could miss his gold Piaget watch. The joke, of course, was that Arabic was a language of implications and ambiguities and truth could only be approached obliquely. In intelligence matters, it was even worse. In their world, no one ever said anything straight out. The Scorpion remembered a classic line religiously recited to all the CTP recruits at the Farm: "Complete paranoids would make good agents if they weren't so trusting."

"Very good . . . why not just ask him?" al-Amir snickered.

"You see . . . it's more than just the blonde. P-p-pepper on a hen's belly . . . that's all that is," Braithwaite said, his false teeth clicking like a geiger counter. Like most old desert rats, he had more than a touch of the Puritan in him. That's why when Lowell Thomas had once asked T. E. Lawrence why he liked the desert, Lawrence had replied: "Because it's clean."

"Not for her," the Scorpion said. Braithwaite looked at him blankly, his face ridged with seams like a radial tire. The British SIS must have been really desperate to bring the old retread out, the Scorpion thought. He hadn't been in Bahrain two hours and the needle was already in the red zone.

"I suppose not," Braithwaite said at last. When he picked up his glass again, his hand was shaking. He quickly put the glass down and pulled the offending hand out of sight.

"What about the girl?" the Scorpion asked. Al-Amir sighed and fingered his beads.

"T-t-tummy friction, that's all . . . rub, rub . . . pepper on a hen's belly," Braithwaite shrugged, trying to smile like a man of the world. Something was frightening him all right, the Scorpion decided.

"Nuruddin," al-Amir said, dropping the name like an Alka Seltzer tablet into water, then he sat back waiting for it to fizz.

"Big man . . . import-export . . . knows everyone. His daughter is married to Sheikh al-Khatifa's nephew," Braithwaite said, rubbing his thumb against his fingers in the universal sign for money.

The Scorpion nodded grimly. So that's what happened to the girl, he thought. Import-export was the classic cover in ports like Bahrain for illegal smuggling. Except that with his money and connections, this Nuruddin probably could have taken her off the plane with a brass band playing. No wonder Braithwaite was scared.

"Does Nuruddin have a connection with Prince Abdul Sa'ad?" the Scorpion asked. Now he knew why they needed an outsider and why no one wanted to touch it with a ten-foot pole. It was the kind of log that might come crashing down on you if you weren't careful, and if you did manage to turn it over, God only knew what slimy things might crawl out.

"Do you know the Place of the Tombs near Sar?" al-Amir asked.

The Scorpion nodded.

"Nuruddin and the prince are meeting there tonight . . . secretly. Perhaps you might find what you're looking for," al-

Amir said. His face revealed nothing, as though he wore one of those black face-masks still worn by the older Gulf women. The Scorpion flushed angrily.

"Is that where Chambers went?" he demanded. Al-Amir looked as shocked as if the Scorpion had reached for food with his left hand, the most unforgivable breach of manners possible.

The color drained out of Braithwaite's face as though a plug had been pulled in his neck. "Now . . . now . . . hardly cricket, old lad," he stuttered.

"Just checking," the Scorpion grinned. He felt like the commander of the Light Brigade who's just been given his orders and knows it's a fuck-up and that there isn't a damn thing he can do about it, except go charging like an asshole into the Valley of Death. "This isn't a business for heroes. Guts stand about as much chance against brains and logistics as a rabbit in a tiger cage," Koenig had told them once. Well, what would Koenig do if he were here now, the Scorpion wondered. He didn't really want to think about that, because he suspected that Koenig would be looking for the emergency exit at this point. Almost superstitiously his fingers touched the pocket where he kept the girl's photo. Although she didn't know he existed, he was really all she had. He took a deep breath, because it was time to show his hole card and he didn't know whether he was holding an ace or a deuce.

"Just remember, it's the girl I'm after," the Scorpion said.

"Allah be praised," al-Amir murmured, piously raising his hands.

"Quite . . . quite," Braithwaite said, nervously pouring himself a glassful. His eyes were teary and the Scorpion wondered if Braithwaite was remembering him as a skinny teenager in the desert, all those years ago. The Scorpion nodded at the old man and stood up. They looked at each other for a long moment, both of them remembering their first meeting in the flat searing plain near Wadi er Rumania. They had both changed so much since then, it was something of a miracle that they could still recognize each other. Or perhaps old friends don't really recognize each other, perhaps they just acknowledge the walking images of their memories, he thought.

"Good seeing you again," the Scorpion said.

"*Salaam, asayid* . . . Shaw," al-Amir murmured.

"G-good luck!" Braithwaite called out, looking as if he knew the Scorpion might need it.

Place of the Tombs

STARS FILLED THE DOME of night as though it had snowed diamonds on the sky. High over the distant Sar Mosque floated a perfect crescent moon, gleaming like a shaving from a new silver coin. The crescent was upturned, horns pointing at the Milky Way, a silvery bowl to catch stars. The minarets of the mosque were shrouded in scaffolding like cobwebs. The Scorpion remembered the scaffolding from the time when he was a small boy and his father had taken him to see the ancient Place of the Tombs. The repair work was still going on and might go on yet for centuries. It didn't really matter how long it took. God was in no hurry.

The Scorpion stood in one of the shallow graves opened by archaeologists and trained his binoculars at the campfire. He had carefully piled the bones to one side so he wouldn't step on the skeleton and reveal his presence by cracking any of the brittle bones. He didn't think whoever's grave it was would mind. The skeleton had been in the dry earth for thousands of years, since the days of the fabled kingdom of Dilmun.

Long ago in humanity's springtime, Dilmun was said to be an earthly paradise. Some even claimed it was the Garden of Eden. It was mentioned in the *Epic of Gilgamesh*, the first

45

narrative ever written. According to the story, the Sumerian King Gilgamesh crossed the sea from Mesopotamia to Dilmun in his quest for the "flower that makes men immortal," so old are mankind's dreams, he mused. Perhaps the skeleton had lived in that happy kingdom, of which the tablets say:

> The land of Dilmun is holy,
> The land of Dilmun is pure.
> In Dilmun the raven utters no cry,
> The wolf snatches not the lamb.

Now, nothing remained of the dream but the ancient words and tens of thousands of mounds in the desert. Squatters lived in cardboard and tin-can shacks among the mounds. They dug holes in the sides of the mounds and used them for open kilns to make cheap pottery, feeding the fires with cast-off lumber from the construction projects around Manama. The night was illuminated by the firelight from the ovens, as though from thousands of red eyes, lighting the darkness with a twilight glow. It gave the Scorpion excellent visibility, as well as shadowy cover; ideal conditions for a surveillance.

He could see them clearly through the binoculars. Prince Abdul Sa'ad and Nuruddin, whom Braithwaite had described to him, and several others were politely drinking coffee from a copper pot gleaming in the firelight. They were engaged in intense conversation and he'd have traded his Swiss account for a bug that would let him hear what they were saying. But he was too far away. No sound reached him on the faint sea breeze which carried only the salt tang of the sea, smoke from the kilns and the medicinal scent of the eucalyptus trees from the direction of the beach reclamation project. In the distance he could make out the shadowy forms of a small herd of wild camels grazing among the mounds. There was a vast sense of desolation, of endless vistas of sand and ancient tombs. It was as if Bahrain was the center of the desert, instead of a sandy dagger-shaped island barely ten miles wide and twice as long.

He considered moving closer, but that was too dangerous,

even with the cover provided by the black *bisht* he wore over western clothes. The area was heavily patrolled by armed tribesmen and it hadn't been easy to slip through. The fact that they felt they needed armed guards instead of retainers disturbed him. Were the guards there to protect them from prying eyes, or from each other, he wondered. Then too, he pondered why they hadn't had the meeting in Nuruddin's house, or some other private place. That bothered him. They had gone to far too much trouble if what they were doing was merely business, or even criminal. Their connections made them virtually immune from any charges, he reflected. So it could only be political.

He pulled the Nikon F3 camera with the special 1.2 lens from his robe and began to snap photos of the men around the campfire. He took his time and made sure of telephoto close-ups of all of them. One of them wore a lightweight suit and looked like a Latin, which seemed wildly preposterous. Another wore the shirtlike *fuuta* of a Yemeni, a boomerang-shaped *jambiyya* dagger at his waist. His cheek bulged like a chipmunk with a wad of *khat* leaves. What the hell would a Saudi prince be doing with a Latin and a social inferior like a Yemeni? he wondered. Well, he would send the film to Macready and maybe George could ID them. The important thing was that he had verified a close link between Abdul Sa'ad and Nuruddin. Assuming—and that's a hell of an assumption, *habibi*—that Nuruddin had sold the girl to Abdul Sa'ad, who liked his blondes, he could try to pick up the trail in Riyadh.

Except that Harris hadn't set him running like a rat in a maze just to find the girl, he thought. That could have been handled through channels by mid-level types. The station chief in Riyadh would have given it to the ambassador, who would have whispered it to King Salim. The king would have denied it, but the message would have been delivered and the Crown Prince would have passed the word down. There would have been a little titillating gossip within the byzantine tangle of the royal family and a few might cluck over Abdul Sa'ad's wicked ways, but they would keep it in the family and the prince would be forced to give up the girl. He figured Abdul Sa'ad wouldn't want it to get to the *ulama*. Not even the king would want to face any criticism from the strict Sunni religious council and if Kelly was still alive, she'd be delivered in due course, after a stern warning from the Company to keep her lid shut on her little Arabian adventure. That was how it should have gone down.

But watching the firelight play on the faces around the campfire, the Scorpion knew that getting the girl wasn't the mission at all. He should have realized it before, he thought, cursing his own stupidity. "Things are a little dicey in Arabia," Harris had said. The Scorpion's thoughts had returned to that sentence time and again, like a popular tune you hear on the radio in the morning and can't get rid of all day. But if finding the girl wasn't the mission, what was? "Sometimes, when hunting rabbits, one puts up a lion," Koenig used to say, rocking on the balls of his feet in the Quonset hut during their paramilitary training at the Farm; what the trainees used to call "the boom-boom course."

The answer to the riddle was in front of him around the campfire, like a gift-wrapped package waiting to be opened. There was no way to signal Macready, his nominal case officer on this one, because he was already in the red zone and it really didn't matter anyway. He would have to get closer and find out what they were up to.

"Might as well," Sergeant Walker used to say as they saddled up for a patrol in Indian country in Quang Tri province, "that's what they're paying us for." But his feet didn't want to move. He felt safe in the grave, that "fine and private place." If they spotted him, he didn't think they'd just pour him a cup of coffee and hand him a bowl of *mansuf*. Not after what they had done to Chambers.

He knew that the answer to the girl's disappearance was in Riyadh and he could just slip away now, pass the photos

48

on to Macready and let all the IA computer types in Langley analyze the pictures to death. That was the smart thing to do. The only thing stopping him was the thought that he was the Scorpion, a professional. He could just picture Koenig's incredulous glance and hear him say, "You mean, they were all right there and you didn't try to get closer? You just fucking stood there and snapped photos like some little old lady from Iowa on the Capitol steps?" He would have to get closer. We are all the prisoners of our own self-images, he thought as he opened the camera and slipped the film cartridge into his jockey shorts, where it rested uncomfortably next to his groin. As Koenig used to say, "It's the safest place. That way they've got to jerk you off before they can take it away."

He hid the camera and binoculars under the jumble of dry bones. There was no need to hide a gun. He hadn't brought one. It was better that way. There were too many guards to outgun and if they did nail him he would have a chance to lie his way out of it. Packing a camera and a gun was an amateurish giveaway, like wearing a trenchcoat. Besides, guns tended to limit the conversation. When the Mutayr were first teaching him to shoot with those old British Enfield .303s, Sheikh Zaid had told him, "Words are better weapons than guns, little *dhimmi*. The Prophet conquered Arabia with a book, not a sword." Still, it felt pretty damn antsy jumping into the middle of an armed camp packing nothing but a film cartridge in his jockey shorts, he thought. He rolled over the stone ledge of the grave and, crouching, moved on cat feet through the shadows.

He played tag with the shadows, moving silently from mound to mound. Armed guards carrying AK-47s formed a ragged defense perimeter that gazed outward from the campfire and the Scorpion had to remind himself that they didn't know he was there and that he was virtually invisible in his black *bisht*. He moved slowly in a careful zig-zag pattern, wondering if they could hear the pounding of his heart that sounded so loudly in his own ears. They'd cut off Chambers' arms and legs! Don't think about that, blinking the sweat from his eyes. Think about the next step.

He was almost within arm's length of one of the guards and briefly debated taking him out. It wasn't worth the risk, he decided. The slightest sound would be suicidal. He went around the mound until he glimpsed the campfire again. The ground was flat and without cover from here to the fire. He could get no closer. He silently sank to one knee, because the eye of an observer would tend to look for a face at full height. Another edge was that their night vision would be reduced by the firelight. They were about fifty feet away and he could just make out the soft murmur of conversation. He cupped his hand behind his right ear to help catch the sound and pointed it towards the fire. The right ear was preferred because it fed a fraction more directly to the left hemisphere of the brain, which processes all sound data.

"His death will be the signal," the Latin said. "Unless he dies immediately . . ." the rest was unintelligible.

So it was a hit, the Scorpion thought. But who was the target?

One of the Arabs said something about the "Israeli dogs" and he saw Prince Abdul Sa'ad dismiss the notion with a wave of his hand.

"Can their ground forces cross the Nefud?" Abdul Sa'ad said and there was a murmur of agreement from the others mingled with a few chuckles at the insanity of any land force attempting to strike across the hundreds of miles of sand dunes that were the Nefud desert.

The Scorpion stiffened, unable to believe what he was hearing. It was the craziest thing he had ever heard. What on earth could ever make the Israelis want to cross the Nefud? To go where? Riyadh? And for what purpose? To get to the Nefud, the Israelis would first have to conquer all of Jordan and a good chunk of the Middle East besides! Not even the most fanatic religious nut of the right-wing Israeli Likud party would ever even conceive of the idea. Yet, here were powerful intelligent men actually discussing the bizarre notion. It was crazy!

Even before he had consciously identified the sound of a scraped pebble, he was already rising in a twisting motion to face the Arab guard. The guard motioned with the AK-47 and then made the mistake of grabbing the Scorpion's right sleeve near the wrist, presumably to drag him into the light. Without thinking, the Scorpion was into the sequence which Koenig had drilled into them so often that they could do it in their sleep (and sometimes did, because the training included being attacked in bed in the middle of the night). He splayed the fingers of his right hand, to loosen the grip on his wrist, and rotated his hand up. At the top of the arc, he twisted his hand to grab the Arab's wrist, brought his left hand up to lock the hands together and continued the counter-clockwise motion, breaking the Arab's wrist. The Arab had a fraction of a second to scream before the Scorpion thrust the knife edge of his left hand into the Arab's throat, smashing the Adam's apple.

The Arab was dead before he hit the ground, the Scorpion already plucking away the AK-47 and running through the shadows, because in those few seconds all hell had broken loose. Yet even through his fear, anguish stabbed at his heart, because in the Arab's scream he saw two lives, Kelly's and his own, sizzle into nothing like two specks of spit on a hot griddle.

Scattered shots were fired and there were shouts as guards ran wildly about, milling in confusion like insects in a broken anthill. Prince Abdul Sa'ad, Nuruddin and the others stood uncertainly, caught for a moment in the flickering light. For the briefest instant, Abdul Sa'ad's eyes scanned the ancient mounds, trying to seek out the intruder. Then they ran towards cars parked nearby.

"He's there—to the right!" the Scorpion shouted to two guards, who began running towards the mound where he was pointing. He ran behind them for a moment, then peeled back towards the mosque, where he had parked his rental car. He stopped because guards had already closed off that direction, then broke towards a small cluster of potters' shacks. Someone shouted and dust skipped around his feet as the bullets ricocheted off the ground. He had been spotted!

He sprang into a forward roll in the direction of the open grave, perhaps because that had been the last safe spot for him. He leaped over a stone ledge and circled a large mound. If he could just get far enough away he might lose them among the mounds, he thought, his breath coming in ragged gasps. He swerved as he heard them coming around the other side of the mound. As he turned back, he saw the rifle butt out of the corner of his eye and started to duck, but it was too late. He felt a terrible thud above his right eye and then the diamond-bright stars were sliding into darkness, as though the sky was a black velvet jeweler's tray that someone had tipped to one side.

Sar

THE SMELL OF AMMONIA was thick in his nostrils and he watched an enormous hand recede and then it was back, slapping his face from side to side. He tried to slip back into the darkness, but they doused him with cold water and when he finally opened his eyes and tried to move, he found that he was tied to a chair. A round moonfaced image floated just out of focus and when it came closer it looked grotesquely flat and stretched, like a face painted on a child's balloon. Then he heard a swish and he grunted involuntarily as his side erupted in pain. The balloon became a reddish moon and finally resolved itself into the piggish face of a giant Arab with a wrestler's build and the dull mechanical eyes of a mental defective. The brute stepped away and the Scorpion could see a large rubber hose dangling from his huge hand. His sides ached as if a troupe of flamenco dancers had been using him for a stage floor and he wondered if any ribs were broken.

He could no longer pretend to be out and looked around. He was in a small room with blue walls, painted blue to ward off the evil eye, no doubt. The room was lit by a single naked bulb, dangling from a twisted ceiling wire like a gibbet. There were four of them, all Arabs. Except for the brute, they were all cut from the same pattern of slender builds, hawk noses and caramel-colored skin. Two of them were dressed in white *thaubs*. The one by the closed door covered with blue handprints to protect against the evil *afreet* spirits had an AK-47. The other off to his side had one of those cheap Italian automatics. The leader was a small, slim Arab with a thick moustache and a pointed parrot's beak of a nose. He wore a shiny western suit and there was a swagger in his shoulders which suggested that he was more accustomed to wearing a uniform. His eyes were black and empty, like chunks of coal stuck in his face. The Scorpion recognized him as one of the men sitting around the campfire with Abdul Sa'ad and Nuruddin. The Arab sat on the edge of a crude wooden table scored with notches and the Scorpion tried not to think about how those notches got there, because as Harold Gallagher, the fat, bespectacled agent who had run the Phoenix operation in Nam, once told him: "The subject's anticipation is the key ingredient in the interrogation process."

Harold always looked like the kind of perpetual loser who might be found in an adult movie theater on a rainy night, but in fact he was a sadistic psychopath who had found his true vocation in Nam. He used to brag that he could get the most dedicated VC to give him Uncle Ho's phone number in less than twenty minutes.

The Arab studied him carefully, pensively stroking his

moustache. The Scorpion understood him perfectly. Torture created an almost obscenely intimate relationship between the interrogator and the victim.

The only other object in the room was a large iron cauldron sitting on the tiled floor. A strong chemical odor filled the room and suddenly the Scorpion's pulse began to pound. He took a *kiya* breath to control his pulse rate, because he couldn't stop thinking about what they had done to Chambers.

The only good thing was that they were amateurs. He knew it because they hadn't done a complete body search. He could still feel the film cartridge resting uncomfortably in his shorts. That and the fact that they couldn't identify him. He had only just arrived in Bahrain and, of course, he carried no ID. He was a professional.

"God is Great," the Scorpion declared. The interrogator looked at him curiously.

"By the beard of the Prophet, this is a terrible mistake, *asayid*. I am Mahmud the potter, from Aali . . ." the Scorpion broke off, because the interrogator was laughing. The interrogator looked at the others and they too began to laugh. Just one merry band, the Scorpion thought, chagrined. He shrugged and they laughed even harder. Still, it had been worth a try. Anything was worth a try. He had seen too many men die because they had given up. The interrogator wiped the tears from his eyes and shook his head.

"Truly, *asayid* Shaw. You are most amusing," the interrogator said with a wide smirk. The shock of hearing his cover name rippled through the Scorpion like something indigestible. Your point, he thought and inclined his head to the Arab. "The interrogator's objective is best achieved if he can convince the subject that he knows more than he really does," Gallagher once told him. They were drinking at Madame Wu's, that bar on Tu Do Street in Saigon where the MPs never came because according to the story, Madame Wu had once had "razor girls" service a squad of MPs. Razor girls were VC women who reputedly placed razor blades, edge out, inside the one part of their anatomy a male was most interested in. The Scorpion didn't know whether the story was true or not. Personally he had always figured the MPs never came around because President Thieu got a cut of the profits. "Give the subject a tiny bit of information that he doesn't think you know and you can get him to believe you know it all," Gallagher had said, his wash and wear suit hanging gray and wrinkled like an elephant skin.

"By the beard of the Prophet . . ." the Scorpion began again.

"Enough!" the Arab screamed, his voice climbing into a register usually reserved for hysterical sopranos. "Do you think we are children, that you play with us?"

The Scorpion shrugged. It looked like the Arab was going to play Good Guy/Bad Guy all by himself. The Arab got off the table and stood before him. He looked even shorter standing up than he had sitting on the table.

"You will tell us please, who you are working for and why you were spying on us," the Arab declared sharply, ominously slapping his leg with a swagger stick to show his impatience. He was an army officer, all right, the Scorpion thought. The kind of bullshit martinet who would've been a prime candidate for "fragging" in Nam. Prick the little Napoleon's pride and something interesting might tumble out, he thought. It was essential that he identify the interrogator, who spoke Arabic with a Palestinian accent. But he had to be sure.

"I don't talk to camel turds descended from a long line of pig slime mated with dog droppings," the Scorpion said contemptuously.

"Your mother's diseased cunt!" screamed the Arab, slashing the Scorpion's face with his swagger stick. "I'll teach you how to address a major in . . ." a sickly, embarrassed flush crept over the Arab's face and the Scorpion smiled despite the searing pain streaking down the left side of his face. Drops of blood trickled down, staining his *bisht* with red spots that disappeared into the black cloth.

"Very good, *asayid* Shaw. Most ingenious," the major said, shaking his head, as though the Scorpion had just scored with an impressive slam-dunk.

"All praise belongs to Allah," the Scorpion said piously.

"Who do you work for? I assure you I will not ask again."

The Scorpion muttered something unprintable, but this time the major (major in what?) restrained himself and ordered the big Arab to bring over the cauldron. The big Arab put on outsized heavy rubber gloves that reached all the way up his arms and a big rubber apron. Then he picked up the heavy cauldron and set it in front of the Scorpion. The cauldron was filled with a clear liquid. It looked like water and the Scorpion began to get a very bad feeling.

"Show him," the major ordered. The big Arab pulled a piece of chicken from his pocket and tossed it into the cauldron, which began to bubble and hiss like a basket of snakes.

"Concentrated sulphuric acid," the major remarked conversationally. "It will dissolve skin, flesh, even bone . . . but slowly. Not like Arabia where mercy is shown to thieves by using a sword. That is too quick. For spies something slower is needed," the major declared, his eyes gleaming. He snapped his fingers and the big Arab stuck his glove in the cauldron and fished around until he brought out the piece of chicken. All that was left were a few strands of white flesh and a partially eaten-away bone.

The bastards, the Scorpion thought wildly. They hadn't cut Chambers' arms and legs off, they'd burned them off! The bastards, he thought, his gorge rising up at the thought of it. He forced himself to take a *kiya* breath, because unless he could come up with something, and fast, he was next.

"Now I asked you in all seriousness and for the truly last time, who are you and who do you work for? I would hate to subject you to our little bath," the major said sympathetically, using the old torturer's trick of implying that he was being forced to do the dirty work against his better nature, only because of the victim's pig-headed recalcitrance. He stroked

56

his moustache, waiting as if he had nothing better to do. The Scorpion had to come up with something. Anything to delay that acid bath that made his skin crawl.

"My name is Carlos. I work with Dr. Habash of the Popular Front for the Liberation of Palestine," the Scorpion declared arrogantly. Switching sides to make the interrogator believe that you're on his side is the surest way to confuse things.

"Impossible! Habash knows this is an Al-Fatah . . ." the major broke off in horror. Got you, you fucker! the Scorpion thought exultantly. The interrogator was a major in Al-Fatah, the striking arm of the Palestine Liberation Organization. That tied Prince Abdul Sa'ad to the PLO, Nuruddin and the Yemenis, who had also been at the meeting. The only piece missing was the Latin.

Except that it didn't look like the information would ever do him much good, because the Palestinian major was glaring at him, realizing his error. Even if the Scorpion was the infamous terrorist Carlos, no one would fault the major for getting the truth out of him. And if he wasn't Carlos, so much the better. The Scorpion shivered as he watched awareness dawn on the major. Either way, they would never let him leave this room alive. What was left of him, he mused bitterly.

"I don't believe you," the major said, a crazy glare in his eyes. "You are perhaps right-handed? Fine. It is your right hand that you will lose first. When you are screaming, then you will tell us the truth."

"Your mother's diseased cunt came from a syphilitic Zionist pig's cock!" the Scorpion shouted, spitting at the major.

"First, his right arm . . . all the way!" screamed the major in that high-pitched voice. The huge Arab and the one with the automatic were galvanized into obedience. They were furious with him, which was what he wanted, because you don't want your enemies thinking clearly.

The Scorpion's eyes darted furiously, measuring angles, which were going to be critical. Everything depended on where the Arabs were standing in relationship to each other when he moved. The real problem was the Arab by the door with the Kalachnikov. He figured the Arab wouldn't shoot with all the bodies tangled together, but even if it all worked perfectly, there would be a moment when he would have a clear field of fire and the Scorpion didn't know what he could do about that. Underneath it all was the queasy question about why Chambers hadn't put up more of a fight. What was the missing factor? But there was no time to think about that, about anything, because they were already moving. He began the rhythmic *kokyu no henko* breathing to clear his mind, remembering how Koichi would stand in the middle of the *do-jang*, oblivious to anything but the sound of his own breathing.

He got his answer about Chambers when the huge Arab grabbed his head in a choke hold with one arm and his right wrist with the other. The man was incredibly strong. The major cut his bonds with a gleaming stiletto. The Scorpion's eyes never left the dagger as the major put it on the table. The Arab with the automatic put the gun away and moved closer to the cauldron to lend a hand as the huge Arab lifted the Scorpion out of the chair like a baby. That left only the Arab by the door with a gun at hand, the Scorpion thought, relaxing his legs so they had to half-drag him to the cauldron. He tried to move his right arm against the strength of the big Arab, but it was impossible. It was like pushing against the side of a truck and now he knew for sure why Chambers had bought it. It would have to be right, he knew. He wasn't going to get a second chance. The major leaned against the table, smirking as they pulled him over to the cauldron.

He took one last breath, remembering how Koichi would lecture them in his pedantic oriental way, hardly raising a sweat as he tossed them around the *do-jang*. "The more stronger, the more better," Koichi would say. "The essence is to use your opponent's own strength to defeat him." That was the theory, at least.

"Forget the others, concentrate on the one," Koichi would

say. The choke hold is one of the easiest to break, he remembered. All that is required is to jerk the head back in a line perpendicular to the plane formed by the opponent's arm. It helps if you have a free hand to push against your opponent's arm, as well. Except that he wished Koichi were here to test the theory against the big Arab instead of him, because his neck and right arm felt as if they'd been set in concrete. Instinctively he pressed away from the cauldron, the liquid darkened by their shadows, as they forced him to bend towards it. As he exhaled, the rage exploded inside him like a bubble popping. They were going to do it to him . . . to him! Even as his hand's reflection in the acid almost touched his own flesh, he had begun his move.

He jerked his head out and jammed his right foot into the back of the big Arab's knee, followed by a knee to the coccyx, breaking the Arab's balance. At the same time he spread his fingers and yanked his right arm sideways in the same direction the Arab had been pushing him, their combined forces knocking the big Arab into the cauldron, which tipped over, splashing the acid on to the major's feet. As the big Arab lost balance, pulling the Scorpion with him, the Scorpion kicked the other Arab in the knee, tripping him into the spreading acid puddle.

The major was howling as he hopped around the room in a bizarre jig, jerking his burning feet like a marionette. The Arab he had kicked was flopping on the wet floor like a fish and screaming as the Scorpion struggled with the big Arab underneath him who, despite the acid, still managed to jam his massive forearm against the Scorpion's throat and hang on. The Scorpion pushed with everything he had at the big Arab's arm, but this second choke-hold was solid. The Scorpion's breath was gone and his eyes began to fill with light as he felt consciousness trickling away. With a last effort, he jammed his right elbow into the big Arab's ribs. The Arab just grunted and held on. It was like hitting a solid wall. He tried it again, at the same time slicing with his left hand into the Arab's groin. The big Arab screamed and he sliced again with the left, as he brought his right forearm around and smashed a back fist into the big Arab's temple.

The Scorpion rolled free and grabbed at the table, knocking it over as the Arab by the door began to fire. He felt something stab his neck as he grabbed the dagger from the floor and whirling, threw it at the Arab with the gun. Then his balance was gone, as the big Arab grabbed at his leg. He fell in a heap, kicking wildly and rolled towards the door, where the Arab with the gun still stood, stupidly staring at the handle of the dagger sticking out of his belly.

The Scorpion sprang at the door, launching into a flying *tiuchaki*. From somewhere in the corner, he heard the sound of an automatic as the major fired, but that didn't matter. He began the reverse kick in mid-air, feinting with the left knee, but as the Arab tried to weakly block with the AK-47, the Scorpion caught him in the neck with the ball of the right foot and they both crashed against the door. The Scorpion grabbed the Kalachnikov and shot the major in the head, then raked across the room killing the Arab crawling towards the automatic. The big Arab loomed like a truck as he charged across the room. The Scorpion fired point blank. Three obscene red flowers blossomed on the big Arab's chest and he crashed at the Scorpion's feet.

He heard the sound of shouts outside and backed against the wall near the door as two Arabs, guns drawn, ran into the room. He shot them both from behind. One of them tried to turn and fire and as the Scorpion squeezed the trigger, there was only an empty click that reverberated to the bottom of his stomach. As the Arab struggled to aim, the Scorpion swung the butt at the side of the man's skull, cracking it with the sound of a well-hit baseball.

The Scorpion threw away the empty AK-47 and grabbed the major's Walther PPK automatic. Then he dropped into a two-handed firing position aimed at the doorway, but there was nothing else in the room except for the sound of his own labored breathing. He glanced down at his arms and saw that his left arm was covered with blood. His right arm burned with pain where the acid had eaten through. The side of his neck felt like someone was turning a corkscrew in it and he felt lightheaded. Loss of blood, he told himself stupidly. Got to get out of here, some part of his mind was screaming at him. He bent down and used one of the Arabs' *kaffiyehs* to wipe off his arms, then he tore off a clean strip and tied it around his neck like a scarf. His hands were slippery with blood and he kept wiping them on his *bisht*, already growing stiff with drying blood. He heard shouts from outside, checked the clip and cocked the Walther. It was time to perform the classic military maneuver known as "Getting the fuck out of here," he told himself.

He charged out through the doorway with a forward roll —luckily, as a bullet split the air where his head would have been had he been upright. The gun fired again from the center of the courtyard and he spotted the muzzle flash coming from inside a dark Ford Mustang. He snapped into the kneeling two-handed firing position, squeezing off three shots at the open car window. Without waiting for return fire, he ran to the car and opened the door. A body slumped out, its head shattered and pulpy, like a split-open melon. He pulled out the body, started the Mustang and slammed it into gear. He was already rolling as he pulled the car door shut, bullets buzzing into the wing like metal wasps.

Automatic fire turned the rear windshield into a dense white spider's web. He ducked his head and hit the gas, aiming for the locked steel courtyard gate. As he smashed through the gate he heard a roar behind him as a big white Mercedes started in pursuit. The road was a narrow black tunnel, the hot air roaring through the windows. Insects spattered against the windshield like brown rain as he tore through the darkness.

He risked a glance out of the window behind him. The house where they had held him was floodlit, a giant white marble slab that looked like a modernistic tomb, and he shuddered. Nuruddin's? He wished he knew where the hell he was. The Mercedes was closing up fast, sparks of light popping from the side window like a series of flashbulbs, and he floored the accelerator. The Mustang's transmission whined and then surged into high gear. He glanced at the tachometer and the fuel gauge. It was half full, which gave him a little added lightness, yet provided him with enough fuel to go around the island twenty times, if he knew where he was going. Then out of the corner of his eye he caught sight of the lighted gantry that was the BAPCO refinery and the reflection of the big dish of the Earth-satellite station far off to the left, so he knew he must be somewhere near Awali. Unless he could get away soon, he would find himself on the beach at the end of the island with nowhere to go. He glanced back again, almost swerving off the road. The Mercedes was only a few yards behind.

He was edging up to 100 on the speedometer, but it wasn't doing much good. The Mercedes was faster and heavier and all they had to do was bump him anywhere off-center to send him careening out of control. If the road wasn't a straightaway, driving skill could come into play, but it was straight and he was running out of time. He memorized the road ahead and flicked off his lights, making it a little harder for them to aim and follow him. A single bullet in his gas tank or one of the tires would finish it right then and there.

There was a loud cracking sound, like a frozen river breaking up in spring, and the rear window disappeared. A roar of rushing air blasted through the Mustang as it surged forward, the air resistance suddenly reduced. Now he could see the headlights of the Mercedes instead of a white film in the rearview mirror. It was a wonderful break, except that the Mercedes was only inches from his rear bumper. He flicked on the headlights and watched the front end of the Mercedes swerve and recede as the driver braked to avoid what he had assumed from the rear lights to be the Mustang's sudden braking. The driver should have realized that braking, given the Mercedes' heavier mass, would have been suicidal, the Scorpion thought. But it hadn't bought him much. Even worse, the Mercedes was coming up again on his left side and it wasn't a trick you could use twice.

The two cars sped like bullets through the night. Ahead, he spotted a fork, one road curving off to the right to Zallaq, the left twisting into Sakhir all the way down towards Ras al-Barr at the southern tip of the island. Left, he decided, perhaps because it was a longer road. He needed every edge he could get. His Walther was virtually useless against the AK-47 in the Mercedes and it was all wrong, anyway. Something kept nagging at him and then he had it. They'd used his cover name! They'd known all along.

The glare from the Mercedes' headlights filled the rearview mirror and he felt the bump on the left side, like a gentle push from behind, and he lost control. The headlights raked across the side of the road as the Mustang slid on to the dirt shoulder. He turned the wheel to the right, fighting the skid, and the front of the car rocked forward and back like a metronome. A palm tree loomed on his right, seeming as wide an obstacle as a mountain and then he was flying off the road on to the mushy sand surface of the desert, just barely grazing the tree. If he stuck in the sand, he was a dead man.

He used the momentum to throw the Mustang into a diagonal skid back towards the road. The Mercedes had dropped back to watch and now it came on again as the Mustang buckled over rocks and slammed back on to the concrete in a series of small bounces, like a stone skipped across a lake. Just ahead were other cars moving sedately through the narrow main road of Sakhir. He could see people on the pavements, and lights from the cafés and *dars* along the street. The street was too narrow to pass the other cars. He was plugged like a cork in a bottle.

He hit the horn and bounced up on the pavement, honking savagely as he weaved through the pedestrians who were

63

jumping for dear life. He smashed through the tables and chairs of a sidewalk café, the scream of metal grinding against the bumper, then swerved back on to the road to avoid smashing into a telephone pole. He floored it again and when he checked the rear-view mirror, the Mercedes had fallen about a hundred yards behind. A number of cars ahead were making a right turn and he angled off the road to cut them off, bouncing like an old flivver on the bumpy track. He saw lights ahead and suddenly found himself on an old abandoned air strip, filled with cars slowly wheeling in a giant oval pattern.

It was the *après*-dinner promenade, Bahraini-style, a kind of Middle-Eastern Van Nuys Boulevard complete with Egyptian music blasting from the car stereos. All the young blades in their shiny American and German cars were driving around the giant circle to spy the girls, many of whom were daringly unveiled. The girls came in giggling groups, or with a somber-faced male relative. There were lots of smiles and waves, but any real conversation or dating was unthinkable. In some of the men's cars, faces were lit by the flickering blue light of a television, a further advertisement of affluence. In a way, with its buzz of engines and the headlights, the promenade reminded the Scorpion of the mating flight of fireflies.

The Scorpion weaved in and out of the lanes, the Mercedes right behind. He figured that with so many influential young Bahrainis around, they wouldn't dare to shoot. A dark-haired Bahraini girl in a red Caddy waved seductively at him and she was so lighthearted he almost waved back. The Mercedes had dropped back a few feet and now he could see that there were two men in the car. The AK-47 was out of sight.

The Scorpion suddenly turned into the empty center of the oval and hit the gas. He tore down the runway as though he were taking off. The Mercedes' lights flashed in the rear-view mirror, coming fast behind him. As he neared the inevitable collision at the end of the oval, he spun the car 180 degrees and headed back. Behind him he heard the gratifying sound of tearing metal as the Mercedes ploughed into the front end of a white Buick. Driving away, he heard the sounds of furious arguing, as the Bahraini from the Buick pounded his wing and called upon Allah to witness the perfidy of German cars. The Scorpion was grinning as he turned up the road to Manama, while behind him dozens of angry fists were shaken at him, cursing his descendants for a hundred generations.

Manama

BRAITHWAITE LIVED IN A TINY FLAT in the old Arab Quarter, near the arches of the Bab al-Bahrain which had once been the gateway to the ancient walled city. It was in a small stone house on a narrow street, hidden in a warren of adobe houses and shops. The Englishman was well known in the quarter and he would spend hours at a small *dar* next door, sipping tea and smoking his pipe, its stem gnawed away as though by a rat, while the men of the street would puff at their *narguilehs* and discuss the latest gossip. Although it was almost midnight and the dusty street was dark and empty, the Scorpion wasn't surprised to see a light in Braithwaite's curtained window. He could hear the sound of the BBC's Overseas Service on the radio. The announcer was saying something about a meeting in San'a between the representatives of North and South Yemen, mediated by the Russians. The Scorpion knocked on the door and the radio was turned off. When Braithwaite saw who it was, he just stood there blinking in frustrated confusion, the way a tennis player who's completely missed the ball looks at his racket.

"Nicky . . . My G-G-God! What happened?" Braithwaite said, using a name the Scorpion hadn't heard in a long time.

"It was a rough party," the Scorpion shrugged as Braithwaite led him into the room and closed the door. Braithwaite's worried face seemed bright, almost festive as he bustled around the sink, fetching a basin, antiseptic ointments and bandages. His color was high and the Scorpion could have sworn that the old rogue had applied rouge to his cheeks and outlined his eyes with *kohl*. The effect on his wrinkled skin was grotesque, like lipstick on a corpse. Passing a mirror, Braithwaite paused to smooth his hair and flick a speck of lint from his white *thaub*, like a girl primping for a date.

The room was crowded with enough antique junk to have enabled Braithwaite to open a shop on Portobello Road. A long cobra coiled on a low coffee table raised its hooded head to glare at the Scorpion with its unblinking gaze. Braithwaite hurried over and affectionately picked up the snake. He stroked the head with his finger.

"Naughty Zahabi . . . Nicky's our friend, isn't he?" the old man clucked. "If my baby's hungry, he should have let D-D-Daddy know," he cooed and placed the snake next to a saucer of milk by its reed basket. He came over to the threadbare divan where the Scorpion was sitting and began fussing over his wounds.

"D-d-don't mind Zahabi. He's just c-c-curious about strangers," Braithwaite said, his false teeth rattling like a metal chain.

"I'm glad to hear it," the Scorpion said, wincing as Braithwaite bandaged his neck. When he finished, Braithwaite brought out a bottle of cheap Scotch and filled two glasses. One of the glasses had a chipped decal of the Queen that read "25th Jubilee British Railways SR" in white letters.

"Cheerio, lad," Braithwaite said.

"Cheers."

Braithwaite leaned forward, his *kohl*-accented eyes shiny with concern. In the corner, the cobra's long tongue fastidiously lapped at the milk, its tail wagging like that of a cat.

"What h-h-happened, lad?"

"I almost died of snakebite," the Scorpion said, using an old Beduin expression for treachery.

"Now, now. You'll hurt Zahabi's feelings," Braithwaite said winsomely, then turned towards the cobra. "Nicky didn't mean you, p-p-precious," he told the snake.

"It was a setup," the Scorpion said.

"P-p-perhaps you were spotted. It's been known."

"I wasn't spotted," the Scorpion declared flatly. "Give me some credit."

"Of course you weren't," Braithwaite said placatingly, implying that of course he was. For a long moment they sipped their drinks.

"Why'd you do it, Ralph?" the Scorpion asked quietly.

"I d-d-don't know what you mean, lad," Braithwaite said, glancing nervously at the door. The Scorpion slammed his drink down, sloshing whisky on to the coffee table.

"For God's sake, Ralph! There's no time to play footsie. They're after me. I've got to get off the island."

"What makes you think it was me?" Braithwaite blustered.

"They knew who I was. They called me 'Shaw,' for Chrissakes. The only ones who knew me were al-Amir and you and he could have arrested me any time he wanted. It was you, Ralph. Just you."

"Oh Nicky," Braithwaite shook his head sadly and gulped his drink, his hand trembling with what could have been the palsy of age, or just fear.

"Who were you all tricked out for, Ralph? It wasn't me."

Braithwaite straightened his *thaub* self-consciously, with the fussy mannerisms of an old bachelor who has lived alone for too long.

"It's no one, Nicky. R-r-really."

"Tell me, goddamit," the Scorpion shouted. In the corner, the cobra stirred uneasily. Braithwaite's lower lip trembled nervously, its painted surface rippling like a fleshy worm.

"It's Amair. He's a Shiite," Braithwaite explained. Shiite Moslems were a despised minority in most of orthodox Sunni Arabia.

"He's a handsome lad, a bank clerk," Braithwaite offered with an odd defiance. "It's no good you're t-t-telling me he's just an empty-headed clothes-horse, or that he's just using me. I c-c-can't help myself, Nicky. Love's not so easy, you know. It c-c-costs so bloody much . . . the price in self-respect alone . . . don't you think I know?" Braithwaite pleaded, his eyes watery and unfocused.

"Jesus, Ralph. At your age . . ." the Scorpion began.

"At my age . . ." Braithwaite snapped. "At my age, it's . . . why it's like a m-m-miracle . . . The last burst from a star. For God's sake, Nicky . . . don't you understand? Romance is a f-f-farce, a stupid bedroom joke . . . but it's the only answer . . . to death, don't you see?"

"Look around you," Braithwaite gestured at the junk-filled room. "The odd bits and tag-ends of a life. Once . . ." he mused, his eyes misty as he gazed down the corridors of time. "Once, I crossed the Empty Quarter with the Beit Kathir all the way to the Hadhramaut, where only Philby and Thesiger had gone before. I saw places that no white man had ever seen b-b-before and met Bedu who had never seen a Christian. There were nights in the sands bright as day from the stars. I became a Moslem, Nicky. I made the *hajj* to Mecca. I circled the Sacred Ka'aba and walked the *sa'y* between Safa and Marwah. I performed 'the standing' at the Mount of Mercy, praying on the blazing plain of Arafat. I served, Nicky. I have ridden with p-p-princes, boy. I have walked with kings. All gone . . ." his voice trailed off.

"Don't ever get old, Nicky . . . they'll just throw you away, like trash. Don't you see? Before Amair, there was n-n-nothing . . . nothing except . . . Oh God, Nicky . . . I was so bloody lonely," the old man finished in a wheezy quaver.

They sat silently for a long time. In the corner, the snake slept.

68

"You do believe me, don't you lad?" Braithwaite asked at last.

"I believe you, Ralph. Nobody ever lies about being lonely."

"Amair said if I didn't t-t-tell . . . he'd leave me. He swore they wouldn't harm you," Braithwaite said pathetically. The Scorpion poured himself a drink and took a long, slow swallow, trying to delay what was coming. When he was a boy, the crumbling ruin before him had been someone to reckon with, someone who had ridden out from Buraida into the Nefud to bring him water.

"They tried to torture and kill me," the Scorpion said quietly. Braithwaite shook his head and looked down at his feet. His head hung awkwardly from his neck like a broken fixture.

"I'm sorry," Braithwaite said.

"Sorry doesn't cut it, Ralph," the Scorpion growled. "This is Company business. They don't play by Queensberry rules. According to the book, I'm supposed to bring you around the corner," using the intelligence slang phrase for killing.

"I don't give a d-d-damn about your bloody Company rules, Nicky. I don't give a damn about the bloody Yanks, or the bloody FO and their rotten little pension. I don't give a bloody hoot for the UK and Watney's Ale and thatched villages and shepherd's bloody pie. Here is where I belong, Nicky." Braithwaite looked up, his eyes gleaming. He pulled a snapshot out of his pocket and gazed at it longingly, then showed it to the Scorpion. A smooth-faced Arab with brown puppy-dog eyes stared soulfully out of the photo.

"Amair?" the Scorpion asked.

Braithwaite nodded. He glanced again at the photo, put it in his pocket and straightened a little.

"You d-d-do what you have to, Nicky," Braithwaite said.

"God, Ralph," the Scorpion breathed, leaning forward.

The two men stared at each other, then Braithwaite closed his eyes and swallowed, his Adam's apple bobbing like a fishing float. The Scorpion drew closer, the edge of his right hand

69

tingling. A single slice to the temple and he'd have covered his ass. Braithwaite's lips moved silently. Perhaps he was praying.

"Aw, fuck it," the Scorpion muttered. He slumped back on the divan and sipped his drink. Braithwaite opened his eyes and squeezed the Scorpion's arm with bony fingers which trembled like a high-tension wire. Through the whisky, the Scorpion saw the room as amber shadows.

"Did Nuruddin sell the girl to Abdul Sa'ad?" the Scorpion asked.

"I don't know. But there have been stories about Nuruddin d-d-dealing in white females . . . and everyone knows about Abdul Sa'ad's . . . appetites," Braithwaite shrugged.

"Yes, tell me about Abdul Sa'ad's appetites," the Scorpion murmured, almost to himself.

Braithwaite opened a tin of Dunhill's and stuffed the tobacco into his pipe. A strand of tobacco fell on the floor. He picked it up and placed it carefully back in the tin. He lit up and puffed until he was wreathed with smoke.

"When Abdul Sa'ad was a baby it was rumored that he was born with t-t-teeth, so that it was almost impossible to find a wet-nurse who could bear the p-p-pain. What made it even w-w-worse was that he was such a greedy little eater that a s-s-single wet-nurse wasn't enough for him," Braithwaite said.

"What are you trying to tell me?"

"Who was at the m-m-meeting?" Braithwaite asked. As he puffed, his sunken cheeks made his face look almost skeletal.

"Abdul Sa'ad, Nuruddin, the PLO, Yemenis and a European, probably a Latin," the Scorpion ticked them off on his fingers. Suddenly, he straightened.

"They talked about a hit. It's a coup, isn't it?"

"The m-m-man who would be k-k-king," Braithwaite murmured.

The Scorpion put down his drink and stood up, casting his

shadow across Braithwaite's face. He took a deep breath and the smell of the eucalyptus tree from the tiny courtyard filled his nostrils. He put his hand on the old man's bony shoulder. It was like holding a broom handle.

"So long, Ralph. *Salaam.*"

Braithwaite looked up, his eyes red and teary.

"What are you g-g-going to do about me, Nicky?"

"I'm turning you in once I get to Arabia. You've got about twenty-four hours' head start. Hide, Ralph. Just don't let them find you."

"Where would I go, Nicky? God, I love this place . . . the *souk* . . . the *dar* . . . the women veiled like ghosts, the men puffing at their *narguilehs* . . . Amair. I love the bloody wogs and I think they l-l-love me too," Braithwaite said breathlessly.

"I know, Ralph," the Scorpion said quietly.

"There's nowhere to g-g-go, Nicky. Don't you know that?"

"I know, *habibi*, I know," the Scorpion said, closing the door quietly behind him.

After a moment Braithwaite went and stood by the window, listening to the footsteps fading in the darkness. In the distance he could hear the faint barking of a dog. He poured himself another drink and swallowed it with a shudder. It had been a close call; only he knew how close. He had survived because the Scorpion thought he was too old.

He paused in front of a small bronze-framed mirror speckled with yellowing spots and patted down a stray hair. Old isn't dead, he thought. He liked the sound of that and said it out loud.

"I may be old, b-b-but I'm not d-d-dead yet, am I, darling?" he said, pausing to stroke the cobra. The snake flared its hood and stared back with its unblinking gaze.

The Scorpion sat cross-legged on the prow of an old wooden *dhow*, its lateen sail bellied out with the breeze. The deck rolled as the fishing boat slid through the dark waves. The night was full of stars and the wooden deck was rank with the oily smell of barracuda, the usual catch. Back at the stern, the old *nakhoda* kept one arm on the tiller while he brewed coffee on a small primus stove. The only sound was the young boy, the *nakhoda*'s son, singing an ancient shanty in a clear voice, punctuated by the slapping of the waves against the hull.

> Oh Allah, be my guardian,
> Oh Allah, watch over me always,
> Oh Allah, bring me home again,
> To the one who waits for me.

It had cost him plenty of *baksheesh* to persuade them to take him to the coast near Doha in the middle of the night. But he knew that with Abdul Sa'ad and Nuruddin after him, he was definitely *persona non grata* and couldn't just fly in to Riyadh. When he'd gone back to the hotel, he found that the hair he'd stretched across the doorposts was broken. The keys he'd left in a careful pattern in a drawer had been moved. The keys themselves were of no use to anyone. One of them opened the trunk of a car he'd sold six years ago and the other was for the apartment of a young lady in Georgetown who'd told him she never wanted to see him again, back in the days when he was still a CTP trainee.

He was almost spotted when he left the hotel and had to bribe a night porter to show him out through the kitchen to a back exit. He had reversed on foot through the *souk* to make sure he was clean, before making his way down to the wharves, where he had finally roused the boy and the old man.

He tapped his pocket where he kept the film cartridge. The next step was to get it to Macready in Doha. They'd be ringing alarm bells like crazy at Langley, trying to figure when the balloon was going up. Harris, of course, would act as if he knew it all the time, and would try to pressure him into finding out when and where Abdul Sa'ad would make his move.

He wondered if he had made a mistake letting Braithwaite live. Koenig would have said so, but Koenig didn't owe Ralph a life as he did. Nor had Koenig ever been schooled in the harsh desert code of treachery and honor. Only once before had he been soft-hearted and it had cost Tuyet her life. Forget Saigon, forget Braithwaite, he told himself. Concentrate on the mission.

His excitement quickened as they approached the shore. Whatever was going on, the answer lay in Arabia. It was a strange excitement, part danger, part contentment, because in a certain sense he was coming home. Ever since he was a boy, he had known that Arabia was his destiny. "There is only the desert for you," Sheikh Zaid had told him when he had first decided to return to the States. At the time, he hadn't understood what Zaid had meant and had thought that the old man was full of hot air. Later, in Nam, he had discovered that it was a kind of prophecy. And now, his *kismet* was bringing him back.

He reached into his pocket and pulled out the photo of the girl, studying it in the faint light from the primus stove. There was something very fragile about her healthy young beauty, almost as if she were pleading for help with those wonderful eyes. Or perhaps he was just creating his own fairy tale, a romantic fantasy that had nothing to do with the real flesh and blood woman at all.

"Kelly love," the Scorpion said to himself. "I sure hope you're worth all this."

The young sailor fell silent as he began to work the ropes. The boat creaked in the night like an old house full of secrets. Ahead, like a low dark cloud brooding against the stars, lay the mainland of Arabia.

Arabia

OUTSIDE THE NIGHT WIND stirred the desert to silent life, spinning dust devils that the Bedu believe are the visible manifestations of evil spirits called *zars*. It was that dark hour before midnight when men are moved by a strange restlessness as old as firelight on cave walls and shadowy sexual fantasies dance across the mind.

In the bathroom of her quarters, Kelly marked the seconds with the rhythmic stropping of the gold letter-opener she had stolen from Abdul Sa'ad's desk. Relentlessly she scraped the blade against the edge of a pried-up floor tile. Every so often she would test the edge, honed to razor-sharpness, on her finger. Finally satisfied, she went back into the bedroom. She hid the letter-opener in her handbag and walked aimlessly around the room, as though she were waiting for a phone call. In the light of a gold and ivory lamp her eyes appeared to be hollow, like bottomless blue holes in her skull. Soon, she knew, he would send for her.

"How good a slice of bread tastes depends on how hungry you are," Kelly's father once told her. They were sitting in his den, the walls covered with plaques and civic awards. Even in a sports shirt he looked distinguished, as if he never sweated. His face was attractively tan and glowing from a recent "fact-finding" trip to the French Riviera with his latest mistress, who was younger than Kelly. He jokingly told her that the trip had been arranged by the famous Congressional travel agency: Boon & Doggle.

That was the time when she had discovered that in exchange for a large campaign contribution from a building contractor, he had agreed to push an important contract the builder's way. What made it doubly hypocritical in Kelly's view was

74

that he was running on a reform platform, accusing his Democratic opponent of underworld ties.

"In the real-world jungle, morality is a luxury of the well-fed," her father had declared in that self-righteous tone of voice she had associated with his lectures ever since she was a little girl. No matter how hard she tried, that tone always made her feel as if she could never do anything right.

"You don't look like you're starving," Kelly had retorted, her eyes darting blue flames, like a gas jet. She felt that he had betrayed her. God, she had been so naive, she thought. Robert had shown her the truth. But that was a secret she would never reveal, no matter what they did to her.

She went to the night table and picked up the compact Abdul Sa'ad had given her and began to do her make-up. The compact was solid gold and on the lid her new name, Saria, was spelled out in Arabic letters made of perfect blue-white diamonds. Abdul Sa'ad was generous that way, she conceded as she brushed her cheeks with powder. Her face revealed no more emotion than a doll's face as she worked on it.

The name might be Saria, but the face was still Kelly, she thought, studying her features in the compact mirror. Like a soldier seeing to his equipment, she adjusted those ridiculous tassels hanging from the bodice of her belly-dancing costume. Fatma, another of Abdul Sa'ad's concubines, had told her to put it on this evening. Abdul Sa'ad liked to have her wear it when she danced for him to disco records. While she smiled and danced, she would think about the one idea that had become an obsession with her. As her thoughts grew increasingly darker, the only image she could seem to focus on was murder.

In the end, the only choices we have are murder and suicide, Kelly thought, wondering if she was still sane. If they really wanted to prepare students for the real world, that's what they should have been teaching in Philosophy 101, she thought grimly. The fact that she could even contemplate the idea astonished her. Ever since she could remember she had always been so squeamish that she couldn't stand to squash a bug. Perhaps it was all this religious crap she had been getting from Fatma, because Kelly had correctly gambled that her treatment would be better if she expressed interest in becoming a Moslem.

Well, religion was a pretty bloodthirsty subject, she'd discovered. Something Fatma had said about the Koran had triggered a Sunday-school memory. She was sure that a woman in the Bible—was it Jael, or Judith?—something with a J—had slept with her enemy and then murdered him by pounding a tent spike into his head, thereby delivering the Israelites. The blood pounded in her temples as the idea struck her. But if she murdered Abdul Sa'ad, whom would she deliver? Because if she did it, they would kill her. Abdul Sa'ad had explained that early on.

"We Arabs are a simple people," Abdul Sa'ad had said in perfect Oxford-educated English.

They were in the tiny whitewashed hut in the courtyard which had been her cell when they first brought her to this place. The hut was hot as a furnace and her clothes clung wetly to her body like a clammy outer skin. That was in the first phase, what he called her "education."

"All our laws are also simple, as are the punishments. The only law is the Koran, which is the Word of God and the only court is the *ulama*, which is the council of religious elders. If a man is a thief, we cut off his hand. If the man commits libel, we cut off his tongue. If a man commits a violent act, we cut off his head. You see, it is very simple," he explained.

"What if a servant escapes?" Kelly asked, her eyes flashing. She still couldn't bring herself to say the word "slave."

"For a male servant, flogging. For repeated escapes, death."

"What about females?" she prompted.

"Females cannot escape," Abdul Sa'ad declared, raising an eyebrow to let her know that he knew what she was driving at. "We are well-guarded here, but even if you should manage it, where could you go? If you went into the desert, you would die. If you went into a city, anyone who saw a lone woman would turn her over to the religious police, who are everywhere," he said.

That was true enough, she thought. She had seen the religious police during her brief ride in the Cadillac through Riyadh. They wore white *thaubs* and black-checked headcloths and carried long wands to whip anyone who violated a religious law. The slightest infraction, a woman unveiled or wearing short sleeves, a shopkeeper who didn't close up the moment the muezzin called to prayer, a man who passed a beggar without dropping a coin, resulted in a few taps from the switch, or worse.

"What would they do?" she asked, licking her dry lips with a tongue that rasped like a file.

"They would return you to me," he said.

For a long moment they looked at each other. The bright sunlight from the open doorway dazzled her eyes. It reflected off Abdul Sa'ad's white robe, seeming to clothe him in a nimbus of light.

"Why are you doing this to me?" she asked.

His answer terrified her.

"Because I can," he said.

And then he was gone. The fat eunuch assigned to guard her locked the door and once again she was alone in the dark oven of her cell.

She lay curled in a ball, as far away as possible from the stinking hole in the corner which served as a toilet. It had been days since they had given her anything to drink and her mouth tasted as foul as that disgusting hole in the corner. She no longer had any spit to swallow and thought of begging for water again. But all her cries had been ignored. When the fat eunuch did come in once, she had pleaded for water in the one Arabic word she had learned.

"*Maya . . . maya,*" she begged, going down on her knees, but the eunuch simply shook his head and left the bowl of bland *hummus* paste which she had learned not to eat, because it only made her thirstier. Her tongue felt enormous. It seemed to completely fill her mouth. She licked at the sweat on her forearm like a cat, but it didn't help. Now and again she gagged with dry heaves, her body wrenching like a half-crushed insect. If she didn't get some water soon, she would die. In her fevered mind she saw flowing streams sparkling in the sun, pouring endlessly into a clear lake the color of the sky. Her body was a useless burden to her, she thought desperately as she tossed like a restless sleeper. This water torture was worse than drugs, worse than anything she had ever imagined.

She felt herself losing consciousness again, but some part of her was screaming inside, warning her that if she let go she would die. She looked down at her lifeless hands. They were dirty and clammy. It was as if they belonged to a stranger. How could this be happening to her? And then, a more insidious question. What could she have done? Nothing, she tried to tell herself over and over. She had been helpless from the moment she drank the champagne. And after they had raped her, she had been a virtual basket case.

She remembered only the occasional pinprick of the hypodermic during the trip. There was a haze of people and jets, but no matter how hard she tried to call out, nothing came from her throat. She remembered seeing Gerard, a nasty smile on his face, looking as if he was very far away, as though seen through the wrong end of a telescope. And then she was surrounded by Arabs and people speaking a strange guttural language that she couldn't understand. She didn't know what drug they had used, but it made her skin tingle with electricity and try as she might, she couldn't move. Through the plane window she saw a vast brown plain far below that seemed to go on forever and then blackness came.

She remembered how everything seemed to be moving in slow motion when they took her down the rear exit of the jet. Her legs were wobbly and the blinding light and heat almost knocked her over as they walked across the tarmac to a waiting limousine. It was like walking through boiling water. Inside the limo, a fat middle-aged Arab took her face in his hand and turned her this way and that, inspecting her as if she were a horse, even poking his fingers in her mouth to examine her teeth. They loaded her on a private Lear jet, its interior thick with oriental rugs and painted with intricate arabesques, looking like a flying Moroccan seraglio. The furnishings were covered with velour upholstery and the jet was filled with expensive stereos and electronic gadgets. It was as if Hugh Hefner had employed Sanford the Junkman as an interior decorator.

Once the jet took off, she was taken in tow by two veiled women, who led her behind an ornate screen, chattering away in the language she couldn't understand. The women bathed her in a solid silver tub, splashed her with enough perfume to float a good-sized ship and dressed her in a black robe and veil. By the time they landed, her mind had finally begun to clear from the effects of the drug, except for the strangeness of everything around her and the sweet reek of the perfume which enveloped her like a cloud. They led her from the plane to a Cadillac parked on the tarmac and drove her through an immense modern city, thronged with Arabs in western clothes, which she later learned was Riyadh, the capital of Saudi Arabia.

The Cadillac sped past squat adobe huts on the outskirts of the city and turned on to a modern two-lane asphalt road which led straight into the al Aramah desert. The road was virtually empty and the honey-colored desert lay flat as a table as far as she could see. Through the tinted windows the desert sped by, unpopulated by houses or any living thing. There was only the flat land and sky and the endless highway unrolling before them.

After several hours they turned into a dirt side road that led to a large featureless house surrounded by a thin border of grass and palm trees. It looked like a giant yellow brick on a billiard table. There were barbed-wire fences and soldiers in gun emplacements all around the house. It was a fortress.

The car pulled into a courtyard where two Mercedes and a gold Rolls-Royce were parked. In the center of the courtyard stood a stone fountain that was dry as a bone. A fat eunuch with a hairless face and pendulous female breasts waddled out to the car and led her to the small stone hut, her cell. They left her there for days, apparently to die of thirst, until Abdul Sa'ad came and explained what he wanted.

Prince Abdul Sa'ad was a strongly built man in his thirties. He was dressed in a simple white linen robe. At his belt he wore a beautiful gold-handled dagger. His brown face with its trim black beard and desert hawk's nose was striking against the contrast of his white headcloth. His eyes, under thick black brows, were impressive. Liquid brown, they were at the same time both expressive and implacable. He looked like a prophet! In truth, he was almost handsome, she thought.

He told her that she was his slave and would remain so for the rest of her life. When she argued and demanded that she be allowed to go and that he contact the American Embassy, he almost smiled. Later, of course, she realized how ridiculous she must have seemed. A woman claiming her rights in Arabia was like a hen claiming parental jurisdiction over her eggs.

"Be careful, mister. I'm an American. The daughter of a congressman," Kelly warned.

"I know who you are," Abdul Sa'ad said.

Then he left her alone with her thirst.

She lay curled on the dirt floor, her eyes filled with visions of sparkling fountains, water spurting wastefully from hoses as people washed their cars, cans of beer in ice and sunlight sparkling on the surface of Lake Tahoe, where her family would go for the summers when she was a girl. She was dying, dying because Abdul Sa'ad wanted a little nookie, she thought grimly.

Everyone likes to think he's unique, she thought. Whenever she had read about people dying of panic in a fire, or heard on TV about a POW who had succumbed to brainwashing, an inner voice would reassure her that they had been weak, that she would have been able to resist. That was all nonsense, she now realized. Anyone can succumb. It didn't even require any sophisticated technique. She was willing to sell her soul, for that was surely the price, for a glass of water. You're easy, Kelly. You come cheap, she accused herself.

Later, she woke and lay staring into the darkness, shivering despite the burning heat. Her throat felt so dry she could barely breathe. She was waiting, she realized. Waiting for something to happen, or—tell the truth, Kelly—waiting for someone to save her. That's what women do; we wait, she thought, blinking eyes so dry her lids felt like sandpaper. We spend our lives waiting for a man to rescue us, from home, from being single, from boring marriages. We wait, forever going on diets, buying clothes, fixing ourselves, so that the label will be so attractive that we'll be the one piece of goods he picks off the shelf.

And then it struck her. There wasn't going to be any rescuer, no knight in shining armor. There was no one to wait for and never had been. The only person who could save her was herself. The thought was like a bolt of lightning, galvanizing her into action.

She sprang to her feet in the center of the dark cell, her teeth clenched, her fingernails digging into her palms. The pain in her palms felt good, shocking her mind to clarity. I'm going to get out of this, she vowed, her eyes gleaming defiantly in the darkness. No matter what it takes. Now we'll see what a woman can do. And she would use a woman's only real weapon, her wits, she thought craftily. And patience. Somewhere along the line, her chance would come.

She raced to the cell door and pounded on it, screaming for Abdul Sa'ad. When the eunuch finally opened the door she kept screaming and gesturing until he brought his Master to her. As soon as she saw the prince, she dropped to her knees, bowed to the ground and kissed his shoes, again and again. She swore that she would be his slave forever and

81

begged him to allow her to become a Moslem. When she said that, he raised her up and embraced her with an odd look on his face, as though he knew she was acting, but that he didn't care. Taking her hand, he led her to the luxurious apartment in the women's quarters which would henceforth be her home.

Prince Abdul Sa'ad's "country house," as he called it, was built around a central atrium green with flowers and date palms, where the women were allowed for two hours every afternoon. The garden was exquisite. A crystal clear stream fed a waterfall which tumbled over rocks into a lovely pond surrounded by trees and grassy banks bordered by beautiful wildflowers. Goldfish darted like flecks of sunlight in the cool water. It was as if a tiny piece of Hawaii had been somehow dropped into the middle of the desert.

The house itself, or at least the *harim*, or women's quarters was extraordinary, an incredible mixture of opulence and bad taste. The walls and floors and ceilings were covered with intricate mosaic arabesques. Some of the designs were exquisite, while others were outlandish. Semi-precious stones were inlaid in every room. There were rooms filled with expensive TVs and stereos that rarely worked. Many of the furnishings were made of pure gold. Even her own bathroom had gold accessories including a solid gold toilet bowl. It was an incomprehensible place, where money was truly no object. Once she asked Abdul Sa'ad how much money he had and he had replied with an eloquent shrug: "If we all did nothing but spent it lavishly every single minute, we could never spend it all."

Abdul Sa'ad had three other concubines living there. There was Fatma, a beautiful sloe-eyed Arab girl from a poor family in Jidda, a sprawling port on the Red Sea. The other westerner was Inga, a stolid Swedish girl with blue eyes and long blond hair, whom Abdul Sa'ad had purchased from a brothel in Beirut. Her mind had long since been dulled by drugs and now she spent her days chewing *khat* leaves with the bland expression of a cow chewing its cud. Then there was Yasmin, a lithe, sensuous Negress, bought to add a touch of spice to Abdul Sa'ad's *harim*. She was a Somali and had been purchased from her father, a refugee in the lower Shabelle region near Mogadishu. Her purchase had saved the family from starvation, she told Kelly tearfully. In addition, she learned that Abdul Sa'ad had four wives and eleven children, whom he kept in an apartment in the Royal Palace in Riyadh.

At first she thought it might be bearable. Her room was comfortable, the walls covered with colorful tapestries and the lamps and accessories were made of solid gold. The floors were covered with exquisite oriental rugs. The fat eunuch brought her a catalogue from Harrod's in London and told her she could order anything she wished. The other concubines were kind and friendly. Abdul Sa'ad even gave her a diamond necklace which looked like something featured in Tiffany's window. But that first night convinced her that she wasn't going to make it.

Fatma brought her a lacy white pinafore, white stockings and a big white bow for her hair and told her to wear them. When she put them on she looked like a ten-year-old. Then Abdul Sa'ad sent for her. When she entered his apartment, he was sprawled naked on a mound of gold satin cushions, smoking a water pipe. His body was covered with a dense mat of black hair. He looked like an overfed chimpanzee. In the corner a tethered falcon shifted its position on its perch and stared at her with its cold savage eyes as if she was just another kind of prey. Then the craziness began.

He handed her a large doll and told her to play with it and talk in baby talk. Uneasily, she prattled and played with the doll, occasionally stealing a glance over at him. He told her to bend over, her short skirt hitching up, and stared at her lacy panties. The only sound was the gurgling of the water pipe. Her eyes grew round with horror as she began to realize the reality of the fantasy she was acting out for him. In a strangled voice, he called her over. She couldn't help noticing his erection, standing out red and taut.

He told her that she had been a naughty child and that she would have to be spanked. He ordered her to bring him the hairbrush on his dressing table, then took her across his knees, her long legs stretched out across the cushions. He paddled her furiously, her bottom burning like fire until she couldn't stand it any more. She whimpered and pleaded for him to stop, but he seemed possessed. Suddenly, he ripped the pinafore off her and ordered her to pull off her panties.

But instead of mounting her, he gave her a large solid gold phallus, realistically carved down to the smallest detail.

That was her initiation into what it meant to be Abdul Sa'ad's concubine, she reflected, grimly fingering the edge of the letter-opener.

Night after night he sent for her, each night more bizarre than the last. It was like mating with a demon and she breathed great sighs of relief whenever she learned that he would be away in Riyadh or Bahrain on business.

Lately, that had been happening more often. In fact, she would be with him tonight for the first time in days. Often his phone would ring at odd times, and yesterday the courtyard filled with armed men making a great racket, who just as suddenly disappeared. Something was up and when she asked Nasir the eunuch what was happening, he clutched his bald head in his hands and exclaimed that the Master was in a terrible mood. Then he reminded himself that politics were not a woman's concern and shooed her away.

She checked the handbag one more time, although she had gone over its contents a dozen times. In it she had a skirt and blouse, the letter-opener and the keys to one of the Mercedes, which she had filched from Abdul Sa'ad's pocket. He had made a fuss about it when he missed the keys and her heart pounded at the thought that he might suspect her. In the end, one of the servants found a spare set of keys. Kelly distracted him with kisses and he just shrugged and forgot about it.

Under the guise of her education, she had asked Fatma,

84

her unofficial teacher, to show her a map, and had planned an escape route. Kelly figured that she could head east on the road towards the oil fields, near the coast around Dhahran. Where there were oil fields, there were bound to be American workers and she hoped they would help her to get away. All she had to do was murder Abdul Sa'ad so he couldn't stop her, sneak past the guard to the courtyard and steal the car. In her mind, it was easy. Just a few minutes and she would be free.

But the idea of actually sticking the blade into him while he slept, even after all he had done to her, sickened her. She had to do it, she told herself. She had to. Otherwise she would never be free. She remembered the words of an old Janis Joplin song. Something about how "freedom's just another word for nothing left to lose." Well, she had nothing left to lose all right, she thought, and grimly closed her handbag clasp.

Fatma came in to take her to the Master's quarters. She followed the concubine down the hall to Abdul Sa'ad's apartment, her belly-dancing costume swishing and tinkling like coins as she walked. Her palms began to sweat. She wondered how she would ever get through this night. You've nothing left to lose, she told herself. All she had to do was let him do whatever filthy things he wanted one last time. Just till he finally fell asleep. Then it would be all over, one way or another.

Abdul Sa'ad was still wearing his robe when they entered, bowing to him. With a flick of his finger, he dismissed Fatma and started the stereo. The room exploded with the sound of hard rock and Kelly mechanically began to dance, grinding her pelvis in erotic rhythms. Abdul Sa'ad lit a cigarette and slumped back on the cushion. There were circles under his eyes. She had never seen him so distracted.

She rolled her belly and bumped her hips faster and faster, the tassels on her costume bobbing wildly. She began to strip slowly and sensuously in time to the music. Abdul Sa'ad nervously tapped his leg in rhythm with the beat. Sweat glistened on his forehead, but his eyes were heavy-lidded as if drugged. She removed her bra and bent forward so he could watch her breasts swaying above his face. A pearl of sweat dripped from the curve of her breast down on to his face, but he seemed not to notice. His eyes were closed. He was either asleep or in a trance.

Was it time? she thought wildly. The letter-opener was still in her bag. If he opened his eyes now he would order them to kill her. But she felt she couldn't stand it another second. It made her skin crawl to be near him.

She picked up the bag and opened it. The letter-opener gleamed in the light. She crouched over him, her hand clenched around the opener poised over his throat.

A single stab and she was free, she thought. But it was so horrible to stick it into him. He was beginning to come out of it. She had to do it now, she steeled herself.

She had started to raise the opener when there was a commotion in the hallway outside. Quickly she slid the opener under a silk cushion and stepped away to resume her dance.

Suddenly a half-dozen Arabs in military uniform barged in and began jabbering excitedly in Arabic. Kelly stopped dancing in confusion. As the men glanced at her, she covered her naked breasts in embarrassment. One of them, an evil-looking man with a cataract in one eye, stared at her and a cruel smile lifted the corners of his mouth. Kelly covered her face and scuttled into a corner. She sat beside the cushion under which the opener was hidden.

Then the fat Arab who had examined her teeth came in, followed by a westerner with a Latin moustache, wearing a white suit.

"Our friend called. The intruder has been identified," Nuruddin said in English, so that the westerner could understand.

"How fortunate for you," Abdul Sa'ad said. The Arabs glanced uneasily at each other.

"He is an American agent," Nuruddin said.

"Brilliant! I never could have guessed," Abdul Sa'ad replied, looking skyward to Allah for assistance.

"He's not in Bahrain any more. He seems to have disappeared," the westerner added.

"Perhaps he's hiding," Nuruddin said. He gave a *Ma'alesh* shrug, as if to say "So what?"

"He hasn't been hiding, you idiot!" Abdul Sa'ad shrieked, slapping Nuruddin across the face. The Bahraini staggered back, clutching his face. Abdul Sa'ad grabbed him and pulled him close.

"Don't you understand? He could destroy us all. I want every airport watched. Every harbor and hotel. Most important, every foreign embassy, especially every American embassy. Not just in Arabia, but throughout the Middle East," Abdul Sa'ad said.

He let go of Nuruddin, plucked a sugared fig from a gold bowl and ate it thoughtfully. Nuruddin stood stiffly, red fingermarks imprinted on his face. Abdul Sa'ad came over to Nuruddin and embraced him. He kissed Nuruddin's bruise and stepped back.

"I know you think me harsh; but you are merely soldiers and businessmen. I must be a king," he said softly to no one in particular. He picked up his prayer beads and fingered them thoughtfully.

"I have a feeling about this man. A bad feeling. We shall have to stop him before he stops us," he said.

"My life is yours, your Highness," Nuruddin said, and bowed. He wore the bruise on his face like a medal.

"What else do we know about him?" Abdul Sa'ad asked.

"They call him 'the Scorpion,' " Nuruddin said.

At this the one-eyed Arab gasped. Abdul Sa'ad made a mental note to question him later, then turned to Nuruddin.

"Allah watches us. Even this very moment. You have the chance to redeem yourself. This Scorpion must be destroyed."

Nuruddin kissed the tip of Abdul Sa'ad's nose as a sign of respect. "He won't get away this time," he said.

"He had better not. Moscow does not like mistakes," the westerner said.

"Neither do I," Abdul Sa'ad said.

MOSCOW

THE JUNE MORNING was bright and clear. It was already growing warm. A gauzy veil of gas fumes shimmered over Moscow, giving the city the steamy illusion of a tropical capital. The trees in the little park in Sverdlov Square were in full leaf, a bright splash of green providing a sylvan background to the outline of the Sobakin Tower as seen from the Kremlin. *Apparachiki* taking an early lunch hour and *babushkas* with swaddled infants strolled among the trees, snacking on ice cream and greasy *pyshki* doughnuts served hot from the fryer by pavement vendors, oblivious to the thick tension in the Arsenal building in the Kremlin, where the Politburo was beginning its regular Thursday morning meeting.

The Politburo meets in a medium-sized room which sits at the heart of the vast Soviet empire like a spider at the center of its web. The room has white marble walls and is bare of any decoration except for a portrait of Lenin, his profile gazing stonily in the direction of the onion-shaped dome of St. Basil's Cathedral across Red Square. Around the long oak conference table, its surface polished like a mirror, twelve of the men who ruled half the planet uneasily waited for Fyedorenko to take his place at the head of the table. In front of each member was a blank note pad and pen, an ashtray, and according to his preference, a carafe of ice water or *kvas*, the pungent brown drink made from fermented rye bread that is the Coca-Cola of Russia. In one corner sat three stenographers ready to take down every word. After the meeting their notes would be compared and a definitive transcript would be distributed among the participants. In the opposite corner, two KGB operators readied a tape recorder. The doorway was blocked by two six-footers at rigid attention. They wore the green uniform of the Kremlin Guard, their leather holsters gleaming with polish.

The twelve glanced uncomfortably around the room avoiding each other's eyes. With the Byzantine instinct for the jugular that had taken each of them to the very pinnacle of power, they collectively sensed that this was to be no ordinary meeting. From time to time one or another of them would furtively glance at the empty Penal Chair, at the far end of the table, hoping that wherever the axe fell, his head wouldn't be under it. If the party secretary had planned to increase their uneasiness by making them wait, he had certainly achieved his end.

To help ease the tension, Korchnoi, the roly-poly minister of agriculture, who concealed a ruthless nature under the jovial exterior of a Russian Santa Claus, was telling the latest joke. Two *apparachiki* meet on the street and the first *apparachik* asks the second if he's heard about the shop in Kalinin Prospekt that just got in a fabulous shipment of shoes. "Everyone is lining up," he says. The second *apparachik* replies that he's going to Minsk to buy shoes.

"But there are no shoes in Minsk," the first *apparachik* objects.

"I know," replies the second *apparachik*. "But that's where the line from the Kalinin Prospekt ends."

The ministers were still chuckling over the joke when Fyedorenko burst in and stalked over to his chair, Svetlov close at his heels. As he took his seat, Fyedorenko made an offhand apology about being late and gazed intently at the other members. Despite his famous poker-faced impassivity, they noted with astonishment that Fyedorenko was obviously keyed up. For a moment he studied them, impatiently drumming his fingers on the glossy table.

In fact, only once before had Fyedorenko been so nervous before a Politburo meeting. That was the time shortly after he had earned his place on the Politburo by betraying Gugalov, ostensibly because of his alleged black-market activities with a ring of *fartsovshchiki* who ran prostitutes out of Komsomol Square, but in reality because Gugalov opposed the old man's China policy.

He had first become alerted to a new development when the old man had hinted that he was going to do some weeding out at the next Politburo meeting and then left him dangling. It was essential that he learn who it was: Petrovsky or Ivanenko, because whoever wound up on the Penal Chair would leave the Kremlin on a one-way trip to the Black Wall in Lubyanka prison, along with anyone who supported him. It would have been so easy for the old man to let him know which way to jump, but he hadn't and, walking into the meeting, Fyedorenko still didn't know whom to denounce.

Soon after the meeting started, he decided it had to be Petrovsky, who kept licking his lips and nervously chain smoking those old-fashioned *paprossy* cigarettes, his shirt collar wilted with sweat, while Ivanenko sat there with the self-righteous smile of a club member whose dues are paid in full. The meeting dealt with the latest miserable agricultural forecasts until the old man nodded at Fyedorenko. He took a deep breath and was about to denounce Petrovsky when a horrible thought flashed across his mind, like a spark jumping across a gap. Petrovsky knew! That's why he was so nervous! He knew what was going to happen and Ivanenko didn't. That meant that Petrovsky's information sources were better than Ivanenko's. Before he exhaled his breath, Fyedorenko had revised his denunciation speech, shocking them all with his sudden vehement attack on Ivanenko. Fyedorenko never forgot the appraising glance the old man had thrown him at the end of the meeting, as the guards led Ivanenko from the Penal Chair. The old man had been a real *sukin sin*, all right, a son-of-a-bitch from start to finish, Fyedorenko mused.

He studied each of the ministers in turn, trying to calculate from his expression which way he would go when the crucial vote came. Just to his right sat the President of the Soviet Union, Nikolai Bulganov, a rubber-nosed old *apparachik*. Although he was nominally the chief of state and senior to all of them, in reality his position had become largely ceremonial. Bulganov had survived by going along and he would undoubtedly vote with the majority.

On Fyedorenko's left was Yuri Suvarov, son of the nephew of the great field marshal, whose famous maxim, "Train hard, fight easy," had become the watchword of the Red Army. Suvarov had a gray anonymous face made even more anonymous by the shapeless gray suits he always wore. Once Irina, Fyedorenko's late wife, had said of Suvarov, "Put him in a field of ashes and he'd be invisible." As Premier, Suvarov shared the top of the table with Fyedorenko and Bulganov, thereby maintaining the fiction that since the death of the old man, the Soviet Union was ruled by what the western press called "the three-man *troika*."

Of the three of them Fyedorenko, as general secretary of the CPSU, was nominally the most junior. And in theory they were all equal, each Politburo member having only one vote. But nothing is ever as it seems in Russia. In reality, Bulganov had little power and in the months since the old man's death, Fyedorenko had severely undercut the scope of Suvarov's authority. As party secretary and chairman of the Central Committee, Fyedorenko, like the Pope, was *primum inter pares*, "the first among equals." Once Suvarov had been a superb in-fighter, who had helped to depose Khrushchev after the Cuban fiasco. Recently he had been in ill health and seemed to lack the stamina to withstand Fyedorenko's incursions, yet he was still a formidable presence, for all his face-lessness, and Fyedorenko had no idea whether or not he would support the Molotov Plan.

The remainder of the ministers were seated down the length of the table. Nearest to Bulganov sat Alexei Andreyev, the head of the KGB and at fifty-nine, the youngest minister in the room. He was stylishly dressed in a three-piece suit and was considered attractive by the KGB secretaries among whom he cut such a wide and democratic swathe that he was face-tiously called "the Father of Soviet Intelligence" among the KGB small-fry. Fyedorenko knew he could count on Andreyev's support, since the Molotov Plan had been a KGB operation from the beginning.

Directly across from Andreyev, Marshal Orlov, defense minister and head of the Red Army, was nervously drumming his pen against the note pad, impatient for Fyedorenko to begin. He was the only other man in the room who knew of the Molotov Plan and was its strongest supporter, having maintained for years that the outcome of the revolutionary struggle against the West would inevitably require a military solution. A tall, grizzled, but still powerful man in his seventies, he had fought under Marshal Zhukov, whom he regarded as the savior of Mother Russia, during the Great Patriotic War against the Nazis, and it was no secret that he thought of himself as Zhukov's natural successor.

Next to Orlov sat the foreign minister, Ivan Kishinev, a suave diplomat in banker's pinstripes, his salt and pepper hair slicked neatly back. He had the sleek air of a fat cat, the kind who would be equally at home at an embassy party or a conference of businessmen in Brussels. Indeed, the slang expression for a fat cat, *nachalstvo*, occurred to Fyedorenko. Kishinev was "smooth enough to piss down your back and convince you it was raining," as the old Russian saying went. His was the face most familiar to westerners, always providing a façade of reasonableness to the zigs and zags of Soviet policy. In truth, Kishinev was a bit too enamored of the West, Fyedorenko thought with a frown. If he was to have opposition, it would come from Kishinev.

Across from Kishinev, Myshkin, the rapier-thin senior party theoretician, the scourge of "deviationism," which had become the latest buzzword in *Pravda*, the philosopher whose gushy celebrations of the ideal *stakhanovite* worker were a regular feature of *Izvestia*, was anxiously glancing around the room, as if seeking out the slightest crumbs of revisionism even here in the Holy of Holies. Fyedorenko thought that Myshkin would go along with Molotov Plan as the next stage in the historically inevitable course of Marxist-Leninist destiny.

Next to Myshkin was Uri Arbatov, the minister of industrial development and across from him sat Nikolai Suganin, the tough head of the trade unions. Next to Arbatov sat Korchnoi, the bouncy minister of agriculture. Opposite him was Vladimir Komarovsky, Comintern secretary and liaison to Communist parties worldwide. He was nervously licking his thin lips, upset by the unmistakable sense of crisis in the room. He had grown increasingly more uneasy during the last months, as Fyedorenko had nibbled away at Suvarov's authority. A certain No vote, Fyedorenko decided.

At the foot of the table was Cherkassy, the Ukrainian party secretary from Kiev and across from him, Liepka, his Latvian counterpart from Riga. These last two were the required token non-Russians. Despite many ruthless tests, they had proven their loyalty to Moscow over and over, but still, the Soviet soul is incapable of ever truly trusting anyone who isn't a Great Russian by birth. Well, they would get another test today, Fyedorenko mused.

"Comrades," he began and everyone in the room stirred at the unmistakable note of urgency in his voice. Kishinev and Myshkin looked significantly at each other, their suspicions confirmed. Like the sharks they were, they immediately recognized the scent of blood. Fyedorenko took a deep breath before proceeding. He had no doubt whatsoever that he was about to make history.

"I request that we dispense with today's agenda in order to deal with a matter of some urgency," Fyedorenko said.

There were affirmative nods around the table. The scent of blood was in the air and no mistaking it.

"I am as anxious as the rest to hear what the party chairman has to say," Arbatov interjected, "but I would remind the members that final approval of the new Five-Year Plan cannot be delayed much longer."

"Your point is well taken, Uri. But I'm sure the party secretary would not dispense with the agenda unless the matter was fully urgent," Kishinev put in smoothly. Fyedorenko smiled his thanks to the foreign minister. Your point, you bastard, he thought.

"Also the plans for the forthcoming Trade Union Congress must be finalized," Suganin said.

"Duly noted, comrade. But I know that we all want to hear the party secretary's views," Suvarov said. Fyedorenko leaned forward and stared intently down the length of the table.

"Over the last decade our confrontation with the West has degenerated into stalemate," he began. "It is true that we have had our successes, notably in Latin America, Southeast Asia and the Third World. Most importantly in the improvement of our defenses and the expansion of the Red Army into the most formidable military machine the world has ever known."

Marshal Orlov nodded in acknowledgement of Fyedorenko's praise. He took full credit for the build-up and everyone knew it.

"But candor forces us to admit that we have also had our reverses as well, comrades. The space race, Afghanistan, Poland, the U.S.—China alliance, and most importantly, the massive military build-up in the West," Fyedorenko ticked them off.

"Comrades, let us face facts," Fyedorenko's cutting voice jolting them to attention. "We have reached the high-water mark. Our industrial capacity is strained to the limit. The cost of our military build-up has been high, very high. Our satellites are restive, the forces of revisionism, hooliganism and dissidence grow more impudent daily. This year, for the first time in history, we shall have to import oil. And we cannot hope to match the western military build-up indefinitely. Time"—Fyedorenko let the word hang in the air like a bird of ill omen—"is no longer on our side, comrades."

There was an uneasy stir around the table. Fyedorenko's remarks sounded uncomfortably close to personal criticism of virtually every man there.

"During the last months of the late party secretary's rule," Fyedorenko went on, "it became apparent that the status quo was no longer tenable, despite the nuclear impasse between us and the Americans. With the old man's full approval, a top-secret operation designed to break the ice-jam"—he used a coarse Russian expression that evoked a thrusting penis—"and bring the West to its knees once and for all was put into effect. In honor of the late and may I say, visionary, foreign minister, this operation was code-named the Molotov Plan."

The room was as hushed as a cathedral. The members who were hearing about it for the first time glanced at each other in shock. It was inconceivable. A full-fledged operation being launched without prior Politburo approval. They looked with fear at Fyedorenko, who seemed to have grown suddenly taller. Not since Stalin had anyone dared to assume so much power.

"The Molotov Plan was conceived as a joint KGB-GRU operation, in association with the Red Army. The objective of the plan is to bring the West to heel once and for all, while achieving our age-old foreign objectives of total dominance, secure warm-water ports and control of worldwide resources. I have asked Comrade Svetlov to provide an overview of the operation," Fyedorenko said, summoning Svetlov with a flick of his finger. While Svetlov stood anxiously by the wall, Fyedorenko's secretary set up a large wall map. The room buzzed with conversation as each minister tried to be noncommital about whether he had any foreknowledge of the operation.

95

"Comrades," Svetlov's bull-frog voice boomed out. With his squat body, shapeless gray suit, bulging eyes and a face pitted from a terrible case of childhood chicken pox that had almost killed him, Svetlov looked like a talking toad. But that deep frog's voice of his was unmistakable and despite his evident nervousness at addressing the Politburo, it had authority and power. Turning to the map, Svetlov gestured at the Straits of Hormuz at the mouth of the Persian Gulf.

"This is the Achilles' heel of the West. Through these waters pass the oil lifelines of the major western powers. Roughly three quarters of Japan's oil, sixty per cent of Western Europe's oil and about a third of America's imported oil comes from the Persian Gulf, most of that coming from Saudi Arabia. Whoever controls this oil, controls the world. Make no mistake about that, comrades," Svetlov said, his eyes boring into them.

"The Molotov Plan was designed to place control of this oil into our hands," he declared. The room buzzed with excitement.

"The plan was coordinated in the Middle East by a mole recruited by the KGB when he was a student," Svetlov went on. "Today, he is a wealthy and influential Bahraini businessman. Under our orders, he established contact with Prince Abdul Sa'ad of Arabia and together they began to plot a coup against King Salim. Abdul Sa'ad leads a fanatically antiwestern Wahabi faction in the Saudi royal family. He is also Deputy Commander of the Royal Saudi Army, numbering some fifty thousand troops, who are loyal to their commanders. The object of the coup is to give us control of the oil. In exchange, we will support Abdul Sa'ad as King of Arabia.

"We expect Abdul Sa'ad's army to be opposed by the Saudi National Guard, which is fiercely loyal to the king. In a one-to-one fight they would be an even match for the army, but Abdul Sa'ad won't be fighting alone.

"As you can see by the map, control of Arabia really rests upon the control of three key areas: the Hejaz, particularly the holy city of Mecca, Riyadh the capital, and the oil facilities at Ras Tanura. The Molotov Plan will place all three areas under our control," Svetlov declared.

"To begin with, troops from the People's Democratic Republic of Yemen spearheaded by Cuban units, under a secret protocol with North Yemen arranged by us, are to march up the coast of the Red Sea and take Mecca. They will not be opposed by the Saudi Army which will be busy fighting the National Guard. Other Yemeni units will move against the tiny states of Oman and the Arab Emirates, which although weak are strategic.

"Secondly, the capital city of Riyadh will be taken over by the Saudi Army, supported by armed PLO guerrillas and Shiite cells in Riyadh and Hofuf. These have been despised minorities in Arabia and we can properly proclaim our support of these 'liberation' forces.

"Finally, the oil facilities around Dommam, Dhahran and especially Ras Tanura are to be taken by special commando units of the PLO who will be ferried across Iraq to the oil fields by Syrian aircraft. Both Iraq and Syria are client states and there will be no trouble from either of them. As a matter of fact, Iraq's President Hosnani is taking advantage of the situation and is moving ten thousand troops from Basra to the border with Kuwait. We anticipate that he will take Kuwait, which he has long coveted. Kuwait has only a token army, about enough for a military band," Svetlov joked.

"The signal for the coup will be the assassination of King Salim. Without the king to lead them, the National Guard will be fragmented and the royal family divided between Abdul Sa'ad and other factions. Everything depends upon a clear swift removal of the king. We estimate with high probability that with Salim out of the way, Abdul Sa'ad will need only one week to take over Arabia and shut off the oil faucet. The Americans, including most of their military, have enough oil stockpiled to last about sixty days. After that, their only option is surrender."

The members of the Politburo sat in stunned silence, then Premier Suvarov's voice sputtered like a balky engine.

"But surely the old man didn't approve this operation. This kind of adventurism is against everything he ever stood for," Suvarov blustered.

"It was his idea," Fyedorenko said calmly. It was an absolute lie, of course. He imagined that the old man must be spinning like a gyroscope in his grave behind the Lenin mausoleum at the very thought of the Molotov Plan.

"Well, if it was his idea . . ." Bulganov said doubtfully. Not one of them believed Fyedorenko about the old man, but if the KGB and the Red Amry were involved, Fyedorenko was in too strong a position to be challenged.

"This is preposterous," Foreign Minister Kishinev broke in. "Does any of us think for a second that the Americans are going to just sit back and allow us to slit their throats like chickens and not do a damn thing about it?"

"Marshal Orlov," Fyedorenko prompted.

"If it becomes necessary for us to intervene, the Red Army has twenty-four divisions of the Caucasus Army Group deployed south of Lake Sevan and along the Iranian border from Erivan to Baku. An additional fifty thousand troops can be airlifted from Afghanistan and we have the twenty-six-ship fleet of the Sokolov missile cruiser battle group already in position near the Gulf of Oman. We are ready to slice down through Iran with armor and armored infantry. I can be in Abadan in seventy-two hours and in control of the Arabian oil fields in a week to ten days," Orlov declared flatly in his deep basso voice.

"What about the Americans?" Myshkin, the party theoretician, asked Orlov nervously, sensing like the others that the operation would take them into dangerous and uncharted waters.

"The American Persian Gulf fleet is headed by the U.S.S. *Nimitz* carrier task force. They would be an even match for the Sokolov battle group, but under combat conditions it would be impossible for them to keep the Straits of Hormuz open. But the important battle will be waged on the ground, as always. They could move a token force, say a battalion, into combat within twenty-four hours, but that is meaningless. It would take them nearly two weeks to move their Rapid Deployment Force of two divisions plus support units into position. If necessary, they might be able to move in two Marine divisions, as well. But even so they would be too late. We would already control the oil fields and if necessary, blow them up, so that in any case the West would lose the oil. The Marines have no support facilities and the temperature in that desert is one hundred and twenty degrees in the shade, comrades. And there is no shade. Not to mention the fact that their supply lines would stretch around half the world.

"Besides it doesn't really matter. We would already be in position and we outnumber them in men and equipment by at least twelve to one. It would be a massacre," Orlov declared in that rumbling voice that left no room for argument.

"What about the Israelis?" Cherkassy the Ukrainian asked.

"Their ground forces would be a serious factor, but they don't have the airlift capability to move so many troops into a distant battle zone," Orlov replied.

"Suppose they move their troops on the ground?" Liepka the Latvian asked.

"Across all of Jordan and the great Nefud desert?" the field marshal said, amused, his famous bushy eyebrows raised quizzically.

"But is it possible?" Liepka insisted.

"Is a pig kosher?" Korchnoi called out and a nervous laugh rippled around the table.

"Then if I understand you correctly, Comrade Marshal, if it comes to a limited Persian Gulf war with the Americans, you are saying that we cannot lose," Myshkin put in.

"That is correct," Orlov said, his arms folded complacently over his bemedalled chest.

"But what if it isn't limited?" Kishinev put in.

"What are you saying?" Andreyev of the KGB asked.

"I'm saying, comrades, that this plan outlined by Comrade Svetlov is brilliant. In fact it is so brilliant that it leaves the Americans with only one option. Nuclear war, the insanity that we've been working all our lives to prevent," Kishinev said.

"You don't think they would actually—" Komarovsky muttered nervously.

"Nonsense," the urbane KGB chief countered. "Given the choice between nuclear holocaust and higher oil prices, the capitalists will make the only sane decision. As a matter of fact, their oil companies will even show larger profits."

"I disagree. The Americans have never hesitated to use force whenever their interests have been threatened, despite all their pious platitudes about peace," Kishinev objected, wagging his finger like a schoolteacher.

"My God," Komarovsky muttered, in his shock actually pronouncing the forbidden word. He looked up at them, his face drawn and bloodless. "We're on the brink of nuclear war," he said, his voice confused and stunned.

Fyedorenko could sense them hesitating. Now was the time for him to intervene.

"By the time the West can react, it will be too late. You see, comrades, the coup has already begun. The PLO is crossing Syria into Iraq at this moment. Troops from the People's Democratic Republic of Yemen have begun to mobilize. The assassination plot is already in motion," Fyedorenko said with studied nonchalance, conscious that every eye was riveted on him. He expected a murmur of surprise, and got it, but what startled him was Suvarov's air of indifference. Fyedorenko was instantly on guard.

"You dared—without Politburo approval!" Komarovsky sputtered.

As Fyedorenko rose to crush Komarovsky as he had planned all along, Suvarov gestured to an aide, who came forward and handed Suvarov a message. Suvarov smiled.

"I have some news that pertains to our discussion, comrades," Suvarov said. The silence was total. Their careers hung by the thread of what he would say next, Fyedorenko thought with a sickening feeling.

"Perhaps the West will have more time than Comrade Fyedorenko anticipates. It seems this Arab conspiracy has been penetrated by a western agent. According to the GRU," Suvarov said, putting on his bifocals to read the note, "the final meeting was broken up by this agent, who managed a remarkable escape. They call him 'the Scorpion.' "

Everyone turned towards Fyedorenko, sensing weakness. But Fyedorenko smiled and leaned calmly back in his chair. Years of training masked his inner turmoil. That damned Marshal Orlov had allowed Suvarov GRU access, playing both ends against the middle, the gutless bastard. His turn would come too, Fyedorenko thought. Not even a single bead of sweat broke the perfection of his calm exterior.

"That is old news, comrade. Orders to terminate this Scorpion have already been issued," Fyedorenko said, looking intently at Svetlov.

Svetlov nodded. Check and mate, he thought, watching Suvarov develop a sudden intense interest in his fingernails. Fyedorenko had recovered beautifully.

As for this Scorpion, Svetlov mused, he was as good as dead.

Doha

SOMETHING IN THE PATTERN didn't fit. It was like one of those puzzles where you have to find the images of animals hidden in the illustrated foliage.

Macready was right on time, carrying a copy of the *Gulf*

Times folded under his left arm to signal a clear approach. He should have been able to just walk up and join him at the Juice House bar, but still the Scorpion held back. Everything was just as it should be, but there was danger hidden somewhere. The animal in the foliage. He carefully and methodically checked the rendezvous again.

Shiny Buicks and Cadillacs were parked outside the row of Juice Houses, each painted a different color of the rainbow. The cars were filled with young Qataris in jeans and punk T-shirts, sullenly sipping the milky juice made of fruit, sugar, powdered milk and ice pulverized in a blender, to which some of the bolder blades added a shot of illicit gin. Their eyes smoldered dangerously, yet futilely, in this womanless world, money burning in their pockets and no place to spend it.

Cars roared along the Corniche, skimming through the shimmering Gulf heat like brightly painted water bugs. *Dhows* and yachts crowded the distant harbor, their reflections perfectly mirrored in the clear still water. The mud huts which used to cluster along the quays were gone. Instead, white concrete and cinder-block buildings lined the waterfront. The rectangular National Monetary Agency Building, its glass turned to gold in the late afternoon sun, towered over the shops and cafés along the Corniche. Offshore, the oil rigs which had changed everything dotted the horizon like steel islands. Only the rancid mud smell from the fishing quays and *El Khalij*, the clear green Gulf itself, were as the Scorpion remembered them.

Macready sat at the bar of the Sphinx Juice House, meticulously chewing a deep-fried Palace bread roll. His every movement was deliberate and slow, almost ritualized, as if to slice time into smaller chunks of boredom. He stared without seeing at the big yellow sign that gave the Juice House its name. The lopsided face of the Sphinx on the sign looked like an unhappy beagle, as if it had been painted by a faintly disturbed first-grader.

Macready sighed and took another slow bite. That had

changed, the Scorpion thought. He remembered Macready's restlessness in Saigon, his foot always tapping, his eyes always darting about as if wanting to dash around the next corner. He had put on a lot of weight, too. His lightweight linen suit stretched in tight folds across his sagging belly. Maybe it was the hurt look in Macready's eyes that made him nervous, the Scorpion thought.

Still, it should've been all right. After all, Macready was famous for his paranoia about security. There was even a joke that had once made the rounds at Maclean: "I overheard George calling his grandmother yesterday. Of course he ran an in-depth check on her first." After Saigon fell, they didn't tell it any more. Instead, it was "poor George," or "that fucking Macready," depending on the speaker's politics. The Company had shipped him to Doha station hoping he'd resign. Qatar was the ultimate backwater in those days. But Macready had just hung on and on.

Harris must be pissed as hell to have to use Macready for something as hot as this, the Scorpion thought with a grim smile.

His eyes ran over the scene again. Besides Macready's gray Chevy, there were three other cars parked outside the Sphinx. In one a couple of Qatari women sipped juice through the mouth-holes in their facemasks. Four Arab boys in a Cadillac next to theirs bobbed their heads in time to the whining amalgam of quarter-tones and rock that passes for pop music in the Gulf. The music blared so loudly it could have been used to mask jet takeoffs. The third car, a black Pontiac Trans Am convertible, was empty, the door open. Two Arabs in white *dishdashas* sat at the bar near Macready, as the Pakistani barman worked the electric blender. That was normal, too. The Pakistanis were cheap labor. They were to the Gulf Arabs what Mexicans were to white Californians.

That was all. Traffic on the Corniche was light and moving. There was no surveillance. Then he noticed Macready's license plate. Damn! The idiot had used an embassy car. It was an amateurish mistake; the kind of thing Macready never would have done in Saigon. But that was another world, the Scorpion thought.

The Scorpion thought of calling it off, then changed his mind. He had to get the data and the film to Maclean. Besides, Macready had signaled the safe sign. And in his *dishdasha* and *kaffiyeh*, the Scorpion knew that he himself was fairly anonymous. To any but the most careful observer, he was just another Arab. Still, his sense of foreboding grew as he crossed the Corniche. He ordered a *mishmish* and sat next to Macready.

"*Ya Allah,* if it isn't *asayid* . . ." the Scorpion began, smiling broadly.

"Smith," Macready put in hurriedly. He placed the newspaper on the counter. "And you are Sheikh Ahmet's cousin, dear Mister . . ."

"Abu ben Adam, may my tribe increase," the Scorpion said drily. It was a game anyone could play.

"Yes, Mister ben Adam, of course," Macready winced. "Perhaps you might be interested in a spare shipment of air conditioners. Very good price," he added, rolling his eyes as if to suggest that the Qatari Customs would give their left nut to get their hands on it.

"Ah, how sly you westerners are. But Allah sees everything," the Scorpion said with a wink. He picked up the folded newspaper and they carried their drinks back to the car. As Macready was getting behind the wheel, the Scorpion shoved him over and took the driver's seat.

"What's up?" Macready asked.

"Something stinks, George—and it's not the mud-flats."

"Are you hot?" Macready asked, looking around nervously, as if they were already trapped.

"I shouldn't be. Am I?" the Scorpion said, slipping the new I.D. and money out of Macready's newspaper. When he passed it back to Macready, the film cartridge was folded inside.

"I was watched as I left the embassy. I'm sure I shook them in town, but it's a little unnerving," Macready said with a nervous laugh. "This is the first time it's ever happened. It's always been live and let live here. No one cares and everyone makes a few bucks on the side. That business about air conditioners is true. It's amazing how much you can make with a little fiddle on the side."

"Save it for the Junior Achievement Club, George," the Scorpion said and was pleased to see Macready's cheeks color. The hurt look was back in his eyes. Macready looked back at the Juice House.

"What's all this about a hit?" Macready asked glumly.

"You don't need all those players for just a hit. It may be tied to a coup," the Scorpion said.

Something was wrong. He could feel it, like watching a wire being stretched tighter and tighter, waiting for it to snap. The animal part of his brain, honed by a million years of hunting and warfare, had recognized a danger signal, but had been unable to transmit what it was to his conscious mind.

"Who's the target?" Macready asked.

"With Abdul Sa'ad in on it, my money is on King Salim," the Scorpion said, checking the rear-view mirror. There were no new arrivals; no one stopping along the Corniche to see the view or pretending to have car trouble.

"What about the girl?" Macready asked, lighting a cigarette. His hand trembled and he had to shake the match twice.

"It all leads back to Abdul Sa'ad," the Scorpion said.

"When and where is this alleged hit to take place?" Macready demanded. He stabbed out the just-lit cigarette as if he were crushing a bug. His thoughts were obvious. The Scorpion was putting him on the spot. The data was too thin. Washington would ream his ass on this one.

"I don't know—yet. But it's soon. They may have even moved their timetable up because I broke up their little pow-wow."

"You don't really expect me to transmit such crap, do you?

It's all speculation, damn it!" Macready exploded. He looked suspiciously out of the corner of his eye, as though the Scorpion was trying to pass him a bad check. "What are you up to? Is this something you and Harris cooked up?" he demanded, his voice going up a full octave.

"You've grown fat, George," the Scorpion said mildly, unable to keep the distaste out of his voice. With Macready as the case officer, the way he was now, it was hopeless. He'd have to dump Macready and let Washington handle it.

"I know. I'm not the man I was," Macready said suddenly, looking at him with that even-featured American face that would remain boyish well into middle age. "Ever since Saigon," he added softly.

Now how do you deal with a man like that? the Scorpion thought. One minute he had you going and the next he had you feeling sorry for him.

"This is the way back," the Scorpion said. "You've got to convince those assholes that a coup is going down—and soon."

"It's too thin. They won't believe me," Macready said pathetically. Macready looked down at his hands as if they didn't belong to him. He picked up and smoothed the half-crushed cigarette. He didn't relight it.

"Send a CRITIC, George. Wake them up."

"I'll pass it on. That's all I can do," Macready said glumly.

"I was in Nam, too. Remember. I'm not the enemy," the Scorpion said.

He was sweating, but it wasn't the memory of Nam that did it. He had to get away. Now. Something inside him was screaming that it was all wrong. But what was the missing piece, the face hidden in the foliage?

He touched the ignition key, hesitated, then started the car.

"What is it?" Macready asked, startled.

"Who are they after—you or me?" the Scorpion murmured aloud, almost to himself. Macready didn't answer, but his hands began to shake again.

Then the Scorpion suddenly realized what was wrong. The two Arabs in white *dishdashas* hadn't returned to their Pontiac. He had checked out the Corniche in the rear-view mirror again and when he had looked back at the Juice Bar they were gone. Even before he had completed the thought, he had thrown the car into reverse. The wheels spun wildly and he caught a powerful whiff of burnt rubber. Macready was jerked forward almost into the windshield. The tires howled as the Scorpion backed out on to the Corniche and slammed into drive. The Chevy fishtailed as he floored the accelerator, then straightened as he raced towards the harbor. The Juice Bar began to recede in the rear-view mirror.

"What the hell . . . ." Macready began.

"Hang on!" the Scorpion shouted. The rest of his words were lost in a deafening roar as the Pontiac exploded into a brilliant fireball. A blast of fiery air almost knocked them off the road.

The Chevy skidded against a traffic circle curb, the shock almost wrenching the wheel from the Scorpion's hands. They bounced off the circle, grazing a blue Cadillac which had gone out of control. The driver, a Qatari businessman, stared in horror as his car started to roll over. The Cadillac turned on to its back, smashing into a gaudily painted van. The two vehicles slammed into a parked truck, just missing a car full of wide-eyed children. As the Chevy slued towards the pileup, the Scorpion twisted the wheel to fight the skid, sliding halfway across the road before straightening out.

As they pulled away, the accelerator jammed against the floorboard, he risked a glance at the rear-view mirror. The Pontiac and one of the Cadillacs were gone, obliterated. The other Cadillac where the women had been was a sheet of flame. The Sphinx and the Juice Bar next door were black twisted rubble. Only the sagging back walls remained. Another Juice House was burning rapidly. Black smoke built an immense column that could be seen for miles. Broken glass littered acres of ground.

And there was something else. A couple of hundred yards behind them and gaining fast was a black BMW 733i. Inside it were the two young Arabs from the Pontiac at the Juice Bar.

"My God! They tried to kill me," Macready said, his face white. He grasped the dashboard so tightly, pools of blood collected under his fingernails.

"Not you, me," the Scorpion snapped bitterly. Macready's carelessness had put them on his trail again. What was worse, there was no way the Chevy was going to be able to outrun the BMW. Although he was flying down the Corniche, passing cars going sixty as if they were standing still, the BMW was still creeping closer.

The Scorpion turned the rear-view mirror so Macready could use it.

"Recognize either of those guys in the BMW?" he asked.

"No," Macready said. Then he added "I'm sorry," although the Scorpion wasn't sure what he was apologizing for. Life, maybe.

The Scorpion remembered Koenig in his neat khaki uniform, balancing on the balls of his feet in that stifling Quonset hut in Virginia, telling them: " 'Sorry' is a word for children and lovers' quarrels. If you ever have to say 'sorry' in this business, it'll mean somebody died because you fucked up."

"What makes you so sure it's you they're after?" Macready asked.

"Because we're close, damn it. This is the second time in twenty-four hours that they've tried to kill me. There's your proof, George. They're going to hit the king. Or do you play these car games all the time?" the Scorpion said, whipping around a slow-moving red sedan and slipping neatly into a gap in the traffic ahead. Traffic began to thicken as they approached the waterfront. The BMW was only a few cars behind.

The Scorpion's mind raced. Assume that they were after him. Macready was just along for the ride. Then if he could peel them off, Macready would be free to get the data to Maclean. On the plus side, they probably hadn't expected him to survive the blast, so they were playing it by ear. There would be no traps lurking for George at the embassy. On the minus side, they knew their way around town better than he did and the Chevy was no match for the BMW.

In the gospel according to Koenig, you could always break a single tail. The theory was that action is faster than reaction and since (assumption) they don't know where you're going, any surprise combined with average driver reactions in normal traffic flows ought to break you free long enough for them to lose line of sight, etcetera. He could just drop Macready off somewhere near the embassy, and hide after dumping the Chevy.

That was the theory, anyway. But a glance in the rear-view mirror convinced him that it wasn't going to happen that way. By this time only a single car separated them from the BMW. But that wasn't the problem.

He had seen the Arab in the BMW's passenger seat speaking into a car phone.

"I don't suppose you have a phone or a CB in this thing?" the Scorpion asked as they went around the last traffic circle before the quays. The setting sun gilded the crowded shops and street cafés with their brightly-colored umbrellas with a golden glamor, as though it were the Riviera.

Macready shook his head. "Budget," he said, as if that covered everything in life.

Macready's sense of futility was beginning to grate. The Scorpion hoped the prick could find his zipper when he needed it.

"The embassy still near the bank?" the Scorpion asked. He had to make a move quickly, before whatever reinforcements the BMW had called were in place.

Macready shook his head.

"Just two blocks from . . . What are you going to do?" Macready asked, suddenly pale.

"When I yell 'Go,' don't argue. Just get out of the car and run like hell for the embassy. With any luck, Mr. Smith will get a call from Abu ben Adam to confirm the assassination," the Scorpion said, his eyes darting as he calculated the traffic flow. Ahead, near the white-filigreed façade of the Royal Bank of Qatar, a one-way street jammed with traffic fed into the Corniche.

A rear-view mirror check showed the BMW right behind them. One of the Arabs was pulling what looked like an AK-47 out of a gun case. In this traffic, Macready and he were sitting ducks. If only the car in front of them—a rheumatic old Citroen belching black exhaust and driven by an elderly Qatari sitting bolt upright behind the wheel as if he had been nailed there—did not move immediately when the van ahead of him, striped red and green like a candy cane, started up, they might have a chance.

The Scorpion wiped the sweat out of his eyes with his sleeve. Even with good luck, it was going to be close.

He made one last check. The traffic on the Corniche was stop and go. Dodging pedestrians played chicken with honking cars at intersections. The street cafés were beginning to fill and the pavement swarmed with the flotsam of a dozen nations, drawn by the smell of money to Qatar like flies to a corpse. The Scorpion hoped they would all add to the confusion at the right moment.

"Suppose you're wrong. Suppose it's me they're really after?" Macready demanded petulantly.

"Then I'll apologize—afterwards."

"By then I'll be dead. It'll be too late," Macready pouted. He really was a little prick, the Scorpion thought.

"Apologies always are," the Scorpion replied.

Come on, come on, he thought, the wheel slippery in his hands from sweat. Just then the candy-striped van's brake lights went off. As the van lurched forward with a jerk, the Scorpion made his move.

The Chevy leaped forward in a sideways curve as he slued

the wheel to the left while stepping on the accelerator as though he wanted to put it through the floorboard. He sandwiched into a gap in the oncoming lane, then swerved back into line ahead of the Citroen, smashing its wing as he angled across its front. As he had anticipated, the panicked old Qatari driver jammed on the brake and froze, giving him the precious inches he needed to cross the lane. Horn blaring, tires screaming, he swerved broadside to the one-way side street feeding cars into the Corniche traffic. Bracing hard, he deliberately allowed the Chevy to smash sideways into the front of a truck filled with frizzy-haired Baluchi laborers. Metal grating and ripping, the Scorpion then rammed almost head-on into a pink Cadillac filled with Qatari women, their eyes bulging wide behind their veils.

"Go!" the Scorpion shouted as he pulled the key out of the ignition and flung himself out of the car. Out of the corner of his eye, he saw Macready jump out of the other side and run with a fat man's bouncing gait up the one-way street, now jammed with traffic completely corked by the accident. He looked back for the BMW as he watched Macready turn the corner and disappear. The Arabs had abandoned the BMW. He felt a sense of grim satisfaction that he had been right, they were coming after him, not Macready.

A symphony of noise exploded as angry Arabs pounded on their horns, cursing and calling upon Allah. The Scorpion headed up the one-way street, his spine tensed for the bullet that might come any second. He started towards the pavement, then hesitated for an instant. The narrow walks were jammed with bystanders swarming towards the accident. Instead, he began to weave in and out of the blocked cars, jumping over wings and locked bumpers. He risked a backward glance over his shoulder. They were still coming. He had to get off the street. Then he spotted the entrance to a small department store.

Just before he dodged through the crowd into the store, the Scorpion spotted the Arabs from the BMW shouldering their way through the crowd in a serious way. They were good, making way without raising too many eyebrows, he thought. They would try to bracket him. Get him to an isolated killing-ground, where hunter and prey would play the oldest game on earth.

At least they hadn't brought the AK-47 because it was too conspicuous, he thought, waiting until he was sure they spotted him before he entered the store.

After the street the store was an oasis of quiet. The coolness of the air conditioning was like a caress. The store had just reopened after the midday siesta and there were only a few customers, mostly women veiled in black from head to toe, flitting among the racks like dark ghosts. Except for the signs in Arabic and that indelible scent of the Gulf made of mud and decay, he might have been in a suburban shopping mall anywhere.

It was difficult to force himself to walk not run as he made his way through the men's clothing area. Time was short. The Arabs from the BMW would be in the store any second. He had to change the image, he thought, his eyes running urgently along the endless racks of overpriced suits.

Seeing a black-veiled woman chatting with a salesgirl near the opening of the partitioned women's clothing area gave him an idea. It was the element of surprise he needed, because it was the one thing no Arab would ever think of. He was debating whether to try it when he saw the outside door begin to open, and before the two Arabs came in he was on his hands and toes, crawling crab-like between the racks of clothes towards the women's partition.

If only they didn't come this way first, the Scorpion thought, sweat streaming down his face. He crouched by the partition, hesitating. Now luck was everything, because if anyone spotted him on the women's side, they would raise an outcry that would wake the dead.

The sound of a carpeted footstep on the other side of the rack he was crouching behind froze his blood. Without thinking, he slipped silently behind the women's partition. The footsteps had stopped and he could visualize the Arab standing there, listening.

He cautiously peered over the top of a rack of women's black full-length veils. A fat woman shopper in western dress was heading right towards him. Fortunately she hadn't seen him yet. In desperation the Scorpion grabbed one of the veils marked Extra Large and threw it over his head. He cautiously straightened up. The veil covered him from head to the bottom of his trousers. Because of his height he would have to walk with his knees bent, but only his man's sandals might give him away.

He began to walk openly down the aisle, counting on the notion of a man in a woman's veil being too outlandish for Arabs to even consider. But his security was as flimsy as the veil itself, he knew. He had to get something to cut down the odds, something quieter than a Walther automatic. What made it harder wasn't just that there were two of them, but that he needed to get one of them alive. They only had to kill him.

He headed for the kitchenware section and began to examine the kitchen knives. A salesgirl started to come over. The Scorpion turned away, his heart pounding. He faced a display of plates with a French country pattern, no doubt mass-produced in Korean sweatshops. The salesgirl was still heading towards him. She looked at him oddly, as if trying to make up her mind about something. He was sure she had spotted something wrong. He had to do something.

"What is that on your face? Is it lipstick or blood?" the Scorpion said in a falsetto voice.

The salesgirl looked at him wide-eyed, as if he was from Mars.

"What's the matter with your face? Quick, go find a mirror," the Scorpion whispered intently, pointing at her face.

A look of horror came over the girl's face. She scuttled away to find a mirror. No one could have resisted a ploy like that, the Scorpion thought, going back to the kitchen knives.

It took only a second to slip a heavy-bladed butcher knife under his veil. Now the prey becomes the hunter, he thought, heading towards the appliances section.

One of the Arabs from the BMW was standing next to a refrigerator in the home appliances section, his hand around a bulge in his jacket pocket. He began to walk towards the Scorpion, who backed modestly out of his way, as a well-bred Arab woman should. The Scorpion stared blankly at a micro-wave oven with enough dials to fly a space shuttle, his back prickling with sweat. The Arab walked right by him as if he wasn't there. Fortunately for him, women were truly invisible in Arabia, the Scorpion thought, hesitating as he tried to decide whether to take the Arab out or save him for information.

In theory, as Harold Gallagher used to say in Nam, when you have two subjects to question, you intimidate the weaker by making an example of the stronger. Harold invented the technique which became the most widely used by the Special Forces. They would take VC suspects up in a chopper. When they reached an altitude of about 8000 feet, they would question the toughest suspect at gunpoint. If he didn't talk, they'd throw him out without a parachute. It was important to wait till he had fallen all the way, so that the full impact would register before you questioned the next one, Gallagher told him.

Except that the other Arab wasn't in sight and the Scorpion had no idea which of them was tougher. But this one's back was towards the Scorpion and he had to cut down the odds. Before the Arab took another step, the Scorpion struck.

He grabbed the Arab's mouth with his left hand to prevent a cry as he thrust through his veil with his right. The knife slid into the man's back with only a fraction of resistance as the knife glanced off a rib. He felt the Arab's body stiffen and shudder. Although he thought he had pierced the heart, to be sure he sawed with a savage wrench between the sixth and seventh thoracic vertebrae, cutting the spinal cord, as the body slid silently to the floor. The Scorpion wiped the blood off the knife onto the Arab's trousers and hid it back under the veil. He left the body in the aisle. If it caused a commotion, so much the better, so long as he found the second Arab before the police arrived.

The second Arab was a tall thin man with hollow sunken cheeks and a Hitler moustache. He looked like a Hteymi tribesman to the Scorpion. The Arab stalked the aisles of the television section, a Magnum .385 in his hand.

Behind the Arab a bank of television screens all showed the same image, like a pop-art painting. It was an ancient rerun of an American western about a rancher and his sons. It was still popular with the Arabs who liked the close-knit family feeling and the fact that the cowboys lived in a womanless world. The Scorpion had an odd surreal vision as he watched a hundred images of a tiny cowboy stalk someone on a dusty western street while the Hteymi stalked him in an almost identical pose.

The Hteymi came closer. The Scorpion could smell the sweat and fear, although he wasn't sure whether it was coming from the Arab or himself. The Hteymi stared dangerously at him. He had spotted something! Maybe the Scorpion's feet. Or blood. Something. The Scorpion had to distract him for an instant.

"*Ihtaris!* Your friend—over there!" the Scorpion cried out in a falsetto screech which might have come from one of the hags in *Macbeth*. He pointed towards the refrigerators. But it wasn't going to work. The Hteymi just grinned evilly and aimed the gun at the Scorpion's head. The gaps between the Hteymi's teeth made him look demented. That ugly face would be the last thing he would ever see, the Scorpion thought despairingly.

Just then a cry came from the refrigerator section.

"*Alnagda! Otlob al Police!*"

Someone must have discovered the body, the Scorpion thought. The gun in the Hteymi's hand wavered for an instant as he glanced in the direction of the cry. It was all the Scorpion needed.

He slashed with the knife in a wide sweeping curve from under the veil. The blade hit the Arab's wrist, slicing through the veins and tendons to the bone. The Hteymi screamed as the Scorpion grabbed the man's now useless gun hand. The Hteymi's wrist was gushing blood like a faucet. His other hand was around the Scorpion's throat, his fingers digging deep into the Scorpion's neck.

The Scorpion kicked at the inside of the Hteymi's knee, taking them both down. He continued to saw viciously at the Hteymi's hand as they struggled. The Hteymi hung on like a wild animal. The Scorpion was almost out of air. He began to see spots and lights before his eyes. Losing it, he thought desperately.

Suddenly, everything came loose. A hard elbow to the Hteymi's solar plexus slackened the grip on his throat and he was able to put the knife to the Hteymi's throat. He didn't have to worry about the gun. The Hteymi's hand had been completely severed. It lay on the floor like a dead crab, the fingers frozen around the gun.

The Scorpion pried the gun from the still-warm fingers and pointed it at the Hteymi, who stood up slowly, cradling his severed wrist in his good hand. The wrist rhythmically spurted blood like an uncapped oil pump. The Hteymi's eyes were insane.

The Scorpion ripped off his bloodied veil and prodded the Hteymi with the knife in his other hand.

"Quickly. The men's toilet!" he said, motioning with the gun.

"My hand, my hand . . ." the Hteymi began to blubber.

"Hurry! You still have lots of parts I can cut off," the Scorpion snapped harshly, gesturing at the Hteymi's privates with the bloody knife. The Hteymi glanced around desperately.

116

"There's no help. Your friend is dead. Move!" the Scorpion snarled, jabbing lightly below the belt with the knife. The Hteymi stumbled down the aisle, the Scorpion's arm around him, knife at his throat.

They pushed their way into the men's toilet. It stank of urine and cheap tobacco and musk cologne. The only light came from a small open window near the ceiling. A Baluchi janitor was at the mirror, poking at his bushy hair with a comb. When he saw the two men covered with blood he called upon Allah. When he saw the gun, his jaw dropped open and he scuttled out of the door. The Scorpion locked the door and savagely shoved the Hteymi into a stall. The Baluchi was probably too frightened to tell the police, but time was running out, the Scorpion knew. He had to move fast. And he hadn't forgotten all the innocent people killed by the Hteymi back at the Juice Bar.

The Scorpion's icy gray eyes stared at the trembling Hteymi. With an almost casual backhand, he pistol-whipped the Hteymi across the face, smashing the Hteymi's nose and knocking him back against the wall. Before the stunned Hteymi could recover his balance, the Scorpion cut open the man's belt and trousers. The Hteymi stood there in his underwear, his trousers around his ankles, his wrist spraying blood over them both. His eyes were utterly terrified.

The Scorpion stuck the gun into his pocket and with two quick knife strokes sliced off the Hteymi's briefs and wadded them into the Hteymi's mouth. The Hteymi tried to grab the Scorpion's knife with his good hand. The Scorpion reacted instantly, grabbing the Hteymi's privates and squeezing with all his strength. The Hteymi's eyes bulged out as a muffled scream echoed in the stall. The Scorpion placed the edge of the blade against the base of the Hteymi's scrotum.

"Tell me the truth or they're gone. Understand?" the Scorpion demanded, hoping it would work. The police would be barging in any second.

The Hteymi nodded fearfully, whimpering like a child. The Scorpion removed the gag. Sweat poured off the Hteymi as if he were standing in a shower.

"The king is the target, isn't he?" the Scorpion began.

"How did . . ." the Hteymi began, then forced himself to stop.

The Scorpion smiled. He had the confirmation for Macready.

"Does Prince Abdul Sa'ad have the Yankee woman?" he asked.

"Please . . . my hand," the man blubbered. The whimper changed to a scream as the Scorpion squeezed again.

"Yes, yes . . ." the Hteymi cried.

"Where is she?"

"I don't know. No, really," he screamed again, in a panicky voice. "But it is whispered that the Prince has her in his country house in the desert," the Hteymi babbled. His eyes began to roll as the shock and loss of blood began to hit him. The Scorpion shook him like a terrier with a mouse.

"How is the king to be killed?"

"I don't know. I swear to Allah," the Hteymi said. He cried out again as he felt the edge of the blade against his scrotum. "Please, they don't tell me such things. They say only that it must be public—a demonstration!"

"Of course. For all the Shiites and Hteymis and all the downtrodden to see," the Scorpion smiled.

"Yes and soon, very soon, Master," the Hteymi blubbered, his eyes dog-like and eager to please.

"Where and when is this great liberation supposed to take place?" the Scorpion demanded.

He saw fear and a fleeting cunning come into the Hteymi's eyes. Incredible as it was to believe, the man was even more afraid of Abdul Sa'ad than of him. The Scorpion began to get a very bad feeling about Prince Abdul Sa'ad.

"Where?" the Scorpion snarled, putting the bloody knife to the Hteymi's throat.

118

That was a mistake. The Hteymi suddenly arched his head back and then thrust himself forward, impaling himself on the blade. He sank down on the toilet, blood gurgling out of his torn throat.

Outside, the Scorpion could hear voices. Someone cried "Police!" and the sounds came closer. The only way out was through that small window, he thought. He seemed to remember that it was open when he came in. There was no time left for anything else. They were at the door.

The Scorpion leaped up, grabbing at the top of the partition. He pulled himself up and balanced for a second on top like a tightrope walker. The window was near the ceiling and about five feet away. It was going to be a very tight fit. Just then, the door burst open.

The Scorpion leaped headlong at the opening. A shot spattered the plaster just below him as he grabbed hold of the sill and squirmed through the window, propelling himself forward with the thrust of the jump. He looked down at a garbage-strewn alley about ten feet below. He felt something catch his trouser leg. A splinter or a bullet, he thought, jerking his leg away as if stung and diving headlong into the alleyway. As he fell, he went into a tuck position. He landed with an incredible jar at the base of his spine, rolling head over heels in the dirty trash.

He didn't know whether he was hurt or not. All he knew was that he had to get the data to Washington. He had caught a glimpse of the enemy.

Prince Abdul Sa'ad was so dangerous, men would rather kill themselves than betray him. And he had the girl.

Somehow he got to his feet and began to run.

Washington

THE CRITIC FROM MACREADY arrived in the Situation Room in the basement of the East-Wing of the White House at two in the morning. The message was handed to William Page, the Director of Central Intelligence, by Linda Hunnicut, a spectacular redhead whose most prominent assets, Vice-President Larkin once declared, "jutted out like the front of a '59 Pontiac." She was the object of a universal lust and normally one of the men seated around the table, cluttered with coffee cups and a box of doughnuts, would have bantered with her. But this night, the five men sat silently until she closed the door behind her. The tension in the room was so palpable it could have been packaged and sold in drug stores as a diet pill.

"It's a CRITIC from the Qatar station," Page muttered, the light from the illuminated wall map of the Middle East making a harlequin pattern on his bald head, as if he were suffering from a splotchy skin disease. The others glanced anxiously at Page. A CRITIC was a crisis COMINT message, relayed via satellite by the Communication Intelligence radio system operated by the NSA. According to the rules, a CRITIC must be relayed directly to the White House within five minutes of transmission.

"The Scorpion has definitely confirmed. There is an imminent assassination and coup against King Salim of Arabia," Page announced, looking up at them with eyes that were red-rimmed from lack of sleep.

"When and where is this alleged assassination to take place?" asked Secretary of State Wallace. He emphasized the word "alleged" so no one would doubt his position.

Page turned to Bob Harris. "Bob?"

"We don't know yet. So far all we've got is that it's going

to be in a public place, like the Sadat hit, and that it's going down soon, maybe a matter of days," Harris said. Despite the late hour, he looked fresh and unrumpled.

"Why not warn King Salim right away?" Wallace asked.

"Great," Page sighed. "Tell the king his brother might want to kill him, alienate both sides of the royal family, tip our hand to Abdul Sa'ad and maybe make things a hundred times worse."

"War in Arabia. How could things be worse?" Wallace muttered angrily, loosening his tie. A sure sign that he was furious.

"We could lose. That's worse," Page snapped.

"I don't much like the sound of that word 'lose,' " drawled Air Force General Baker, liaison from the Joint Chiefs, in his Tennessee twang.

Secretary of State Wallace, whose handsome face had aged so much during the night it was virtually unrecognizable, opened a new pack of cigarettes and lit up. After a heart attack, reported in the press as an ulcer operation, Wallace had been ordered by his doctors to never touch another cigarette. For almost eight months he had succeeded in doing just that, until tonight.

"The president will have to be told at once," Wallace said.

"Not just yet. You know how he hates to be woken up. Especially when all we have are bits and pieces," said Gary Allen, the president's Security Advisor. A tall man in tweeds, with iron-gray hair cropped short, he dipped a doughnut into his coffee for a single precise dunk, then swallowed it after chewing carefully.

"How much more do you need?" Bob Harris challenged brusquely. "You've seen the Scorpion's photos. The whole thing's got the Kremlin's size elevens stamped all over it."

"We don't know that for sure," Allen replied.

"What about the Scorpion's reports?" Harris said.

Allen dismissed the reports and photos scattered on the table with an offhand gesture, as though brushing away a fly.

"That's evidence, not proof," Allen said.

"What's the difference?" General Baker asked, puzzled.

"Evidence is suggestive; proof is incontrovertible," Allen declared pedantically, as if he were still at his lecture rostrum at Yale. Allen's air of nit-picking arrogance was legendary. When the president had picked him for the job of National Security Advisor, one of his fellow professors had remarked: "Now Allen will be able to give the whole world a grade of C minus."

"Look at the photos," Page insisted. The secretary of state nodded at Harris, who pressed a few buttons on a console. A screen descended on the far wall and the lights darkened. Harris fiddled for a moment with a slide projector and then the faintly blurred image of men sitting around a campfire filled the screen. Everyone in the room stared at the screen. Only Allen looked away pointedly and sighed.

"Have we identified all the players?" Wallace asked. Page looked at Harris, who pulled open his collapsible pointer and went up to the screen.

"That's Abdul Sa'ad there," Harris said, slapping the pointer against Abdul Sa'ad's face on the screen. "He leads a fanatic anti-western Wahabi faction in the Saudi royal family. If the coup succeeds, he would be the most likely candidate for king."

"How did this 'Scorpion'—Wallace pronounced the code name with distaste, as if he were being forced to swallow something disgusting—"come up with Abdul Sa'ad as the ringleader?"

"Actually, he was supposed to be on another op," Page replied.

"What was that?" General Baker asked.

"He was looking for Ormont's daughter. The one who disappeared," Harris said.

"Did he find her?" Wallace asked.

"He says Abdul Sa'ad's got her," Harris said.

"I see," Allen said pensively, his expression troubled.

"Who's this?" Wallace asked, poking towards a face on the screen as if pushing a button.

"That's Nuruddin, the Bahraini millionaire. We think he could be the link to the KGB. Nuruddin was educated at Cambridge in the early thirties. We checked with the British SIS, who report that he was a member of the university Labour Club at that time. The old NKVD did a lot of recruiting from that bunch. They also discovered that he was friendly with Burgess, Maclean and, most importantly, Kim Philby, son of the famous Arabist. They could have recruited him back then," Harris said.

"Could have . . ." Allen intoned like a Greek chorus.

"What else?" Wallace prompted.

"The Scorpion says that this man, the one he terminated, was a major in the PLO. Our Middle East IA section tentatively identified him as Major Habad of Al Fatah. He had close ties to the Arafat faction and we know that they're also tied closely to Moscow."

"Tentatively . . ." Allen sighed.

"The guards at the meeting were Yemenis, Palestinians and Saudis and they carried AK-47s," Harris said, pointedly ignoring Allen's interjection. "The Scorpion identified this man as a South Yemeni and we know that the Russians were having secret meetings in Aden and San'a. We also have a Samos spy satellite recon photo suggesting a movement of Cuban troops from Ethiopia to Aden. Plus, we have unconfirmed reports from both ELINT and Riyadh station about South Yemeni troops moving up the Red Sea coast."

"Unconfirmed . . ." Allen said, his eyebrows raised quizzically.

"Finally, the Scorpion says this man could be a Cuban," Harris said through gritted teeth, tapping the photo as if poking Allen's chest.

"Could be . . ." Allen snapped derisively.

"The Latin desk says he resembled Pablo Huevas, a senior aide to Fidel Castro," Harris said quietly.

"Resembles . . . could be . . . suggests!" Allen exploded. "Can you imagine the president going on television and trying to convince the world of Soviet aggression with such insubstantial crap?"

"That's not the point," Page said.

"What is the point?" General Baker asked, looking around the table for the coffee jug. There was only a trickle left in the jug and he poured it into his cup and swallowed it with a grimace.

"What do we tell the president? That's the damn point," Page growled, rubbing his forehead as if he had a headache.

"I'll tell you what we do. We've got the *Nimitz* task force in that area. We can send in a couple of squadrons of F-14s and bomb the shit out of them," General Baker declared, a boyish enthusiasm lighting his austere face.

"Bomb who?" Wallace asked wearily.

"Them . . . the bad guys," General Baker said lamely.

"Wonderful," Harris muttered sarcastically.

"Don't you understand? There are no battle lines here. So far there's just some talk of an assassination in Riyadh," Page declared. "According to the Scorpion's report, there might be Wahabis, army troops and National Guardsmen, Palestinians, Shiites and Christ knows who else involved in this. You can't even tell the players without a score card and you want to just blast everybody."

"Not to mention the fact that we don't even know who to support. Prince Abdul Sa'ad might be better than having chaos in Arabia," the secretary of state noted.

"Well, we've got to do something," General Baker rumbled, glaring balefully at them.

"Why?" Allen put in. "I mean suppose Abdul Sa'ad wins. So we do business with him. What's the difference?"

"The difference is that he could . . . cut . . . off . . . the goddamn oil," Harris said, enunciating very carefully, as if he were chiseling each word into stone. "And if we're right and

124

it is a major Russian move, then that's exactly what he's going to do, gentlemen."

"My God!" Secretary Wallace muttered in a toneless whisper, the enormity of the threat dawning on him.

At that moment, the door opened and Linda the "Honey Pot," as the White House staff had leeringly nicknamed her, handed General Baker a yellow paper, bending over far enough so that if there were ever any doubt about her bona fides they were erased for ever. But all eyes were on the paper, not on her and she wiggled back out of the door with a vague air of disappointment.

"Oh boy," the general whistled through his teeth and glanced up at the illuminated map.

"What is it?" the worried secretary of state asked.

"It's from naval intelligence. A Soviet naval force headed by the missile cruiser *Sokolov* is moving towards the Straits of Hormuz. This is from a recon patrol from the *Nimitz*," General Baker said in an awed voice, as though he were in church.

For a long moment no one said anything. Each man sat stunned and somehow alone, as though they were in the presence of sudden death. The secretary of state put a cigarette between his lips but forgot to light it. Gary Allen's aristocratic face was drawn and pale.

"Well, Mr. Allen. Do you still think the Kremlin tie-in is pure speculation?" Bob Harris's caustic voice cut rudely through the silence.

The national security advisor got up awkwardly and walked over to the illuminated map. He stared at the narrow inverted blue vee of the Straits of Hormuz like a man in a trance. At last he turned to face them. His eyes were stunned, like a cow that's been killed by a blow to the head from a pneumatic hammer but doesn't know yet that it is dead.

"The president will have to be told at once," he said through bloodless lips.

General Baker crossed to a bank of black telephones on a side table and picked up one of the receivers.

"I'd better alert the Joint Chiefs. What about the Rapid Deployment Force?" he asked to the room at large.

"Tell them to go to Defcon Three Ready status," Wallace said. Baker looked questioningly at Allen who nodded his assent.

"The Marines too," Allen said quietly. "And we'll want a spy ship of the Liberty class in the Red Sea to monitor the Yemenis," he added.

Baker nodded and punched a button on the phone. He began talking in an urgent undertone. Allen went to a separate red phone and hesitated a moment before picking it up.

"Everything seems to depend on the data from this Scorpion of yours," he said to Page, obviously worried.

"Just who the hell is this Scorpion anyway?" Wallace snapped irritably.

"He's an independent. But the boys tell me he's virtually a legend in Arabia," Page said.

"The president will want to know all about him. You know how he is about data on personalities," Allen remarked with a wry smile.

Page nodded. The daily DIA-CIA intelligence report on leading political figures and their sexual peccadillos was said to be the president's favorite bedtime reading.

"Is he an American?" Allen asked.

"Bob?" Page looked questioningly at Harris, leaning back in his chair until it tilted precariously.

"He's an American, all right. Born in Palos Verdes, California."

"What makes him such an expert on the Arabs anyway?" asked Wallace, his brow wrinkled to show his distaste at having to place any reliance on one of the CIA hotshots, particularly an independent, whom he often irritably referred to as "wild men" within the privacy of his State Department office.

"Because he was raised among the Beduin in Arabia," Harris said, an impudent grin creasing his cheeks.

Allen, who had been about to pick up the red phone, turned to Harris, annoyed disbelief written on his face as clearly as if Harris had told him that the Scorpion's real name was Clark Kent.

"Just how in hell did an American kid wind up being raised by Beduin tribesmen?" Allen demanded belligerently, as if he felt he was being used as the butt of a joke.

"I believe it was a family problem of some kind," Harris replied.

Prescribed for you is fighting, though it be hateful to you. Yet it may happen that you will hate a thing which is better for you; and it may happen that you will love a thing which is worse for you; God knows, and you know not.

—The Koran

Arabia, 1951

THE BOY LOOKED DOWN at the man who was said to be his father and wondered if he was dead. The man lay face-down in the sand, a large rust-colored stain slowly spreading across the back of his sun-bleached khaki shirt. In the distance the boy could see the horsemen with the guns rapidly approaching. Tentatively at first, then more urgently, the boy plucked at the man's arm.

"Dad," he said. "C'mon, Dad."

The man didn't move. Was that death? the boy wondered. He'd never seen a dead person before. He looked around for the others, but he was the only one moving. Robby the geologist was slumped over the rig struts as though he was sleeping. Shwayhat, Dad's Arab guide, lay crumpled in an awkward posture. Dad always called Shwayhat his "go-fer," but Nick didn't understand why he called the Arab that. Gramps had told him that a "go-fer" was a little brown animal, like a mouse. Billy, the rigger, was the worst. He lay staring at the sky, his arms flung wide like a picture of Jesus which Gran had shown him in the *Golden Bible for Children*. There was a big red wound on the side of Billy's face and little black things were crawling on it. It made Nick feel sick and he turned away.

The shooting had come without warning and Billy had jumped on Nick, pushing his face into the hot sand. Billy was heavy on him and Nick tried to shove him away, but he couldn't. Billy smelled funny. It was the same smell as Mom when she would come home from a date, bumping into the furniture and saying funny things in a slurred voice. Sometimes Mom would bring home an "uncle" and yell at him because he was still up. He had lots of uncles, but they always left in the morning.

It was just Mom and Nicky then. Dad had left them alone to find something called "oil." Nick figured that it was something he had lost during the war. Mom said Dad was a "bastid" to leave them, but she mixed her words sometimes and he thought she meant "basket." A basket was a bad thing. She always made Nick promise not to be a basket when he grew up. Dad was a wildcatter and all wildcatters were baskets, Mom said.

The worst wildcatters came from Texas. Dad had come from Texas and Mom met him in San Diego. That was during the war when Dad was a "C.B.," whatever that was. Then Mom and Dad got divorced because Dad was a basket. That was what divorce meant: when a dad goes away.

One night Mom left him with Gramps and Gran. She went out with Uncle Stan. Nick remembered that Mom and Uncle Stan were laughing and their breath smelled funny, like Billy. In the morning he woke to find Gran sitting on his bed. Her eyes were puffy and red and she hugged him close. He didn't like being held and tried to wriggle out of her grasp, but she held him tightly.

"Oh my poor baby," Gran cried and Nick's heart beat wildly, like the wings of a trapped bird. He'd never seen Gran act this way before. He wrinkled his nose. Gran didn't smell like Mom. She smelled old. She told him there had been an "accident" and he was afraid she was going to punish him. Sometimes he had an accident at night and woke up with the bed wet and smelling of "pee-pee" and Mom would get mad at him.

She told him that Mom was dead. Uncle Stan too. She said dead meant that Mom had gone away to be with Jesus in heaven. He asked Gran when Mom was coming back and she just shook her head and hugged him again. She asked him if he understood and he said yes. Mom had gone away. That's what grown-ups did: they went away.

When he went down for breakfast, he looked around for Mom, just in case she might've come back. He looked all over the house, but he couldn't find her. The next day, they dressed him in a suit and tie and took him to the funeral home. They said Mom was in a box by the altar, but Gran wouldn't let him look. She said that it wasn't really Mom in the coffin. Mom was in heaven.

They drove to the cemetery in a big black car. The minister, a tall skinny man with a funny nasal voice, talked about peace and heaven and Gran cried. Nick looked down the green slope towards the freeway. The grass was speckled with white markers like stone sheep. The lanes of traffic shimmered in the smoggy sunlight and on a distant billboard, a man and woman embraced against a giant cigarette package.

The minister picked up a handful of dirt and poured it into Nick's hand. He told Nick to throw it into the grave. Nick pressed away from the grave, afraid that if he went too close to the edge he would fall in and be locked in the earth forever. The minister took his hand and tried to make him throw the dirt. Nick's snub-nosed face became contorted and he bared his teeth like a wolf cub. He threw the dirt in the minister's face. The minister stood there blinking stupidly as Gramps took Nick's hand and led him back to the car.

From then on he lived with Gran and Gramps. Esmeralda the maid took him to the nursery every day. At dinner he had to sit still and not speak until spoken to. One night Gran said she wouldn't have that man in her house and Nick's heart began to pound. He somehow knew, although he didn't know how, that they were speaking about his father.

Gran didn't like his father. She said his neck was red and he made loud noises when he ate. She looked disgusted when she said that, like the time when he had found a garter snake in the garden. It was a question of breeding, Gran said, looking pointedly at Nick. You were supposed to keep your mouth closed and chew each bite properly. That showed you had good manners.

That night Nick lay awake for a long time, wondering what his father looked like and whether he really had a red neck.

Rain pattered against his bedroom window and he wondered if it would flood and carry his mother out to sea forever. He began to cry. Then Gran came in and told him about heaven until he began to yawn and fell asleep.

In the morning a strange man came to the house. They were having breakfast in Gran's "breakfast nook" when Esmeralda came in and said there was a Mr. Tim Curry at the door. Nick smiled. That was funny, because Curry was his name too. He was Nick Curry. Gran looked at Gramps.

The man came into the breakfast room. Esmeralda looked at Gramps, who dismissed her with a wave of his hand. The man had very broad shoulders, dark curly hair and gray eyes. His face was dark as an Indian's from the sun and Nick craned his head to see if the man's neck was really red like Gran said.

"I've come for my boy, Marjorie," the man said in a quiet voice, but he wasn't looking at Gran. He was looking at Nick. No one had ever looked at him like that and he felt uncomfortable.

"It's a little late for that now," Gran said.

"Hello Nick. I'm your father," the man said with a smile. It was a nice smile and Nick felt his face grow red.

"What Elizabeth ever saw in you . . ." Gran said.

"It was the war," the man said simply, as though that explained everything.

"I have to tell you that I've already spoken with my attorney. We're taking steps to secure legal custody," Gramps said. Gramps stood up.

"He's my son," the man said.

"You should have thought of that before. Neglecting Elizabeth so you could go tramping all over the world. If you'd stayed where you belonged, none of this would've happened," Gran said, her face twisted like someone about to cry. Her eyes were hard and bright as diamonds.

"Elizabeth wouldn't let me see him. You know that," the man said, wearily shaking his head.

"I want you out of this house now, Tim, or I'm calling the police. If you have anything to say, you can say it in court," Gramps said, crossing to the phone. But the man was quicker than Gramps. He grabbed the phone and jerked it out of the wall.

"It'll take more than courts or the police, Wallace. It'd take a fucking army to keep me from my boy," the man growled.

Nick swallowed hard. The man had used a bad word.

"Get out of here . . . you redneck," Gran hissed.

The man scooped up Nick as easily as if he were a football. His arms and chest were thick and hard as a tree trunk. Nick peered at the back of the man's neck and sure enough it was red, just like Gran said.

"Don't try to stop me, Wallace. Don't anyone try to stop me," the man said, turning to go. Nick clung to the man like a monkey to a tree. On their way out, the man yanked the hall phone from the wall. That was fun. Nick had never seen that done before. The man carried him to a car and as they drove away, the man asked him, "Have you ever been on a plane, Nick?"

Nick shook his head.

"Well, we're going on a plane, little boy. And it's going to fly so high that all the houses and cars will look like tiny little toys," the man smiled. "We're going to a magical land with more wonderful things than you can imagine. And there's oil there. More oil than anyone knows. The greatest treasure in the world! I can smell it, boy!" the man declared with a wink and a sly tap on his nose.

Nick laughed.

Later, on the plane, Nick looked down and saw the houses and cars were small as toys and the people were so tiny he couldn't even see them. The man didn't look out of the window. He just smoked his pipe and kept glancing at Nick. And once, he grabbed Nick and held him tight. He smelled like tobacco. It was a good smell.

"I love you, Nick. There hasn't been a day that's gone by that I haven't thought of you," the man whispered in a thick voice. Nick felt warm all over. It felt good.

Except that now his father was dead. They all were. The black-robed riders had dismounted and were running towards him. He didn't know what to do. There'd never been a time when there wasn't a grown-up around to tell him what to do. The men with the guns came closer and he was afraid. He turned and began to run.

One of the terrible black-robed figures chased him. Nick ran wildly without direction, half-blinded by the sweat stinging his eyes. Around him the sandy plain lay flat and endless and blinding white as a linen-covered table. Glancing over his shoulder, he saw the Arab only a few steps behind him, stabbing the air with a long curved dagger. Nick ran even harder, but it was hard running in the sand and he stumbled. He scrambled on all fours like a monkey and then a hand yanked him off his feet.

He looked up to see the black figure towering above him, the knife blade glittering like fire in the sun. Nick closed his eyes. His ears filled with roaring like the sound of the surf near Gramps' house on the Palos Verdes shore. His body tensed for the blow, but nothing happened. At last, he opened his eyes. The Arab lay beside him in the sand. In the center of his forehead was a small black hole oozing blood. It looked like a third eye.

He became aware of the sound of gunfire. He saw an Arab bending over his dad suddenly straighten up and then crumple to the ground. The black-robed Arabs were running away. Nick turned in the direction of the gunfire but he couldn't see who was firing. The desert was empty all the way to the horizon. When he turned back, the black-robed figures had mounted their horses, spurring them into a desperate gallop. They fled like shadows disappearing in the blinding light.

Nick ran back to his dad, who was lying there exactly as

Nick had left him. Nick had never felt so alone. Who's going to take care of me now, he wondered.

In the far distance, he could see black specks approaching. As they drew closer, he saw that they were Arabs riding on camels. The Arabs approached slowly, as in a dream. The heat haze made it look like the camels were running through water, but he knew there was no water in the desert. It was hard to know what was real.

Now he could see the Arabs clearly. They wore brown robes and carried rifles strung with fringes. Nick pulled the Boy Scout knife his dad had given him from his pocket and opened it. He would kill anyone who tried to touch his dad.

The Arab on the lead camel drew to a halt and looked around. His face was dark and wrinkled like a walnut. His curly beard was speckled black and white and he had a big hooked nose, like a bird's beak. The camel began to sink down on its haunches, rocking back and forth like a boat as it settled to the ground. The Arab slid easily to the ground and stood before Nick.

"*Eenglizi?*" the Arab asked.

"What?" Nick said.

"You—Eengleesh?" the Arab said, pointing at Nick.

"We're American," Nick stammered. Americans were the best, Gramps always said.

The Arab nodded and began to approach Nick's dad.

"Don't touch my daddy!" Nick screamed, his voice thin and wild as a bird's cry. His grip tightened on the knife. The Arab seemed not to have heard and began to kneel by the body. Nick struck.

"*Ya Allah!*" the Arab cried, jerking his hand away. It dripped with blood from the wound. One of the other Arabs aimed his rifle at Nick.

"*La!*" the Arab cried, throwing up his wounded hand and jumping into the line of fire.

"The boy showed courage protecting his own, as a man

should. Besides, we are Moslems, the *khalifah* of Allah on earth. A Moslem does not make war on children," he said in Arabic, then in English to Nick:

"Do not be afraid, little Scorpion," thereby conferring the nickname that was to stay with the boy. "Those who attacked you were Saar, the wolves of the desert. They are our enemies too. I am Sheikh Zaid ibn Bushir of the Mutayr. All that you see is my *dira*"—flinging his arm out wide as if to display the desert like a painting. Zaid squatted down and looked levelly at Nick, his eyes soft and very brown.

"Put away your sting, little Scorpion. I am bound by God to protect you," Zaid said. Nick looked distrustfully at the Arab.

"You won't hurt my daddy?" he asked tremulously, his chin trembling on the verge of sobbing. Zaid looked at the body.

"No one can hurt your *baba* any more," Zaid said.

The two regarded each other for a long moment. Then Nick folded the knife and stuck it in his pocket.

"You are a *dhimmi*, a Child of the Book?" Zaid asked.

"I don't know," Nick shrugged.

Zaid pondered, as though considering a knotty problem. Finally, he shook his head and stood up.

"Where is your mama?"

"She died and went to heaven," Nick said, eager to answer a question he understood. Zaid smiled with approval. A child who believed in heaven was obviously not a pagan.

"You are—orphan," Zaid said, pointing at Nick.

"I don't know," Nick said uncomfortably. He didn't want to be an orphan. One time Gramps had let him stay up to watch a movie about orphans on TV. It was called *Oliver Twist*. Orphans had to wear rags and eat awful stuff called gruel. People were mean to orphans.

"The Messenger of Allah, blessed is his name, taught us to protect the orphan," Zaid declared. He looked down at

138

Nick with his kind eyes, then turned and walked towards his camel.

"Come, you can't stay here. You would die in the desert," Zaid said. Nick stood by his dad, uncertain.

"Come, little Scorpion. You will be hungry," he said and mounted his camel. Nick trudged over to the camel. It turned its great head towards him and drew back its lips, as if it would bite him. Nick froze, afraid to come closer.

"Don't be afraid, little Scorpion," Zaid said.

Zaid leaned down and stretched out his arm. He took Nick's little hand in his and pulled him up. He struck the camel lightly on the neck with his riding whip. The camel rose awkwardly in stages, like a beam being jimmied up. Zaid struck her again and called: *"Hututat!"* Nick almost laughed, because it sounded like he was saying "Hot-hot-hot," and they were off.

At twilight the men of the Mutayr lined up their prayer rugs and bowed their heads towards the dying red sun that lay in the direction of the *gibla,* which is towards Mecca. After the *maghrib* prayers, everyone joined Sheikh Zaid in his tent for dinner. They ate chunks of roasted lamb on a bed of rice called *shawirmu,* served on a single great round brass tray, and dipped pieces of *pita* bread into bowls of *fool* and goat's milk cheese called *gibna beyda min.* Everyone reached into the same bowl with his fingers. Sheikh Zaid plucked choice morsels of lamb and fed Nick with his own hand. The meat was hot.

Sheikh Zaid's son, Youssef, who at ten was much bigger than Nick, taught Nick to reach for the food with his right hand only. The left hand was used to wipe yourself after you went to the toilet, except the only toilet was a hole in the sand. Youssef explained this to Nick in clumsy English and a pantomime that had all the men laughing.

After eating, a veiled woman served thick coffee in a copper pot with a long curved spout and disappeared behind a woven curtain. Then they sat and listened to old Muhammed recite from the Koran from memory.

Nick sat on the woven rug with his legs stuck out straight in front of him. He looked around the tent. From the outside the tent was made of plain black cloth, but inside it was hung with colorful woven rugs, the tent poles festooned with brightly dyed woven hangings. Behind one of the rugs he could hear the clatter and murmur of the women as they cleaned the dishes. The sound of the wind outside was woven into the drone of Muhammed's recitation, as much a part of the saying as the words themselves. The tent ropes creaked in the night. It sounded like a boat in the middle of the sea.

> By the noonday brightness, and by the night
> when it darkens, thy Lord hath not forsaken
> thee, neither hath He been displeased.
> Surely the future shall be better for thee
> than the past; and in the end He shall be
> bounteous to thee, and thou shalt be
> satisfied.
> Did He not find thee an orphan, and give
> thee a home; erring, and guided thee;
> needy, and enriched thee?

Youssef translated the words for Nick in a whisper. The stuff about the orphan was about him, Nick thought, and remembered his dad.

"And the vein, *habibi*. Tell us of the vein," Zaid said to Muhammed. The old man raised his eyes soulfully to the top of the tent and recited:

> Is He not closer than the vein of thy neck?
> Thou needest not raise thy voice, for
> He knoweth the secret whisper, and
> what is yet more hidden . . .
> He knows what is in the land and in

the sea;
no leaf falleth but He knoweth it; nor
is there a grain in the darkness under
the earth, nor a thing, green or sere
but it is recorded.

Youssef noticed the way Nick was sitting with his legs splayed out in front of him, and tapped his legs sharply.

"To show a man the soles of your feet is to insult him," Youssef whispered. He showed Nick how to sit cross-legged. Nick frowned. There was a lot to learn.

Directly across from him, a teenager with a thin scraggly moustache and a cast in one eye was staring at Nick, his eyes narrowed. His lips were thin and tight as a knife edge.

"Who's that?" Nick asked.

"That is Bandar, son of my father's younger half brother, Faraj. You should not have pointed your feet at him. Now he is your enemy," Youssef whispered.

"I didn't mean it," Nick whispered back, a lump in his throat.

"It's too late. You must remember, you are not alone. If you bring dishonor on yourself, you also dishonor your family and your entire tribe," Youssef said.

"Who is my tribe?"

"That is yet to be decided," Youssef replied.

The old man had finished his recitation. Sheikh Zaid took out a pouch, rolled a cigarette and lit it. Then Bandar spoke.

"There is a *kafir* among us," he said, his good eye glaring at Nick.

Sheikh Zaid exhaled a thin stream of smoke which curled in the air like strands of hair.

"The Messenger of Allah said: 'When any man says to his brother "Thou infidel!" one of the two deserves the name.' That is a true *hadith* of Bukhari from Abdullah ibn Umar," Zaid replied mildly.

"The little *dhimmi* is not my brother," Bandar retorted hotly.

"The child is an orphan. We saved him from the Saar dogs and the desert. Are we not bound?" Zaid asked, addressing himself to all of them.

Faraj, a thin man with a beard but no moustache, straightened his back and placed his hands on his knees.

"The boy is a *Giaour*. Better to remove the stone of offense, my brother," Faraj said in a troubled voice. Perhaps he felt called upon to defend his son, Bandar.

"What says the Holy Koran?" Zaid appealed to Muhammed.

The old man closed his eyes and spoke in a clear voice:

> They will question thee concerning the orphans.
> Say: "To set their affairs aright is good.
> And if you intermix with them, they are your
> brothers."

There were nods of agreement around the tent. Nick yawned. He was growing sleepy, but he tried to stay awake. They were talking about him. He looked at the bejeweled *khanjar* dagger in Sheikh Zaid's belt. It was very pretty. He wondered if he could have a knife too.

"Then let him be returned to his own tribe. There are *Americani* at the oil rigs in Dharan," someone said.

Faraj nodded his agreement and quoted the famous proverb of Father Noah: " 'The ploughman to the plough-woman, the retainer to the retainer-woman, and the slave to the slave-woman.' To each according to his own."

There were mutters around the tent. The shadows of the men danced against the tent walls in the firelight as though they were engaged in some ancient pagan rite.

"There has been heavy fighting in that area since the border dispute. The *Ingilizi* are so stupid they cannot tell a Rualla noble from a Hteym slave. They would think we were brigands and shoot at us," said Safooq, a beardless man who was the husband of Faraj's daughter. Although his words were cautious, Youssef whispered to Nick that Safooq was the best marksman among the Mutayr.

"King Abd al Aziz has forbidden any but the Solubba to visit the foreign *kafirs*. The Mutayr are loyal to the House of Saud," said Faisal, a handsome youth who was Zaid's oldest son.

"Even so," Zaid murmured.

"Besides," Faisal declared proudly, "I would sooner die than be taken for a Solubba *sani*." *Asani* was a member of a vassal tribe, Youssef explained to Nick. The *sunna* tribes had to pay a *khawwa* to a noble tribe like the Mutayr. But *sunna* like the Hteym or the Solubba were inviolate from attack. Like women, they were considered creatures too inferior to fight.

"But what would the *dhimmi*'s status be?" Bandar declared, bewildered at the turn of events.

"You should learn mercy, my brother's son," Zaid said sadly. He tossed his cigarette into the glowing coals. "According to the *hadith* of Bukhari from Usama ibn Zaid: 'God has no mercy on those who do not have mercy.' "

"What's a *hadith*?" Nick whispered in Youssef's ear.

"A *hadith* is a saying or action of the Prophet Mohammed, the Messenger of God. The *sunna* or practices of the Prophet guide us in all things. Since some *hadith* are more authentic than others, my father always cites his sources," Youssef whispered back.

"So the boy stays," Farai said.

"His *kismet* has brought him to us. Allah does the writing, we are merely the readers. Perhaps we can bring him to the Truth," Zaid said, patting Nick's head. He gazed seriously into Nick's eyes.

"Would you like to stay with us, little Scorpion?" Zaid asked.

Nick didn't know what to say. He was very confused. He remembered how Zaid had knelt by his dad and saved him

143

from the Saar. Grown-ups knew what to do. He was just a kid. But Zaid's eyes were warm when he looked at Nick. It reminded him of the way Mom looked at him sometimes, and Dad on the plane. He nodded.

"So be it," Zaid sighed. "Listen, little Scorpion, from now on you are a Bedu of the Mutayr, of the family of Zaid ibn Bushir of the al-Amash, son of Abdullah, the son of the great Sheikh Dushan. Do you understand?"

Nick shook his head and yawned again. It was very confusing.

"Well," Zaid laughed, "Understanding will come when it comes."

Later, Nick woke in the night. Everyone was asleep. He lay bundled in a camel robe, listening in the darkness. Outside the tent he could hear the wind singing on the sands. He wondered if it would blow the sand over his dad. Then he slept.

MOSCOW

THE DOSSIER LAY on the desk in a pool of light cast by the lamp. The top page was stamped in bold letters. It read:

TOP STATE SECRET
FOR POLITBURO ONLY
SOURCE: KGB DIRECTORATE 5
NO COPIES TO BE MADE.

It was a remarkable document, Svetlov thought. He wearily massaged his closed eyes with his fingers, blue-white spots swimming across the darkness.

Clipped to the top page was a deciphered telex. It confirmed the worst. Those bungling Arab scum had let the Scorpion slip through their fingers a second time. Now, after reading Directorate Five's dossier he understood why. The Scorpion was no ordinary agent.

He picked up the report and studied it again for a few minutes. It was based on CIA records and provided an incomplete history of the American agent up to his recent gunrunning episode in Afghanistan. The American record ended with the curious computer notation:

"Delete from Files.
Initiate Global Record Search and Purge."

That meant that the CIA didn't even want their own people to know about him.

He drummed his fingers nervously on the padded desk top. He had to assume that the Scorpion already knew about the planned assassination. The disposition of the Arab's body in the department store toilet in Doha indicated that the American had had time to question him. Whether the Scorpion learned enough to interfere or not was debatable. On principle, he had to assume the worst. He had learned never to count on luck. As his grandmother used to say, "Roast pheasant won't fly into your mouth."

Question: Could the plan succeed without the element of surprise?

Like most Russians, Svetlov thought of the Arabs as *Chernomazy* (niggers). If there was a way of pissing in the soup the Arabs would find it, he thought.

What complicated the issue was that they couldn't just send in KGB teams to terminate this Scorpion. Russians would be as conspicuous in Arabia as blackbirds in a snowfield. They would have to use Palestinians, he decided. *Chernomazy*.

They only had to delay the Scorpion for another seventy-two hours. If the Palestinians killed him, so much the better, he thought, pleased with the idea of a countermove to present to Fyedorenko to offset the news about the Scorpion's second escape.

Although it was 2 a.m., Fyedorenko was sure to still be in his office, he thought, slipping the dossier into his briefcase.

Fortunately, Svetlov was in his office in the Great Kremlin Palace and not at KGB headquarters, that yellow monstrosity with the Stalinist wedding-cake façade on Dzerzhinsky Square. Svetlov had long ago learned the virtue of staying close to the Kremlin. Now, he didn't have far to go.

He closed the door to his office located in a corridor off St. George's Hall and headed towards the octagon-shaped Hall of St. Vladimir with its cathedral ceilings. At every door, silent Kremlin guards snapped to attention before opening the door for him. He went down the stairs and crossed Upper Savior Square. Despite the fact that it was June, the night was still very cool and clear. The stars burned with a cold white fire and his footsteps made the only sound. He felt very alone.

He entered the Terem Palace at the Front Hall Chamber entrance and passed through the Cross Chamber to the Throne Room, a gilded chamber with mosaic-tiled walls, its parquet floor covered with a thick wine-red carpet. Floor to ceiling windows stretched along the courtyard side of the chamber, where tsarist petitioners used to stand in line. Lamplight was reflected in the window panes. Where once the tsar himself had sat, Fyedorenko was at work behind a massive desk big enough to be used to land carrier jets, Svetlov mused. Fyedorenko looked up warily.

"Forgive the intrusion, comrade. I came to present the report personally," Svetlov began.

Fyedorenko nodded. As always, his face gave nothing away. Svetlov stood uneasily before the desk like a schoolboy summoned to the principal's office.

"The Arabs have bungled this Scorpion business again. We'll have to move quickly. I've already sent a copy of the

Scorpion's dossier via our contact to Prince Abdul Sa'ad," Svetlov said, placing the report on Fyedorenko's desk.

"Send Marshal Orlov to me," Fyedorenko said, his bloodless lips barely moving.

"Are we mobilizing, comrade?" Svetlov asked breathlessly.

"It's time to move the pieces into position for the centerboard game," Fyedorenko said.

"I have to warn you about the Scorpion. According to the stolen CIA report, he spent his entire childhood studying the Arab culture," Svetlov said.

Fyedorenko gazed at the fragmented image of the room reflected in the Petition window. When he finally turned back towards Svetlov, his eyebrows were arched and a ghostly smile hovered at the corners of his mouth.

"What did he do after the first twenty minutes?" asked an amused Fyedorenko.

Arabia, 1951

IN THE GRAY LIGHT of the false dawn that precedes the sun, Nick woke to the groans of the camels as they shuffled by outside the tent, their forelegs hobbled so they couldn't stray. Ithat, a large pudgy woman with a voice like brass and good-humored eyes outlined by *kohl*, brought him a white cotton robe called a *thaub* and gestured for him to put it on. His shirt and pants were gone. He put on the *thaub*. It belonged to Youssef and was too big for him. She laughed and told him he would grow into it.

Outside, the boys were driving the camels to the nearest

bushes for forage. Old Mohammed gave the call to prayer, his breath like smoke in the cool morning air:

> God is most great.
> I testify that there is no god but God.
> I testify that Mohammed is the Prophet
>   of God.
> Come to prayer!
> Come to Salvation!
> Prayer is better than sleep.
> God is most great.
> There is no god but God.

Sheikh Zaid was by the water skins. They were made of goat skins and quivered obscenely on the sand like giant bloated leeches. Zaid was washing his face, hands and feet before prayer. Iffat gave Nick a twig to brush his teeth with. He watched as the men of the tribe smoothed the sand with their hands and lined up their prayer rugs and bowed their foreheads to the ground, reciting the dawn prayer in unison:

> In the name of God, the Compassionate,
> the Merciful.

Youssef came over and translated for Nick. Allah was God, he said. Allah was God's name just as his name was Nick or "little Scorpion." You made a *ruku* bow when you prayed. Formal prayer was called *salat*. You performed *salat* five times a day. First at dawn, then at noon. The noon *salat* was called *zuhr*. In the afternoon, *salat* was called *ashr*. The dusk *salat* was *maghrib* and the night salat was *isha*. *Salat* was one of the five pillars of Islam, Youssef explained. The others were the *shahadah*, the confession that there is only one God and no other and that Mohammed is the Prophet of God; the *zakat*, which is the giving of charity; the *siyam*, which is the fasting during the holy month of Ramadan; and the *hajj*, which is the pilgrimage to the holy Ka'aba in Mecca.

As the blazing sun rose into the sky empty of clouds, the

148

women pounded coffee beans in a brass mortar, the pestle ringing against the mortar like a bell. Breakfast was *pita* bread and goat cheese with sweet tea called *shay*. Nick was still hungry after breakfast. Yet he noticed that even though the others must have been hungry they refused seconds. Later, he learned that food was often scarce and that the feast of the previous night was a celebration of their victory over the Saar and to honor him because he was a stranger. A guest must always be offered hospitality, even if he is an enemy and you have to slaughter your last camel to feed him.

After tea, Faraj's wife Jawhara, a fat woman wearing a black *milfa* veil over her face, served a very thick black coffee spiced with cardamon called *ahwa*. Each man was served in turn in order of precedence. Nick being the youngest was served last. Jawhara poured a thimbleful into a tiny cup. Each man slurped loudly as he drank. It was bad manners to drink more than three cups. Also, you were supposed to belch after you had eaten. Nick laughed at that, picturing Gran's horror at all the burping.

After breakfast the boys went off to tend the camels, while the girls stayed to clean up and work at household chores. The boys rode the camels, shouting to each other in loud voices that could be heard for miles in the clear air of the desert. But there was no roughhousing. For one Arab to grab or strike another was unthinkable.

Nick tried to mount a camel. Grabbing a tassel hanging from the saddle, he tried to pull himself up as he had seen the other boys do. Sweat blinded his eyes and he fell off. Everyone laughed. His face burned and he kept trying, but couldn't do it till Youssef helped him. Youssef was his friend.

All that day, Youssef taught him how to speak Arabic. In the days that followed, everyone he spoke to corrected him and taught him. He learned at an astonishing rate, as though his mind had been a car idling along in first gear suddenly pushed into overdrive. Even Sheikh Zaid remarked at his ability.

Arabic was very different from English, Nick learned. The most important difference was that everything was either masculine or feminine. The way you said something depended on the gender of the person saying it, the gender of the person you were talking to and the gender of the thing itself. Any word associated with a thing, such as an adjective or a number, was also modified to reflect the gender and number. Usually, if a word ended with "a" it was feminine.

"Why is everything male and female?" Nick asked Youssef.

"Look at the world and show me what is not male or female," Youssef said.

"What about things, like rocks or tents?"

"That's the hard part," Youssef said with a laugh.

That afternoon, Safooq began to teach Nick how to hold a rifle. The old British Enfield .303 was bigger than Nick and he could barely raise it. Safooq held it for him as Nick squeezed off his first shot at a nearby tamarisk tree. The recoil bumped his chin and he began to whimper.

"Crying is not the way of men. If you cry, you should not shoot," Safooq said and Nick choked back the tears. That evening he asked Sheikh Zaid if he wasn't too little to learn to shoot. He was afraid everyone would laugh at him because he couldn't lift the rifle. To be laughed at was a dishonor.

"You are Bedu now. All Bedu can shoot," Zaid said.

"But why is it so important?" Nick asked.

Zaid looked down at the boy with some surprise. "A man who is not a warrior might as well be a woman."

Youssef and Nick became inseparable. One evening after the *maghrib* prayers they swore to be brothers forever. Youssef gave Nick his *khanjar* dagger. The hilt was made of silver and the blade was shiny steel. Nick gave Youssef the only things he still owned, his Boy Scout knife and his shoes. The shoes were too small, but Youssef wore them unlaced and proudly hobbled around. From then on, Nick went barefoot like everyone else.

The first time he tried to walk barefooted on the hot sand,

the pain seared his feet. It was like walking on hot coals. He hopped around like an awkward dervish and even austere old Mohammed smiled at the sight. He tried to keep up, but soon lagged further behind the others. Faisal offered him a pair of sandals, but the boy refused, his face screwed tight with pain and something else, something in his strange gray eyes that made Faisal back away. Faisal had seen the same savage glare in the eyes of his father's falcon.

It was then that the legend began, because unlike any other *kafir*, the little Scorpion somehow managed to keep up, limping silently into camp. Iffat bathed his scorched and blistered feet with mineral water and looked at the child with wondering eyes. Eventually, his tender feet became calloused and impervious to pain. For the rest of his life, he felt uncomfortable wearing shoes.

Little by little he learned the harsh ways of the Bedu. He learned to be impervious to the pangs of hunger and thirst, to push his body far beyond what he ever thought his body could do. Weather no longer mattered. It was never discussed. He grew indifferent to the intense noonday heat when the sun baked down on the blazing plain as on a frying pan. He learned to sleep in his clothes in the icy chill of night, the darkness blazing with a million diamond chips that were stars, as the temperature plummeted by a hundred degrees in a matter of hours. Pain and discomfort were weaknesses to be mastered, even as the body's pleasures were gifts from Allah to be indulged.

"The body is but a receptacle for the spirit, like the sheath for a shining sword," Sheikh Zaid would say.

Sheikh Zaid gave him a *thelul*, a good riding she-camel. Her name was Jidha and she soon grew as faithful to him as a dog and would come when he called in his boyish soprano. Faisal taught him to ride. He learned to mount her and ride with his leg around the saddle pommel, how to spur her on with a cry and a touch from his whip and how to make her stop and kneel by crooning "Grrr" from deep in his throat.

Riding a camel at a walking pace, which was most common, was like constantly being jerked from a standstill on a sled resting on rough ground. There were many painful falls, but the bruised boy would always remount, his face set like stone. Faisal wondered at the Scorpion's tenacity.

"It is as if the boy knows he is preparing for battle," Faisal said to his father, after seeing the Scorpion climb back up the *thelul*'s neck and perch on the saddle, his leg hooked around the pommel like a monkey's tail around a branch.

"He is Allah's *khalifah*, God's deputy, although he does not know it. Only Allah knows what is written for him," Sheikh Zaid replied in a troubled voice. Silently they watched the Scorpion chase after the other riders.

Even harder was riding at a trot or a gallop. To preserve their bottoms from a terrible pounding, the Mutayr rode squatting, not sitting. The position required an extraordinary sense of balance and it took the Scorpion a long time to master it.

One day Youssef challenged Nick to a race. The boys spurred their camels to a gallop across a vast salt flat, blinding white as snow in the sun and rimmed by *arad* salt bushes, which were good forage for camels. Nick called to Jidha and the she-camel burst into the lead, her long neck stretched out. She held her head up elegantly, like a proper English lady's pinky when sipping tea. The warm wind pressed against the folds of his *thaub* like an embrace. He felt a surge of exaltation, of wild freedom, a boy's dream of heaven come true. When at last they reined in their camels, Nick's face was flushed with triumph. He had never been so happy.

Faisal taught him to ride using only his feet and verbal commands to guide the camel, so that he would have his hands free for fighting. He learned to be a dead shot even while riding at a gallop. Safooq taught him how to feint, slash and thrust with the curved sword and the *khanjar* dagger. Soon while rolling on the ground he was able to throw the *khanjar* at a tamarisk tree from twenty paces and hit a spot no bigger than a man's palm.

"Your enemy will attack you when you least expect him. You must always be ready, for there will be no time to prepare. And you must do the same when you attack him. In fighting, surprise is everything," Safooq said. But learning to survive in the desert meant more than fighting.

He learned to navigate in the desert by the stars at night and by the position of the sun during the day; to always know where he was by distinguishing a thousand tiny landmarks in the almost featureless desert, until he could do it as unthinkingly as a westerner driving a car across town. He learned to see across the immense emptiness, so that he could tell by a barely visible puff of dust on the horizon who or what it was, how many riders and from what tribe, friend or foe. He learned to find his way to distant wells hidden in the sands.

When the Mutayr broke camp and moved to find a new well or grazing, they could never be sure that they would find it or that it hadn't run dry since the last time. And if they made a mistake, there was no second chance: the desert never forgave.

"In the desert the penalty for a mistake is death," Sheikh Zaid would say. And yet, they never really feared. Everything was in Allah's hands anyway. Almost every statement was accompanied by the phrase *"Inshallah"*—"God willing."

He learned to track and hunt with the rifle and the falcon. A Bedu had to know the tracks of every desert animal and of every horse and camel. After a time, Nick could tell by the track of a camel whether it was wild or tame, male or female, whether it was carrying a rider, where it came from, how tired it was and even whose camel it was. Camels from the sandy Nefud had soft soles; those from the rocky plains of the Najd left smooth tracks, their soles polished by friction with the ground. From the droppings you could tell how old the track was, what the camel had been grazing on and when it had been watered last, and from these signs deduce where it came from and where it was going. And the dried droppings could be used for fuel. Nothing was ever wasted.

The desert gave little. It forced a man back upon himself simply in order to survive. Sheikh Zaid said that it was no accident that Allah had revealed himself in the desert. It was the desert's very emptiness, its nothingness of stone and sand and sky, which mirrored the perfection of the Creator. Once Nick asked Sheikh Zaid how he knew there was a God. Zaid reined in his camel and outstretched an arm at the vast empty plain and burning sky.

"No defect canst thou see in the creation of the God of mercy," Zaid declared harshly in the words of the Holy Koran. "Repeat the gaze; seest thou a single flaw?"

By then, Nick had grown conversant in Arabic. At first, he translated everything into English. Later, he simply thought in Arabic without ever translating. He realized he was fluent when he found himself dreaming in Arabic.

It was a language of incredible subtleties and shadings of meaning. Hidden in every phrase was a treasure-house of ambiguities and implications. Every word came from a root, usually made up of three consonants. Vowels, prefixes and suffixes were inserted to provide specific meaning and grammatical context. Thus, words with widely diverse meanings were all derived from the same root and often implied each other.

He discovered that the art of conversation consisted not so much in surface communication, as in the exploration of the metaphors which are the only ways that human beings can truly communicate. Unlike westerners, who are concerned with apparent reality, Arabs, by virtue of the very language in which they thought, turned the most ordinary conversation into the abstractions of poetry. Arabs were not so much interested in facts as in truth, which is quite another thing.

The harshness of the desert forced a discipline among the

Bedu. Their lives were bound by many rules. It was forbidden to drink alcohol or eat pork, to converse with women outside your family, or even for a man to approach his wife during her time of the month. Yet the Mutayr never spanked their children. Nor did a man ever beat his wife. Those were abominations. All that it ever took to discipline Nick and the other children was a reminder of how intimately bound together their lives were.

If a boy did something wrong, he would be told, "That is not the Mutayr way." Once Youssef stood up after the *iftar*, which is the dinner that breaks the day-long fast throughout the holy month of Ramadan, without belching. It was a terrible breach of etiquette, comparable to a western boy spitting out his food in a restaurant. Sheikh Zaid looked at him with disgust and said: "Because of your bad manners I am ashamed to sit with my brothers. I wonder if you wouldn't rather be a Hutaymi instead of a Mutayr." Zaid stalked out of the tent and Youssef followed, his head hanging in shame.

Real learning among the Bedu was accomplished by telling stories. Once Bandar, who was Nick's enemy and never passed Nick without a sneer or a muttered word, snuck up behind Jidha and jammed his dagger between the she-camel's hind legs. Jidha bucked wildly as a bronco, tossing Nick to the ground. Nick rolled to his feet and grabbed Jidha by the lip. He calmed her and, wadding his *kaffiyah* head cloth into a bulky bandage, used it to stem the camel's bleeding. Bandar stood by, laughing.

"Touch her again and I will forget that you are of the *Dar al-Islam*, the House of Islam against whom fighting is forbidden," Nick said, his gray eyes smoky with anger.

"*Ra'iya*," Bandar hissed. *Ra'iya* were human cattle, the lowest form of infidel.

Suddenly, Sheikh Zaid came up and glanced at the two angry boys. He had noticed Bandar's constant abuse of the boy. Yet the little *dhimmi* always kept his temper. Even though he was only a child, he seemed to know that revenge was a dish best tasted cold. It can come to no good. I'd hate to be Bandar when the boy has grown to manhood, Zaid thought. He murmured the old saying: "May Allah make the end better than the beginning."

"Did you hurt the she-camel, my brother's son?" Zaid asked.

Bandar's face flushed and he looked away, his bad eye faintly twitching. Once again, the little *dhimmi* had caused him shame. Sheikh Zaid raised his hand as though surrendering, something he often did when quoting a *hadith* of the Prophet.

"The Messenger of God said: 'While a man was walking on a road, his thirst grew strong. He found a well and descended into it and drank and was leaving, when he saw a dog with its tongue hanging out, licking the ground from thirst. And the man said, "This dog's thirst is like the thirst I had," and he went into the well again, filled his shoe with water and gave the dog to drink. And Allah approved of his act and pardoned his sins. They said, "What, Messenger of God, shall we be rewarded for what we do for animals?" He replied, "Yes. There is a reward on every living creature,"" Zaid said.

Later, Zaid took Nick aside. They walked through a field of stone shingles outside the camp. "It is good you swallow your anger. Bandar is your father's brother's son. But beware how you nourish your revenge. The scorpion, after whom you are named, has a deadly sting. It is said that a trapped scorpion may sting itself rather than be defeated," Zaid said.

"I don't understand," Nick said.

"Sometimes a man is slain by his own weapon, by the very thing he uses to protect himself," Zaid explained.

"Tell that to Bandar," Nick said.

Every Bedu loved stories, especially the tales of adventure. Often at night, after the recitation from the Koran, they would

156

sit around the glowing coals in Sheikh Zaid's tent and listen to old Mohammed tell the famous tales of the *rawi* storytellers. He told of the fabulous Omani sailor, Sinbad, who sailed from Muscat to the ends of the earth and of Khalid ibn al-Walid, the Moslem general who faced the fifty thousand Byzantine troops of the Emperor Heraclius at the battle of the Yarmuk. The Byzantines swore to stand or die and to prove it, they chained themselves together in ranks thirty deep. Shouting *"Allah akbar!"* the Arabs attacked the emperor's soldiers, who fell like ripe wheat under the flashing swords of the Beduin. Heraclius, his army chopped to pieces in the narrow *wadi*, fled to Constantinople. The Moslems went on to conquer the Holy Land.

But of all the tales, Nick's favorites were of Antar, the Beduin warrior of the sixth century. The son of a Bedu sheikh and a black female slave, Antar was dark of skin and born of servitude. But he showed courage and won his freedom in battle. Antar rode a black stallion, faster than the wind, and fought the oppressors of the weak and the poor with his powerful sword. "With my sword will I destroy the oppressors, let Allah's justice fall on me as He wills," Antar vowed.

Once Antar faced an army of forty thousand single-handed. His glittering sword scattered them like chaff in the wind. But no man is invincible. The great warrior was vanquished by a woman, the beautiful dark-eyed virgin, Abla, daughter of a great sheikh. "The eyelashes of my beloved from the corner of her veil are more cutting than the edges of sharp scimitars," swore Antar.

The fire burned low in the tent and even the wind fell silent as in a hushed voice, Mohammed told of Antar's battle with the fiercest lion in the desert.

"To prove his love for the fair virgin Abla, Antar vowed to fight the lion," Mohammed said.

"Ya Allah," breathed Youssef, his eyes wide and full of wonder. Nick took Youssef's hand. The two boys longed to be like Antar.

"But to prevent Antar from escaping the wrath of the lion, his feet were bound by his terrible enemy, Munzar . . ."

"May the raiders get him!" cried a voice in the darkness.

"The lion crouched and sprang, looming larger than the biggest camel, but Antar leapt into the air and cleaved the beast in two with his sword," Mohammed declared.

"*Ya Allah!*" Nick murmured. Like Antar, he too came from a despised background, but his courage might yet win him honor, he thought. Antar was his hero.

Al Aramah

IN THE COOL SHADE, lulled by the gurgling sound of the water as it tumbled down over the rocks to the crystal pond, Abdul Sa'ad tried to return his thoughts to the infinite, the center. Reclining on his prayer rug after the afternoon *salat*, he inhaled deeply of the fragrance of the garden. As he glanced at the tall palms, the wildflowers and watered greens, he recited aloud the poetry of the Holy Koran:

" 'Reclining there upon soft couches, they shall feel neither the scorching heat nor the biting cold. Trees will spread their shade around them and fruits will hang in clusters over them. They shall be served with silver dishes . . . and cups brim full of ginger-water from the Fount of *Selsabil*.' "

He loved this peaceful oasis which sat in the middle of his country fortress surrounded by thousands of armed troops like the eye of a hurricane. How many millions had it cost him? It mattered not the blink of a gnat's eye. Yet like the gnat, this Scorpion intruded on his serenity. With a sigh, Abdul Sa'ad turned his mind back to the report from Moscow.

Those clumsy Russians had all the subtlety of a sledge-hammer, he thought. Their crude Tartar mentality understood nothing of the interplay of plot and counterplot, the intricacies of the arabesque. They had the same answer for everything: more guns.

The Americans were just as crude. Worse. They hadn't even the excuse of being godless barbarians like the Russians. To the Americans, everything was money. They were like spoiled children. Allah had been too kind to them.

He remembered his first trip to America, when he was in his teens. They took him to see Niagara Falls. He stood open-mouthed, his eyes wide as saucers.

"When do they turn it off?" he had asked, unable to imagine that such a torrent of fresh water could be anything other than man-made. He remembered how his face burned as they all laughed.

"Never," they had said. And he knew in that very instant that Allah had damned them with an abundance that made them weak. Then they tried to corrupt Arabia with their evil.

But he would show them the way.

He plucked a sugared fig from a silver bowl and chewed it thoughtfully. Nothingness and sweetness; that is Islam. At the heart of the labyrinth is emptiness and submission. Absolute purity of thought, and physical sensuality. Allah had plucked him out even as he had plucked the fig from the bowl.

Nuruddin had twice failed to destroy the Scorpion because he had not understood the nature of his enemy. An unusual mixture, this Scorpion: half Bedu and half American. But was this Scorpion a romantic who liked running around in a flowing sheet or was he truly dangerous?

According to Moscow's report, the Scorpion was a Moslem. That meant he was committed and therefore dangerous.

He had lived as a Christian with the Bedu for years, and only then converted.

How very odd, Abdul Sa'ad mused.

Arabia, 1956

NICK HAD BEEN LIVING with the Mutayr for nearly five years when war broke out between Egypt and Israel. They first heard the news in the *souk* in al Hasa, where he had gone with Sheikh Zaid, who wanted to buy some gold jewelry. The gold was for Faisal, so that he could offer a *muttra*, the bridal price he would have to pay in order to marry his cousin, Madawi. Sheikh Zaid held up a gold necklace. It gleamed like burning coals in the sunlight.

"How do you know it's real gold?" Nick asked.

"If you don't know the thing, you must know the man," Zaid replied.

"*Ya Amaimi*, weigh and judge, for gold cannot lie," cajoled the gold seller. Sheikh Zaid drew a touchstone from the folds of his *bisht* and lightly rubbed the necklace against the stone.

"It is by testing that we discern fine gold—and more than gold. As is the mold, so will the cast be," Zaid explained to Nick. "Behold, it is as you say," he said to the gold seller.

A battered, colorfully painted Chevrolet rumbled down the dusty street, scattering goats and chickens.

"Devil machines!" muttered the gold seller.

"Soon these foreign machines will drown out the cry of the falcon in the desert," Zaid said, his face troubled.

The gold seller clapped his hands and ordered cups of sweet hot *shay* from a passing vendor. It was as the two men sipped and haggled over the price that the news swept the *souk*, like the breath of hot wind which warns of a coming sandstorm. Sheikh Zaid was thunderstruck. It was inconceivable that Arabs, even the slavish Egyptian *fellahin*, could be swept out of Sinai in only a few days by the lightning attack of the Jews.

"They have won a battle, not the war. Some day we will push them back into the sea," Zaid said.

"What—and pollute the sea?" the gold seller laughed.

On the ride back to their camp Nick pulled his camel alongside Sheikh Zaid and they discussed it.

"Are we to hate the Jews?" Nick asked.

Sheikh Zaid frowned. The world was changing in ways that were difficult to understand. For a time his gaze was lost in the distant burning plain.

"That gold seller was wrong to curse them so," Zaid said at last. "The sons of Isaac and the sons of Ishmael are both the sons of Father Ibrahim. Ours is a family quarrel. But they are wrong to steal the *dira* of the *Falastin*. Without his *dira*, how can a man live? Until they return the land, there can be no peace."

"They are good fighters, though," Nick said.

"It must be admitted. The Jews are exceedingly difficult to get rid of," Zaid said with a rueful smile, urging his camel on.

They stopped for the night in a vast sandy plain. As the sun set in a brilliant slash of red, Zaid performed the *maghrib*. They ate *pita* bread and dried meat, and brewed coffee over a fire made of camel chips. The night was cool and clear and a crescent moon hung like a silver pendant in the starry sky. Zaid, troubled by what had happened, spoke of the Jews in a quiet voice, as they reclined around the glowing embers.

"Honor is due to the Jews. They are the People of the Book. They were the first to whom God revealed the truth, that He is one. Any religion that does not recognize this is not a religion, merely superstition. Their prophets, Father Ibrahim, Moses, Samuel and Isaiah were true prophets. Mohammed, the Messenger of God, was simply the last of the

161

prophets, hence he is called the Seal of the Prophets. But the Jews fell away from God, first because they whored after other gods and golden calves and then because they virtually deified their Law. Also, their concept of being a 'chosen people' is repugnant. All men are equal in God's eyes. No priest or saint is a hair's-breadth closer to the Lord of the Worlds than any ordinary man. No race or people is a particle holier than any other. One of the Prophet's wives was black and he gave his daughter in marriage to a black. Any other teaching is not religion, it is bigotry.

"Another failing of the Jews is that they rejected Jesus, who was a true prophet, who called upon men to love each other as brothers. But the Nazarenes also perverted the teachings of Jesus. They taught that God is three, not one, and that Jesus was his son, begotten of a human female. And the Nazarenes have such strange ideas, such as 'original sin.' How can anyone look at the innocent newborn babe and say that he is guilty of Adam's sin? The very idea is absurd. Every man's sin is his own and no other. If we are not responsible for our own actions, justice has no meaning. They compound the error by confusing this original sin with sex. That too is absurd. Lawful sex is good. If it were not so, God would not have made it pleasurable," Zaid said with a smile.

"Islam is otherwise. With us, there are no miracles to excite the superstitious. The Messenger of God, Peace be upon him, insisted that he never performed a single miracle, except for the improbability of an unlettered man, such as himself, producing the poetic glory that is the holy Koran. Islam is based on man's experience and his reason. If you seek miracles, look for yourself!" Zaid cried harshly, pointing up at the star-scattered night. "Look! Only a fool would cry for a sign when creation harbors nothing else!"

The fire burned low. There was no wind and the camels were still. It was a moment of perfect silence, such as God himself must have known in the moments before creation, Nick thought.

They lay silently for a long time, each of them alone with his thoughts. Nick's mind whirled. His heart burned with thoughts and desires, like a furnace. Yet Zaid's words, like the night, were so clear, so simple. The world only made sense if you accepted yourself. A man was only a man, he thought, his gaze lost in the pinpoints of light which were millions upon millions of worlds, each vaster than our own. They glittered above him, as real as anything could be, in an immutable and perfect order fixed for all time. Understanding lay in seeing that what is real is just that—real. That was the truth and all that was required of him was to perceive it as such and submit. That was what the word "Moslem" meant. One who submits.

"How does one become a Moslem?" Nick asked.

"You only have to say the *shahadah* that there is no God but God and Mohammed is his prophet, and you will be of the Brotherhood of the Faithful forever," Zaid said, his heart beating. He had waited for a long time to hear the boy ask that question.

"That's all?" Nick asked, surprised.

"Well," Zaid replied, a twinkle in his eyes, "you have to mean it."

All that night the boy didn't sleep. He lay awake wrestling with his thoughts. Ideas wheeled around his head like the stars he gazed at. He felt himself pinned to the earth, a whirling rock in space, caught in the same immutable dance as the worlds he could see, burning in the night.

He never revealed to anyone what he thought about that night. But in the morning, as the false dawn broke, he silently knelt beside Sheikh Zaid as he prepared to perform the morning *salat*. As the first rays of morning cast their shadows far across the desert, Nick bowed his forehead to the still-cool sand and said the *shahadah* for the first time.

ABDUL SA'AD IRRITABLY TOSSED the report aside. The Russian plan was nonsense. Idiots! Sending more Palestinians after the Scorpion was like sending an army of men with butterfly nets to capture the wind. The Scorpion was a true Bedu. He could disappear among the desert tribes at will. And should he choose to return to the Mutayr, it would take an army to get at him.

This was a dangerous development, now when everything was poised. A faint breath of desert wind rustled the palm fronds high above him. It whispered of *jihad* and in his mind's eye he saw the desert tremble under the tank treads as the armies of Allah surged across the East in holy war, flags unfurled in the wind.

To calm his mind he sat cross-legged, Bedu-style, on the mossy banks of his pond and contemplated the goldfish gracefully flitting in the cool green depths like sparks of living sunlight. He liked looking at them. They reminded him of women: beautiful, but without souls; useful only for ornaments.

When he had been younger he had allowed his *harim* women to frolic with him in the grass. He felt himself harden as the memories teased him. Later, when that grew boring, he used the naked women as footstools, resting his feet on their soft buttocks as they knelt before him; or as living statues frozen in erotic poses, sweat beading their exquisite skin as they struggled to remain immobile.

But that was before he had heard Allah's call and knew that he was the Chosen One. Although, even as the Prophet, he still enjoyed the delights of women, he no longer defiled himself by entering them. Now he preferred to enjoy his garden in solitude.

That was something those Russian *kulaks* would never understand. They thought to use him, to make him their puppet. But they understood nothing of *kismet*, of the wave of destiny sweeping across the world under the flowing green banner of Islam. The Arab world was awakening after a sleep of centuries to a new dream.

To be king was nothing. He would be *caliph*, even *sultan*! Except for the weapons the West was so good at making, the House of Islam would be purified. Then nothing would resist their armies. What had happened in Iran was nothing. Merely the puff of hot wind which presages the sandstorm yet to come.

As for the Russians, they could be bought with rubles as easily as the West had been corrupted by petrodollars.

He knew it was inevitable that his brother Salim would catch wind of a plot, so he had sent a Palestinian fanatic to assassinate him at a public *majlis* and then made sure that the Palestinian was caught and killed by his own zealous Royal Army guards. Salim now trusted him more than ever. The king had been reassured enough to indicate that the ceremony would go forward as scheduled.

Only the Scorpion remained as a problem, he mused, stroking his beard. If you want to destroy a scorpion, you don't chase after him and stick your finger down into his sand burrow. Instead, you lure him to you.

He doubted that the Scorpion would try to attack him here at al Aramah. It would take an army to penetrate the electronic defenses, minefields and guards surrounding what appeared to be a simple desert estate.

No—the Scorpion would undoubtedly try to learn when and where the assassination would really take place and then try to intercept. That was how to bring the Scorpion to him, Abdul Sa'ad decided. And just to make sure of the Scorpion's appearance, he would set a lure the Scorpion couldn't resist.

Adbul Sa'ad clapped his hands twice sharply. In response,

Nasir the eunuch suddenly materialized beneath the arching cypresses at the gateway to the garden.

"Summon Commander Bandar. Then bring Saria," Abdul Sa'ad ordered.

The eunuch bowed and waddled hurriedly away. Abdul Sa'ad drew a frosted silver goblet from a cooler and sipped iced *Sehha* water. He had not forgotten Bandar's gasp when the Scorpion's name was first mentioned, or the fact that both Bandar and the Scorpion were of the Mutayr tribe.

According to the report from Moscow, the Scorpion had suddenly left Arabia in 1962. That was the same year that Bandar had joined the Royal Army. Something had clearly happened, but whatever it was had gone unnoticed in the general turbulence within Arabia that year.

The only hint of what had happened came from a curious remark in the CIA files dating from the Scorpion's initiation into that organization. In response to a question as to why he left Arabia, the Scorpion had replied, "Because of a woman whom neither I nor my opponent really wanted."

The statement had the ironic ring of truth about it. Abdul Sa'ad sensed a blood feud. His excitement grew. What made it even more delicious was that in addition to years of western military training, Bandar had been secretly trained by the KGB to a level of near perfection in the arts of killing. He had been chosen to represent Arabia in the shooting competition at the Moscow Olympics before the Arab League boycott over Afghanistan.

Abdul Sa'ad felt a sudden prickling at the back of his neck and looked up to see Bandar standing right next to him. By Allah, the man was quick, Abdul Sa'ad thought. He hadn't seen or heard a thing and the man was suddenly there.

Abdul Sa'ad motioned Bandar down to talk. Bandar squatted Bedu-style in a single fluid motion. His body was leathery and spare, yet capable of enormous strength. Abdul Sa'ad studied his face. Bandar had a milk-white cataract in one eye.

There were those who said he had the "evil eye." He had a scar on his cheek. Not for the first time, Abdul Sa'ad wondered how he came by it.

Bandar stared back insolently with his good eye. With his curved fleshless beak of a nose and fierce look, Bandar reminded Abdul Sa'ad of a hunting falcon. But he is my falcon, Abdul Sa'ad told himself.

Unlike the rigidity of western tactics conditioned by such games as chess, Abdul Sa'ad preferred backgammon. His plans were fluid to accommodate an unexpected element like the Scorpion. In a way, it might even improve his plan, he mused.

"I have a new assignment for you on 'the Day,' " Abdul Sa'ad said.

Bandar's good eye began to glitter dangerously.

When you have a pure-bred hunting falcon, you must never allow him to think he is untethered, even for an instant, Abdul Sa'ad reminded himself.

"Am I a Hteymi that you dare look at me that way?" Abdul Sa'ad snapped. He stared Bandar down, allowing a moment for Bandar to remember who he truly was.

Bandar's eye blinked. He looked away.

"You are the *Mahdi*, the Chosen of Allah," Bandar mumbled hoarsely.

First the rod, then the reward, Abdul Sa'ad thought. He petted Bandar's head as he would a faithful dog and smiled.

"*Ya habibi*, I think you'll like this," Abdul Sa'ad began. Just then the eunuch came waddling in, his chest puffed out with self-importance. Four paces behind him came a demurely veiled Kelly. Not even the heavy veil and robe could disguise the lithe grace of her movements. She stood before them, her head bowed as modesty required.

"It seems an American agent with the colorful name of 'the Scorpion' has been sent to rescue you," Abdul Sa'ad said in English and was rewarded by seeing a spark of hope flare in

167

her eyes, only to be immediately extinguished as she realized that if Abdul Sa'ad already knew about it, any rescue was doomed to fail.

"I believe you may know this Scorpion," Abdul Sa'ad said to Bandar.

Bandar's good eye narrowed slightly as if over a gun sight. He nodded.

"Behold the lure for my Scorpion-trap," Abdul Sa'ad said, gesturing languidly at the woman. Even behind the veil and robe he could sense her stiffening.

"If I kill him, sire, what is my reward?" Bandar uttered coarsely, never taking his good eye from the woman.

"Name it," Abdul Sa'ad said, smiling as he plucked a handful of almonds and dates from a silver bowl.

Bandar's good eye wandered over the veiled outline of Kelly's breasts and hips. A shiver rippled through her shrouded body.

"Give me the woman," Bandar muttered, his voice dry and cracked.

Abdul Sa'ad's eyes flashed angrily. Were there no bounds to the man's insolence? Still, what price a kingdom? he thought. By the time he gave Bandar his toy, the one-eyed snake would be expendable. Besides, a brief spell as Bandar's slave would no doubt make the *Americani* woman more appreciative of him when he reclaimed her. Then too, she needed a lesson. With her pathetic female cunning, she thought to lull him; but he knew her spirit remained rebellious.

"She's yours—after the Scorpion is dead," Abdul Sa'ad said.

Bandar bowed and touched the tip of Abdul Sa'ad's nose with his lips. He had chosen well, Abdul Sa'ad thought. Yes, Bandar would kill the Scorpion. And he would smile as he did it.

But Abdul Sa'ad had to be sure there really was a blood feud between them.

"Now, tell me what happened in 1962," Abdul Sa'ad said, leaning back on a silk cushion to listen.

Arabia, 1962

YOUSSEF WAS HEARTBROKEN. He had fallen deeply in love with Aisha, the daughter of Safooq. A bright happy twig of a child, who used to run and play as ably as any boy, she had become the prettiest girl in the tribe. Nicknamed "the Swallow" for her spritely grace and her sparkling dark eyes, at fourteen she was a beautiful woman ready to marry. Safooq was besieged by offers for her, but Youssef and Aisha had eyes only for each other. Both Sheikh Zaid and Safooq favored the match and a bride price was agreed upon, but the marriage could not take place because Bandar refused his consent.

Aisha was Bandar's *bint 'amm*, his father's brother's daughter. According to the *'urf* law of the desert, as Aisha's first cousin, Bandar had the exclusive right of preference to her hand. This tradition is so strong, that the very term "*bint 'ammi*" means "my wife" in Arabia. Bandar wanted Aisha for himself, but she despised him and according to the Moslem *sharia* law, she could not be forced into marriage. Things were at an impasse and the entire tribe was in an uproar over the affair. Everyone took sides. But despite all the efforts and entreaties of Sheikh Zaid, Safooq and even his own father, Faraj, Bandar remained unmoved. If he could not have Aisha, then no one could.

Night after night, Youssef and Aisha would secretly meet to dream and plan, but it was hopeless. Although many in the tribe despised him, Bandar's hatred seemed to feed and grow on the spite he felt. "Aisha will marry me or die an old maid," he had declared.

Youssef became so desperate he even talked of elopement, but Nick dissuaded him. If they eloped, Aisha would be considered merely a concubine, a dishonor that might force her to commit suicide and would certainly compel Safooq to blood vengeance. Nick convinced Youssef to try to reason with Bandar one more time. They agreed to pool everything they owned to make an enormous gift to Bandar. With Sheikh Zaid's help, they managed to put together a million *riyals*, a fabulous sum for a woman.

That Zaid had such a sum at his disposal was a reflection of the enormous changes which had come to the Mutayr because of the oil wealth. No longer nomads, they now lived in concrete houses near the pipeline pumping station on the outskirts of Hofuf. Although the royal family kept most of the petrodollars, enough trickled down to the desert sheikhs so there was no lack of money. Everyone had become car and gadget crazy, although since there was no one to fix them, as soon as they broke they were thrown away and the land behind their houses became covered in enormous junk piles. The towns were full of foreigners—Palestinians, Iraqis, Egyptians, Yemenis, Pakistanis and even western *Giaours* with fair hair and blue eyes that everyone knew were the sign of the evil eye.

As a result of his once-despised western origins, Nick's stature had grown enormously as well. He alone knew what to make of these strange *dhimmis* and their clever gadgets. When Sheikh Zaid first moved into his house, he kept dates and fruits in his toilet bowl because he could not imagine any other use for such an incredible object. Laughing, Nick explained its real function and Zaid turned away, embarrassed. "What a bizarre use for precious water," Zaid muttered into his beard.

Nick had become a strong and resourceful youth and he was acknowledged as a leader among the young men. Mounted on Fidda, his splendid white *mugathir* camel, he had led the Mutayr on a *ghazwa* against the Saar raiders, killing two of them with his own hand. He had well-learned the harsh law of the desert: "Mercy is for women and children; for men, weakness is death."

On the way back, his natural talent for warfare led him to bypass the wadi they would normally have passed through, thereby avoiding a retaliatory Saar ambush. When they returned, the Mutayr honored him with a lavish feast and Sheikh Zaid called him "a true son." His reputation was beginning to precede him, like a shadow when the sun is low. The legend of "the Scorpion" was becoming known among the tribes of the Najd and the Hasa. Only Bandar remained his enemy.

Together with his brother Youssef and Sheikh Zaid, Nick went into the desert with Faraj and Bandar. Ostensibly, they were going on a falcon hunt, but everyone knew that their real purpose was to try one last time to convince Bandar to release Aisha.

At their first camp Youssef, unable to restrain himself any longer, stood meekly before Bandar, his head bowed, and humbly begged Bandar to accept his gift of a million *riyals*. In the sight of his brothers and Allah he swore eternal honor and friendship. Sheikh Zaid and the Scorpion promised that Bandar would be honored in the tribe. Youssef pledged that he and Aisha would name their first son after Bandar.

To all this Bandar listened in silence, lounging insolently, his elbows on his knees. Then he smiled, his good eye gleaming, his teeth shining under the sparse black moustache he had recently grown.

"*Tatahattim!* You cringe like a Hutaymi!" Bandar sneered.

Youssef's head snapped back as if he had been struck. His eyes burned into Bandar as he stood there rigidly, trying to control his anger. Then all at once he broke. With an anguished cry he grabbed a handful of gold coins from the sack he had brought with him as a down payment and flung them into the sand at Bandar's feet.

They all sprang up, appalled. It was a terrible insult.

Bandar's face burned. His good eye rolled in its socket. He looked insane. With a savage growl he leaped upon Youssef, pummeling him to the ground. Zaid and Faraj were stunned. For one Bedu to strike another was an inconceivable sin.

Suddenly the Scorpion was between Bandar and the fallen Youssef. His riding crop slashed at Bandar's face, ripping his cheek open. Bandar staggered back, his hand pressed against the bleeding gash. Howling like a wolf, Bandar tore his *khanjar* dagger from his sheath and advanced upon the Scorpion. Nick's *khanjar* was already in his hand.

"Enough!" Zaid cried, leaping between them. For an endless moment they held their positions, like figures in an ancient tableau.

"No more!" Zaid cried hoarsely. "Or there will be a blood feud that will tear this tribe apart."

"*Kafir* dog, this is not over," Bandar hissed, sheathing his *khanjar*.

The Scorpion smiled. It was not a pretty smile.

That night it was decided to send Bandar to the Royal Army. It was hoped that the discipline he would learn there would teach him how to behave. It was also necessary to separate him from Zaid's sons. As for Aisha, nothing could be done. She too would be sent away—to a girl's school in Riyadh.

"Bandar has turned out like some fancy rifle, all fine inlay and gleaming stock, but which proves not to shoot straight and true," Sheikh Zaid declared sadly. They sat on the rug in a circle, sipping coffee served by Iffat from the old coffee pot. The electric lamps gave off a smoky yellow light. Insects beat against the window screens like rain.

"How could you have struck your cousin?" Zaid asked Nick at last. For a moment the veiled woman, grown immensely fat, glanced compassionately at the young man, then she waddled discreetly out of the room. Nick glanced after her. She was growing old, he told himself sadly.

"You know the saying: 'I and my cousins against the world, I and my brothers against my cousins, I against my brothers.' How could I not? Youssef is my brother," Nick replied in a quiet voice.

Zaid nodded, deeply troubled. "This anarchy has infected all of Arabia. Such people will destroy the world," he said, and they knew he was speaking about more than Bandar. A savage dispute was raging in the *ulama* as to whether King Saud should be deposed and replaced by Prince Faisal.

After some discussion, they decided to send Nick and Youssef on a mission to the Awazim and Rualla tribes, so that all of the noble northern tribes would be in agreement over whom to support for king.

"It is best to send you two away for awhile. Then too, it may be your last chance to cross the Nefud by camel. The old ways are dying. Soon they will pave the sands with *kafir* roads and the Bedu will cross the desert in Tooyooti trucks from Yapan," Zaid said with some bitterness.

"Is there no way to swallow the western machines without choking?" Youssef asked, his voice desperate. The attempt to straddle two divergent cultures was splitting them apart in ways they could not understand.

Zaid gently tapped his son's knee. He knew the boy's heart had been shattered by the loss of the woman. But wasn't their whole world being ripped apart? The little Scorpion more than any of them, he thought. Time and again he had seen the young man torn by some memory of his childhood jogged by an encounter with something western. But what could they do? Oil had brought the entire world to their hearth.

"When a *houbara* is struck by a falcon and lies dying in the sand, you can see the colors of its feathers fade and dull. The beauty is gone. But if you don't kill and eat the bird, how are you to live?" Zaid asked.

Riyadh

SNAKE-LIKE, THE MUSCLES of the dancer's belly began to ripple down from her ribcage to the gold-tasseled skirt which barely clung to her quivering pelvis. As the sinuous rhythm of the *tambor* drum increased, her hips began to move in a graceful simulation of coitus. Sweat glistened on her skin as she thrust her soft young body against her invisible lover. Suddenly, she stamped her bare feet and stood stock-still in the center of the spotlight. The darkness around her was alive, filled with eyes and the sound of breathing.

With a little cry, she began to whip her head back and forth, sending her long black hair flying. She stretched her arms to embrace the smoky light. As the drum went wild, she stiffened and every muscle in her lower body began to tremble in a paroxysm of desire. In a crescendo of drums she thrust her pelvis in a savage series of shudders and groans, then head bowed she sank to the floor, utterly spent.

The crowd went wild. Showers of bank notes were tossed onto the dance floor. The woman jumped up and began scrambling after the money. Then she went up to each table to allow the men to stuff more money down the front of her skirt and bodice.

In all the commotion, no one paid attention to the slim, elegantly dressed westerner in a blue Cardin suit who made his way to a dark corner table. Macready stopped sipping his *kakmar-eldin* long enough to push a plate towards his guest.

"Try the *mezza*. It's not bad," he offered.

"I see Fatima's in rare form tonight," the Scorpion said, sitting down. He selected a piece of *sogo* and popped it into his mouth.

Macready looked carefully around the restaurant, then

174

leaned forward to light a cigarette from the candle on the table.

"I have four men outside, just in case," he said out of the corner of his mouth. The Scorpion thought he had seen one trench-coated B movie too many.

"I saw them. So would anyone," the Scorpion shrugged. Macready might well have used skyrockets to announce the rendezvous, he thought irritably.

"We don't want another Doha. You made a lot of noise. It wasn't easy hushing it up," Macready said, scooping up a mound of *techina* with a piece of *pita* bread. A drop of *techina* landed on his jacket lapel. For a moment he stared at it as if a visitor's dog had just left an unwelcome offering on his best rug.

"Well, at least they didn't use embassy cars this time," the Scorpion said, hoping Macready would stop pushing it. When this was over, he swore never to work with the bastard again.

"Why here? I don't like it. Too public," Macready said, looking uneasily around the restaurant.

The crowd was exclusively male. Although most wore western clothes they sat on cushions at tables that were giant brass trays set low under the arched ceiling. Goat-skin hangings along the walls gave a tent-like intimacy to the dark room, lit by electric candles which added to the atmosphere of a Beduin encampment. Ceiling fans churned slowly through clouds of expensive cigar and cigarette smoke. A small Egyptian orchestra sawed monotonously away at an endless ballad which somehow managed to combine Arabic quarter tones with an occasional melodic foray into Bo bop a lulu she's my baby. All around them, whispered conversations at darkened tables underscored the music.

Everyone in Riyadh knew about Hamid's, the Scorpion thought. It was an information market located near the remains of the old mud wall in the seedier part of Riyadh. Hamid's had become a local institution. The royal family kept it open despite occasional puritanical rumblings from the *ulama* because the young royal bucks would have staged an open revolt if anyone tried to close it. The copious bribes paid by Hamid didn't hurt either, or the fact that Hamid served the best *shawirma* and *mahshee* east of Suez. It was said that on any given day more money was traded over dinner talk at Hamid's than on the New York Stock Exchange.

"How's the air-conditioning business, George?" the Scorpion asked. He sipped an iced *Sehha* water and tried to contain his impatience. Macready's face colored and he looked away.

"I'm sorry," he mumbled. Like a fugue, the expression offered a counterpoint to his life. The Scorpion felt like throwing something in his face. Instead, he ate another *mezza* and leaned forward.

"I chose this place because there's a back way Hamid lets me use. After all, we don't want another shoot-em-up at the OK Corral, do we?" the Scorpion said.

Macready nodded. A bit of *techina* clung to his moustache, the white giving him the odd appearance of a harelip. He began to stuff the *mezza* into his mouth, snatching greedily at the plate like a starving child.

"Your assignment's been changed. Forget the girl. Concentrate on stopping the hit," Macready said, his mouth full.

The Scorpion smiled. "I thought that might occur to Washington. Tell Harris the price is one million dollars in advance, tax-free; paid into my Swiss account," he said, and was rewarded by seeing Macready almost choke.

"Are you crazy?" Macready managed to gasp.

"Not crazy enough to do it without being well paid in advance," the Scorpion shrugged.

Just the thought of so much money stiffened Macready's backbone. He dipped his fingers in scented rosewater and wiped his face and hands on a napkin that hadn't been too rigorously laundered.

"That's a lot of money," he said thoughtfully, as if trying to figure out how he could get a piece of it.

"Just report the price accurately to Harris. Don't get cute, George," the Scorpion said.

"That's still a lot of money," Macready said slowly.

The Scorpion gave a Middle-Eastern shrug, as if to say *ma'alesh*. "What's Arabia worth these days?" he asked.

Macready nodded. He cleared his throat, a sure sign he wanted to get down to business. He looked around suspiciously, then stared at his ashtray as if it were bugged.

"Any idea when the 'incident' is supposed to occur? None of our sources has come up with anything," Macready said.

"Not yet, but you can feel it coming. There are a lot of Royal Army soldiers around Riyadh."

"That's already been reported," Macready said. He leaned forward and half-covered his mouth with the cigarette as he spoke. "They're getting very nervous in Washington. Very. The Russian connection seems very plausible since they found out Nuruddin once knew Philby and Maclean and that crowd at Cambridge. And they think the westerner in the photo is a Cuban. The idea that somebody might cut off the oil has them in a panic."

"Then they won't quibble on the price."

"You've got to come up with something—and fast," Macready added. His left eyelid began to twitch. From another table came the sound of harsh laughter and Macready almost winced. It was hard to remember what he was like in Saigon. Well, they had all changed since then, the Scorpion thought.

"It's not so easy. It could happen anywhere. A deranged gunman at a public *majlis*, in a mosque, a few drops of cyanide in his coffee, a remotely detonated mine under his car. Anywhere. How do you protect a man from the members of his own family—the people he trusts most?" the Scorpion said irritably.

"Washington wants all the stops pulled out on this one. Too bad they're stuck with me," Macready said bitterly. His face was lined with failure, as if etched by acid.

177

"I agree, but then we all have to make do, don't we?" the Scorpion said.

Macready's head snapped back. His eyes were two pinpoints of candlelight. The Scorpion felt better now that their mutual dislike was out in the open. Maybe hate would motivate the son-of-a-bitch. Then Macready blinked as if he couldn't sustain even hate.

Macready looked hangdog again. His face sagged like an old beagle. That way, he was too much of a danger. The only thing the Scorpion had left to motivate him with was fear.

"Don't go all mushy on me, George. I like it better when you hate me. I'm alone out there with you tying one arm behind my back and I can't afford it any more. You know too much, so either you're in or out and I mean permanently out.

"Now, has Riyadh station come up with anything new on Abdul Sa'ad? Anything at all?"

Macready shook his head. Then he looked up startled, as the applause sounded again. The club darkened. Fatima was about to do another number. As the whining quarter tones began, Macready muttered, "Only that his eunuch is in town on some business or other. He's staying at Abdul Sa'ad's new condo on King Abd al Aziz Road."

"Perhaps I should pay him a visit," the Scorpion said.

"He's well guarded."

The Scorpion just smiled. It made Macready shiver. In the spotlight, Fatima was rotating her hips in a way that few vertebrates could match. The tempo began to build. Macready wiped his face and made ready to leave. He left a wad of *riyals* on the tray.

"Come on, I'll show you the back way," the Scorpion said. He timed their exit to Fatima's routine. No one noticed the two shadows make their way between the tables towards the men's toilet. All eyes were glued on the dancer quivering in her grand finale. They started down a dimly lit corridor, the throb of the drum masking their footsteps. About halfway the Scorpion yanked Macready into what apeared to be a broom closet. They went through an old curtain which concealed a dark foul-smelling passage that led to the brightly lit kitchen.

Hamid was swearing amiably at his perspiring cooks and waiters who bustled about clanging dishes and sweating over steaming pots. The fat proprietor caught the Scorpion's eye, but said nothing except to look significantly over at the television blasting unwatched in the corner.

The TV announcer was a dark young man with a moustache so thin he must've measured it with a micrometer. Something he said froze the Scorpion in his tracks. Macready almost bumped into him, but the Scorpion just stared at the screen, which showed a rerun of the King's Camel Race from last year. The race had drawn over four thousand contestants. This year, it was expected to draw more than six thousand riders and half a million spectators. The prize, the announcer declared, his eyes gleaming, was a purse of fifty thousand *riyals* and a solid gold *khanjar* dagger to be presented to the winner by His Majesty, King Salim himself.

What the Palestinian had said flashed in the Scorpion's mind. The hit was supposed to be "public—a demonstration."

It was perfect, the Scorpion thought. The King's Camel Race, where the king was honor-bound to show up whether he heard about a plot or not and where the eyes of all Arabia would be glued. The race was the Arabian version of the Kentucky Derby, the Superbowl, the World Series, the Masters and Wimbledon all rolled into one.

The king would be there, all right. Not to mention the crowds, thousands of riders and camels, a vast course in the open desert, an impossible security problem for the royal palace guards. The Scorpion shook his head in admiration as he led Macready to the kitchen's back door. It was a beauty.

"What was that all about?" Macready said irritably, stumbling over a tin in a back alley behind the restaurant. Suddenly a steel hand grabbed his lapel and pulled him close.

"Shut up and listen," the Scorpion hissed. "I have a hunch about the hit. If I'm right it's going to be in three days."

"Are you sure?" Macready whispered, his eyes reflecting a distant yellow streetlight around which swarmed squadrons of flying insects.

"Not yet. It's just an idea. If it checks out, I'll call you with confirmation at the usual time and place. Tell them to keep the embassy line open. And I want the money now, George."

"I'll try. It's a lot of money," Macready said.

"Tell them," the Scorpion began, then froze. The dead Arab's Magnum was in his hand even before Macready could blink. He had seen a shadow detach itself from the darkness across the street.

Macready suddenly heaved a long sigh, like the sound of air escaping from a balloon. "It's all right. He's one of ours," he said in a shaky voice.

The Scorpion nodded. "Time's running out, you said."

"For both of us. Anything else?" Macready asked.

"Yeah. Braithwaite is working both sides of the street."

For a moment, neither said anything. Macready dug at the rubbish in the alley with the tip of his shoe. "Why'd you wait so long? Do you want to see him get away?" Although he was trying to control it, the Scorpion could hear him grinding his teeth.

"Yes. That's what I want, George."

"You shit!" Macready hissed.

"That's right, George. When you work in a sewer you don't come out smelling like after-shave. You've got the data. All I had to do was betray an old friend."

"What was Braithwaite to you?" Macready asked.

"Minor detail, George. He saved my life in the desert. Come to think of it," the Scorpion smiled, "that all started because of Saud family politics, too."

For the briefest instant the Scorpion looked very young as he remembered. Then he turned away and was gone. His receding footsteps were swallowed in the darkness. At the corner, insects spattered the yellow streetlamp, tiny kamikazis hurling themselves at the light.

Arabia, 1962

"BUT WHY DOES A NEW KING have to be chosen from one of the surviving sons of Abd al Aziz and not the eldest son of Saud who is still king? Neither *urf* nor *sharia* law have such a requirement," Nick asked.

They were camped for the night in a depression on the leeward side of a sand dune in the heart of the vast Nefud desert. The two youths were on their way back from their mission to the Rualla and Awazim sheikhs, where it was agreed that they would join the Mutayr in backing the *ulama* scholars and the *emirs* of the Sudairi family in deposing Kind Saud and placing Faisal on the throne. Youssef smiled, his teeth gleaming in the light from the river of stars above.

"That is some western trick of the Saud family. The Sauds make themselves kings and say we are a country and the West believes them. But we are Bedu. We submit to none save Allah and those who prove themselves as leaders. The king has forgotten this."

"Western tricks!" Nick asked mockingly, but he was uncomfortable. He felt guilty because lately he had been thinking more and more about his lost past. Where did he truly belong? he wondered.

They laid down in their clothes to sleep. Just before dropping off, Nick noticed a faint ripple in the winking of the stars, as if the air was a guitar string which had been plucked. He felt a vague uneasiness. He sensed the coming of a sandstorm.

God help them if it caught them before they reached the well at Wadi er Rumna, he thought.

If it had been an ordinary sandstorm they might have found the well. But it was no ordinary storm. For five days the wind had raged. The air was filled with stinging particles of sand driven by the wind, lancing into their skin like millions of needles. It was impossible to see. By day a vast ochreous cloud surrounded them, shutting out the light. By night, the wind howled on and everything was darkness. The stars could not be seen and the air was a heavy black mass of stinging grains, which swallowed them whole, voraciously flaying their flesh. It was like the end of the world.

Nick's heart fluttered. It was like a supreme test of which Sheikh Zaid spoke and he remembered the terrible prophecy of the Holy Koran:

> When the sun shall be darkened,
> when the stars shall be thrown down,
> when the mountains shall be set moving,
> when the seas shall be set boiling,
> when the heavens shall be stripped off,
> when Hell shall be set blazing,
> when Paradise shall be brought nigh,
> then shall every soul know what it has done.

The two youths lay snuggled against their kneeling camels under a tent formed by their *bishts* half-buried in the sand. During the first day they chattered, for conversation is as natural as breathing for an Arab; but at last they ran out of things to say and each of them was alone with his thoughts. The grinding rumble of the wind thundered in their ears.

Nick's mind wandered. He thought of the politics and the changes that the West had brought to Arabia. Was that part of Allah's plan? He wondered where his *kismet* would lead him. Was he of the West or the East? He gazed for days at the particles of sand clinging to his hand. Their crystalline structure fascinated him. It reminded him of the arabesques on the walls of the Prophet's Mosque in Medina.

How different the concept of the arabesque was from western notions of art, he thought. He remembered the museums his father had shown him in Europe, where they stopped during their trip to Arabia. Western artists made pictures that were pallid representations of nature, he thought contemptuously. They were fascinated by the human figure, as if man was the measure of all things and God was some giant ape in the sky!

The arabesque was infinitely more profound, he thought. The arabesque was more than an abstract design. It was a complex pattern of geometric shapes which reflected not nature as it is perceived by man, but its underlying crystalline pattern. The arabesque is repetitive, symmetrical and yet it has a rhythm which draws the eye ever onward to infinity, for no arabesque pattern ever truly ends. The arabesque is an intuitive expression of the infinite, which is God's nature.

When the storm finally died away, they dug themselves out of the sand and stumbled into the sunlight, rubbing their eyes in disbelief. The wind had changed the patterns in the sand, moved the dunes hundreds of paces and obliterated any tracks. There were no landmarks to guide them to the well, which was probably filled with sand anyway. The camels needed water badly and they had barely enough for themselves. They spent three days in a futile search for the well.

After the third day, Youssef's camel died and they doubled up on Nick's *thelul*. They gave up searching for the well and struck out towards the east, hoping to find Buraida. The heat was relentless, even for these young Bedu. Their throats grew parched and their lips began to crack and blister. Nick's tongue began to swell and a foul taste never left his mouth. He tried to swallow but it was impossible. He had no more saliva left.

Seven days after the sandstorm, Nick's camel collapsed and died. The once splendid *mugathir* lay on her side, her legs rigid, her mouth caked with dried green slime. She had carried the two youths until the last cell in her body had been depleted of its moisture. Towards the end they had tried every trick to keep her going, even pouring handfuls of precious water from their last goat skin into her nostrils. She had been a good *thelul*, Nick thought. Only the best *theluls* went on till they dropped. But with her death, their last hope had died as well. Now they were lost in a vast rocky slope without a landmark to the end of the horizon. The slope was strewn with black stones worn smooth by the wind as far as could be seen. The two young men looked at each other for a brief moment, seeing the hopelessness reflected in each other's eyes.

"*Inshallah*, it is the will of Allah," Youssef shrugged.

Without a word Nick slung the depleted water skin, wrinkled like an old prune, around his neck and began to walk towards the horizon. Youssef scrambled to his feet and followed. The burning sun was directly overhead. They cast no shadows as they walked. The sky was a vast metal plate, blue-white with heat. They had no plan; they were in Allah's fiery hands. Like the *thelul*, they would march until they died.

The endless day wore on. As their shadows lengthened far ahead of them, Youssef began to gag, his body wrenched with terrible dry heaves. After each episode, Youssef would smile apologetically at Nick and they would plod on.

At night they shivered uncontrollably under the icy stars, their bodies too dehydrated to maintain their internal temperature against the cold. At dawn, they shared the last of their water. Then Youssef collapsed during the *salat*. He lay quivering on the hard ground, unable to stand. Desperation in his eyes, he begged Nick to leave him.

Angrily, Nick knelt by Youssef and drew his *khanjar*. "Here!" he rasped, his eyes dried and inflamed. He looked a hundred years old. "Take my blood and drink it! But don't shame me.

Don't make me tell my father that I left my brother to die in the sands," he croaked, the *khanjar* trembling in his hand.

Youssef nodded weakly, his face a weary mask torn by dry, open sores. With Nick's help he struggled to his feet and they went on, facing into the rising sun which was destroying them. Arm in arm they staggered through the watery columns of heated air as though wading through boiling water. One way or another, it would be over today, Nick thought.

At first, he sensed another presence in the emptiness. When he finally saw the distant speck he thought it was just another mirage. He decided not to tell Youssef, whom he was half-dragging by now. It would be too cruel a disappointment. Then Youssef nudged him and gestured, his eyes wild and unfocused. They heard a distant "halloo-ing" and waved wildly. Nick tried to shout, but nothing came out of his throat. The rider waved back and spurred his camel with excitement, shouting as he approached. Nick closed his eyes in thanksgiving and sank to the ground.

Braithwaite supported Nick's head with one hand and held the water skin with the other. Nick sucked greedily at the water. "Like a little n-nipper at the teat," Braithwaite used to say when he would retell the story.

"Easy, lad, easy," Braithwaite cautioned.

"How's Youssef?" Nick asked.

"Fine. Fit as a f-f-fiddle," Braithwaite laughed. He looked shrewdly at Nick.

"They said you were a westerner," he said in English. "Imagine that," he grinned.

"Imagine," Nick echoed in English.

Braithwaite patted Nick's head tenderly.

"Time to g-get you home, laddy-buck," he smiled.

"Home," Nick said, dazed. "Where's home?"

Al Aramah

THE HOODED FALCON stirred restlessly on its perch as if dreaming of the sky. Abdul Sa'ad was asleep, his breathing deep and regular. Kelly was wide awake, her eyes staring into the darkness, her hand clenched around the letter-opener, trying to decide what to do.

This time there would be no going back, she thought. But should she kill Abdul Sa'ad and then try to escape, or just flee while she had the chance?

In three days they would assassinate the king and the whole country would erupt. She had to warn someone. She thought of Bandar, his piggy eye roving over her body, and shuddered. She had to get away. But what about Abdul Sa'ad? If she killed him the conspiracy might collapse. And she would have her revenge, she thought grimly.

But what if she missed in the darkness? What if she struck and he cried out? The letter-opener felt slippery in her sweaty palm. This was her last chance, too. He might not send for her again before the assassination.

If only Robert were here. He would know what to do. She longed for his strong arms around her. "What is most important?" she imagined him asking. Doing the job, getting the information out, she decided.

It was awful. The Middle East was about to explode in a flame that could engulf the world and no one knew about it except her. And even if she could get away and tell them— would they believe her?

She couldn't worry about that now, she thought. Sending the message was more important than anything. That's what Robert would do, she decided. Besides, every fiber of her being was screaming to escape. Abdul Sa'ad was reprieved, she thought bitterly.

She went over the plan again in her mind. The guard outside Abdul Sa'ad's door was used to seeing women come and go. So long as Abdul Sa'ad didn't cry out, he should be no problem. Providing no one saw her in the halls, only the guard by the door to the courtyard stood between her and the Mercedes. He usually fell asleep around 3 a.m. If he was awake, she would have to kill him. Once in the car, nothing would stop her, she vowed.

She had gone over it again and again. At first the thought of the guards and barbed wire and minefields had defeated her. Then the realization had hit her that there was an easy road out. Abdul Sa'ad had built this place as a fortress, not a prison. A fortress is designed to keep people out, not to prevent them from leaving. It would work, she thought. It had to.

Silently she eased away from Abdul Sa'ad and began to stand up. There was a whisper of silk and Abdul Sa'ad shifted position. Her heart pounded wildly and she wondered whether to strike after all. Her arm coiled above his dark form. A soft snore issued from him and she found herself breathing again. Sweat stung her eyes. She picked up her handbag and shoes, pulled her veil down over her head and padded quietly to the door.

She took a deep breath and tried to think of a prayer. The only line that came to mind was "The Lord is my shepherd." She said it over to herself three times, then opened the door. The guard said nothing as she closed the door behind her. He looked carefully at her, as if wondering what to do. She felt his curious eyes on her as she glided like a ghost down the hall, her bare feet making no sound on the carpeted floors. Sweat prickled her spine as she went down the corridor, half expecting a sudden shout from the guard. But everything was still.

As she approached the corridor leading to the courtyard she took off her veil and unbuttoned her blouse so her breasts could be easily seen. If the guard was awake, the sight of an unveiled attractive woman, her breasts exposed, should distract him so much that she ought to be able to get close enough to strike, she thought. She wiped her palm on her skirt and clenched the opener tightly. Then she peeked around the corner.

The guard was asleep, his back against the doorpost. His legs were sprawled across the doorway, an automatic rifle cradled on his thighs. Kelly bit her lip to keep from crying with relief. Then carefully, one silent step at a time she inched her way to the door until she stood beside him, scarcely daring to breathe. She reached across to the big iron bolt securing the heavy wooden door. As she raised the knob an almost infinitesimal sound of scraping metal froze her blood. The guard slept as if drugged.

With painstaking care, millimeter by millimeter she eased the bolt open, sweat prickling out of every pore. Taking a deep breath, she turned the handle, carefully swung the door open, gathered up her skirt and stepped cautiously over the guard.

Once out in the courtyard she sidestepped into the shadows, her back against the stone wall. She took deep gulps of night air. Her clothes were drenched with sweat. She had a terrible urge to run and fought it down somehow.

She waited until she had caught her breath and her eyes had adjusted to the darkness. She could distinctly see the black outline of the Mercedes. It was only about fifty yards away and most of that was in deep shadow. High above the courtyard, stars filled the blackness. There were so many of them. She hadn't known there were so many. It was as if she had never seen stars before.

She got down on all fours and began to cross the courtyard, balanced on her fingers and toes. Lizard-like, she crawled towards the car, one limb at a time. It seemed to take forever. Once she looked up at the stars. They seemed impossibly beautiful, impossibly distant. Like an animal, she looked back down at the ground and pressed on.

When at last she reached up to touch the car handle, she felt as though she had crossed a marathon finish line. The car latch opened with a loud click. Surely someone heard it! Scarcely breathing, she waited for what might have been seconds or minutes, but nothing moved. Her heart throbbed wildly. She was almost free! At last she was in the driver's seat. She quietly closed the car door. She opened her handbag and began looking for the key she had stolen. Then her heart plummeted to her stomach like a runaway elevator.

It wasn't there! It was impossible; it had to be there, she told herself. Desperately she rummaged through the bag. Please, please be here, she prayed.

Suddenly the car light clicked on and a harsh male voice said in clumsy English: "Is thees what you looking on?"

She uttered a little cry of despair. It was Bandar! In one hand he dangled the car keys.

"But how . . ." she began and then it hit her. The eunuch! Yesterday she had discovered him in her room, looking as if he were searching for something. But the handbag looked as if it hadn't been touched, so she had ignored it. What an idiot she was!

Bandar's good eye glinted evilly at her. He seemed delighted with himself. A blind rage erupted in Kelly's brain. With a savage cry she stabbed at him with the opener.

Bandar reacted as quickly as a snake. He grabbed her wrist and twisted it painfully behind her back. She struggled against him, but it was futile. He held her as easily as he would a child.

His body odor was disgusting, as if something had died and rotted inside his skin. It made her gag. He held her close, one hand fondling her breasts as casually as he might pet a dog. He acted as if she was already his possession.

As Bandar led her back to captivity, she cast a last, longing look at the distant impervious stars. A falling star flared briefly in the darkness and she made a sudden wish of death for Nasir the eunuch.

Riyadh

THE FOLLOWING NIGHT Nasir was visited by an evil *zar* spirit at Prince Abdul Sa'ad's Riyadh apartment. Although the fat and womanish eunuch had always considered *zars* a silly Bedu superstition, from the moment he woke up he had no doubt whatsoever that his visitor was not of this earth. Who else but a demon could have slipped by the guards, one of whom was later found outside his door, his windpipe crushed by a single blow? All Nasir knew was that he had awakened with a *khanjar* dagger at his throat and a strange apparition seated on his bed. Even though it was summer, the demon was shrouded from head to foot by a black *bisht*, similar to the cloaks worn by the Mutayr of the Hasa desert. The dark figure stared coldly at him through eyes the color of smoke. Nasir tried to swallow, but his fear was too great.

Without a word, the *zar* rammed a wad of cloth into Nasir's mouth. Then he grabbed Nasir's little finger and bent it backwards till it broke. Nasir screamed into the gag, but only a faint high-pitched squeal could be heard. Sweat poured out of Nasir like a river as an unimaginable pain exploded in his hand. Nasir flopped desperately on the bed like a fish tossed on a dock, but the demon held him down with the strength of ten men. The *zar* calmly pushed the broken finger back till the fingernail touched Nasir's wrist and the eunuch almost swallowed the gag in his agony. His eyes bulged out with horror like a frog's eyes. Perhaps he had died in his sleep and this was hell!

"That was just to get your attention," the demon said softly.

The demon removed the gag and held the razor-sharp blade edge just underneath Nasir's nose, gripping the eunuch's hair with his other hand.

"Tell me what I want to know or I'll slice it off. After all, a man who's already lost one nose should want to hang on to his second," the demon said smiling. It was a cruel joke for the eunuch, alluding to the custom that when a Bedu inadvertently exposed his privates, Arabs would chorus: "Your nose is showing!" to tell him to cover up.

"By the Prophet I will, Master," the eunuch blubbered, his eyes rolling in their sockets as if weighted in the back like doll's eyes.

"Where is the assassination to be?" the demon demanded.

"I know nothing, Master," Nasir wailed. A sudden pain seared his face and he gasped for air as his mouth filled with a warm flush of blood. The *khanjar* had sliced through his septum. The demon held a picture of the western woman before his eyes. Nasir tried to turn away, but the demon held him fast by his curly hair.

"Hear me, slave. I won't ask you again. It's the King's Camel Race, isn't it?" the demon rasped. The eunuch's face collapsed into a fleshy red scowl, like a baby about to cry. The *zar* began to rotate his broken finger like a wheel.

"Yes, the race! Aiee Allah!" Nasir cried.

"How is it to be done?" the demon demanded.

"Please, no more . . ." Nasir pleaded.

"Answer! You needn't betray any confidences. All you have to do is nod. Is it a bomb? Poison? A single rifle . . ." the demon asked in a soft, almost crooning, voice. He looked at Nasir's mutilated finger and smiled.

Nasir nodded desperately.

So, the Scorpion thought. A single sniper with a high-powered rifle; the hardest hit to stop. His shoulders gathered as he made a sudden move. The eunuch's scream was cut off by a strangulating grip, the Scorpion's thumb jammed deep into his Adam's apple.

"Who is it to be? A spectator? A guard?"

Sweat poured out of the eunuch like a sprinkler.

"A contestant. The one-eyed man they call Bandar. He's the one," Nasir blubbered.

The Scorpion blanched. Was it possible? he wondered. Bandar—his childhood enemy? And yet, ever since he had taken this mission, he had found himself rummaging in the past.

"This Bandar, the one-eyed. Is he Bandar ibn Faraj of the Mutayr?" the Scorpion demanded, in a voice he barely recognized as his own.

The eunuch nodded. "He's a Mutayri, Master. A dangerous man," Nasir confided, a desperate dog-like slavishness in his eyes.

The Scorpion's mind reeled. It was as if the entire world was being drawn into the vortex of a single event. After all these years, his *kismet* and Bandar's, drawn at last to a single killing-ground as he had somehow always known it would be.

"Will the prince bring the Yankee woman to the Camel Race?" the Scorpion demanded.

"I am forbidden . . ." Nasir gasped, unable to go on. The pain shot up his nose into the center of his brain as the demon probed with the *khanjar*'s point. Nasir felt his mind drowning in the pain.

"She will be in my master's tent in the royal pavilion," Nasir gasped.

"Is she unharmed?"

"She is my master's new favorite," the eunuch leered. Something about the way he said it bothered the Scorpion.

"What's he done to her?" the Scorpion demanded.

"Nothing, truly. After she was 'trained,' she was willing," Nasir babbled, alarmed at the icy storm cloud in the demon's eyes.

"How was she trained?"

"I never touched her. By the Prophet, I swear. We simply kept her in the hut in the courtyard. When she got thirsty enough, she gave in," he said with a sly grimace that turned to a groan as the Scorpion twisted his broken finger.

"What else?" the Scorpion said.

"It's nothing, Master. Only *harim* gossip," he whimpered.

"Who pays attention to women's babbling?" Nasir tried to shrug it off, man to man.

"Tell me, you camel slime," the Scorpion growled.

"It is whispered that the prince is so debauched that he can only have pleasure by watching a woman using—devices," the eunuch said, a snigger in his voice at such a delicious piece of gossip, despite his fear.

"Bastard," the Scorpion breathed.

"She is only a woman," Nasir muttered placatingly, then comprehension began to dawn and his bulging eyes grew even wider. "She is of your *khamsah*," he whispered in horror. The word *khamsah* was derived from the number five and defined the five patrilineal generations of a person's immediate family. A man was bound to blood vengeance for any dishonor committed against any member of his *khamsah*.

The Scorpion nodded. In a way it was true. After all that Kelly had gone through, he felt as though he had somehow adopted her. He felt a kind of kinship between them that had little to do with them both being Americans. After all, Washington didn't care about her any more. They had bigger fish to fry. No one cared, except him. There was something special about her. He had seen it in the photograph. The mission was no longer business, he admitted to himself. It had become personal. Very personal.

"Did you ever touch her?" the Scorpion asked quietly.

Nasir nodded, his chin trembling like a child about to cry. Who could lie to such a fearsome demon?

"Only once. She was stubborn so my master ordered me to whip her with a riding crop. But it was only that once," he blubbered.

The Scorpion made a sudden move and the eunuch's body thrashed on the bed with jerky motions, like a puppet gone haywire.

"You also only die once," the Scorpion said. He stood up and wiped the *khanjar* on the bedclothes. He had to contact Macready. It was imperative to get the data to Washington.

On the bed, the eunuch gasped his last desperate breaths as the blood gurgled out of his severed throat.

Washington

ALLEN WAS RIGHT. The president was furious at being woken up in the middle of the night for the second time in a week. The chief executive's face was hard and his jaw set, and the others crowded in the room uneasily glanced away. They were meeting in the Lincoln Sitting Room in the southeast corner of the White House, because Allen had suggested that they avoid showing any lights in the Oval Office, which might alert the press corps. The room was the smallest in the mansion, barely thirteen by sixteen feet. It was furnished like a Victorian sitting room and portraits of President Lincoln and his family hung over the marble fireplace.

This room was the president's private retreat, his "*querencia*", Allen thought, the word recalling his junior year at Yale when he had spent the summer in Spain and had briefly become an afficionado of the bullfights. "My Hemingway period," Allen used to drily describe it. A *querencia* was a place in the ring where the bull felt at home. A bull was at his most dangerous in *hisquerencia* and a good part of the *matador*'s skill involved keeping the bull away from it, Allen reflected. Indeed, the president, still dressed in his robe and pajamas, reminded Allen of an old bull as he glared at his advisors from the depths of his leather armchair.

"What the hell took you so long to find out about all this?" the president demanded, fixing Page with an angry glance.

"The CRITIC just came in a few minutes ago, Mr. President. It took the Scorpion a couple of days to find out exactly

194

when and where the assassination is planned to take place," Allen stepped in. He wasn't about to let the meeting degenerate into recriminations. There'd be plenty of those before this crisis was over, he thought.

"All right," the president relented, biting his lower lip as he often did when agitated. "What counter measures have we taken so far?"

"The *Nimitz* is standing by, monitoring the Russian fleet. We've placed the RDF and the Marines on DEFCON Yellow and we're mobilizing transport now," General Baker reported. Defensive Condition Yellow was the highest military ready status except for DEFCON Red, which meant war.

"What about the 'Contingency Plan'?" the president asked.

"It's on its way," Baker replied. The Pentagon had sets of contingency plans drawn up for every possible military situation, up to and including the potential invasion of the South Pole by Hottentots.

"We might want to send SR-71 Blackbirds and AWACs to overfly Arabia and keep us posted on what's happening out there," Secretary of State Wallace put in, lighting another cigarette from a still burning butt.

"We might want to send a few to overfly Russia, if it comes to that," Harris said with a smirk.

Allen quickly turned to confront Harris. His eyebrows were raised in wordless fury. They formed a single ridge across his forehead, giving him the appearance of an angry Neanderthal. Then he apparently thought better of it. Harris, as the Scorpion's senior case officer, was indispensable right now—and the son-of-a-bitch knew it too, Allen thought.

"Just to establish contact with this Scorpion of yours," Allen snapped.

"What do I tell him?" Harris asked.

"We'll have to pay him out of the CIA budget," Allen said.

"A million dollars! Who the hell does he think he is? John Wayne?" Wallace muttered.

"He thinks he has us over a barrel, Mr. Secretary," Harris said.

"Does he?" the president asked.

"Yes sir, I think he does," Harris replied softly.

"Gary . . ." the president looked up at Allen.

"I think if he can pull it off it's a bargain, Mr. President," Allen replied.

"I thought we had lots of oil," the president began peevishly, rubbing his hand against his stubbled cheek.

"We have lots of oil because Arabia wants us to have lots of oil. Abdul Sa'ad and the Russians could change all that, Mr. President," CIA Director Page said.

"Well, why can't we send in our own security—or maybe get King Salim out of the country?" the president asked brightly.

"Might make things even worse. King Salim has to be in Arabia as a focal point for the tribes to rally around, Mr. President," Allen replied.

"All right, suppose they cut off the oil. What's the bottom line?" the president demanded angrily.

"It would make the thirties look like boom times, but it would never get that far," Page answered.

"Why not?"

"Because we couldn't allow the Russians to get away with it," Wallace said.

"In other words . . ." General Baker began.

"In other words 'World War Three,' General," Wallace snapped.

The president slumped back in his chair. Suddenly, he looked very frail.

"What shall I tell the Scorpion?" Harris asked softly.

The president glanced around the room. It was so still for a moment he imagined he could hear the dust settling. "I see no alternative. Tell him it's his mission," he said, his voice sounding old and tired.

"Using any means?" Harris inquired.

"I have no interest in details," the president angrily snapped.

The soft burring of a telephone on the ornate end table was somehow as jarring as a fire alarm. Allen quickly picked it up, listened intently for a moment and hung up, after a "Thank you" muttered in a strangled voice. Everyone looked at Allen as though he were a doctor about to pronounce a life-or-death verdict.

"That was the Air Force Recon Office. They've just received SAMOS photos showing extensive military activity among the Caucasus Army Group along the Iranian border," Allen said.

The edges of Harris' mouth curled up with an I-told-you-so maliciousness. Evidence from one of the SAMOS spy satellites was conclusive.

Each twenty-two-foot satellite was capable of picking up all radio transmissions in its area on all known frequencies and had cameras which could photograph the lettering on a golf ball on a green from a hundred miles up, even through dense cloud and fog cover.

"Does that mean what I think it means, General?" the president asked, fixing Baker with the steely glint which had been known to cow a roomful of political bosses into uneasy silence.

"Yes sir, it means the Russians are mobilizing," Baker said.

The president stood up and ran his fingers through his sleep-touseled hair. The others also stood, at once together and apart in an uneasy, silent group, like people in a lift.

"All right, let's get those spy planes up," the president ordered.

"Russia too?" Page prompted.

"Russia too," the president said, looking around the room. For a moment he gazed at the sad homely face of Lincoln in the portrait over the fireplace. He was another president who had seen his worst fears come true, he thought.

"I want a full-scale alert, gentlemen. And I want a complete press blackout. God help the son-of-a-bitch who leaks even a hint of this," the president declared, and started for the door. Then he turned back for a moment.

"How many Americans are in Arabia now?" he asked, his voice trembling.

"About forty thousand," Harris replied crisply.

The president shook his head. "God help us," he said. He put his hand on Allen's shoulder. It was at once a friendly and a somehow pathetic gesture. "What do you think, Gary? Can this Scorpion pull it off for us? One man alone?" he asked.

Allen thought for a moment. When he looked at the president there was a faint trace of the young Yale undergraduate in his eyes. Allen shook his head.

"Does any man know what awaits him in the desert?" he said.

And when the unbelievers plot to shut
thee up or to kill thee or to drive thee
out they plot, but God plots also, and
God is the best of plotters.
—The Koran

al Hofuf

THE NIGHT WAS FILLED with stars. A new-minted crescent moon balanced like a metal shaving on a shelf of light which was the Milky Way. Beyond the red glow of the campfire the desert sands stretched endlessly, snow-white in the ghostly light of distant worlds. All was silence, except for the tinkling of camel bells which seemed a kind of star music.

The Scorpion sipped a thimble-cup of cardamon-flavored coffee and passed the cup back to his brother Youssef, who refilled it from the long-stemmed coffee pot seated directly on the embers. Youssef refilled the cup and drained it with a loud slurp.

Youssef had changed, the Scorpion thought. Once lean as a saluki, he had acquired a sleek successful look. He had married Farah, Safooq's daughter, and had two boys. As was the custom, he had changed his name from "son of Zaid" to "father of Faisal," his eldest son. No one spoke of Aisha.

Youssef leaned closer. His face glowed like burnished copper in the campfire light. For a moment he seemed ancient, like someone from another time.

"Much of what you say is true, my beloved. These are dangerous things. But what Prince Abdul Sa'ad says is also true. The West corrupts our soul. The noise of the auto salesman grows louder, but Allah's voice is harder to hear every day," Youssef said.

"Now the camel rides in the back of a Yapani pick-up truck as if it were a man. Is that not an oddity, my brother?" said Faisal, Zaid's eldest son.

"Abdul Sa'ad has spoken against this insanity of educating females. In Riyadh women ride buses with men and even work in banks," Safooq said in a peevish tone.

"What women want is what they have always had," Sheikh

Zaid said. His shiny new false teeth gave him the peculiar look of someone who smiles for a living.

"What is that, my father?" asked Faisal, an air of amusement hovering at the corners of his mouth.

"Their own way, of course," Zaid wheezed triumphantly and they all laughed.

"Still, something must be done. We don't want an Iran in Arabia," Faisal put in seriously as the laughter died down.

"Allah forbid!" muttered Zaid.

"Let the royal family fight it out among themselves. What is that to us?" Safooq grumbled.

There were murmurs of approval from some of the other tribesmen gathered around the fire.

"But with Abdul Sa'ad comes the *Roosees*," the Scorpion said softly.

"And with King Salim the *Americani*. Which is worse? It is still dog and master," Faisal said, holding up his little finger when he said "dog" and his fist when he said "master."

"In Riyadh it is said that when America sneezes the king gets pneumonia," Youssef said.

"*Sa*, it is even thus," Zaid grumbled.

"These *giaour* treat us like strangers in our own home. They are like lice. No matter how you scratch you cannot get rid of them," Safooq snapped irritably.

"What would be so bad about the *Roosees*? At least they support the *Falastin* against the Jews," someone called out.

"The *Roosees* are atheists," the Scorpion murmured.

"Abomination," a voice rumbled in the darkness. The Scorpion thought it might have been old Turki, father of Safooq.

"I too have heard this said of the *Roosees*," Faisal said.

"What sort of men are they? To think all this is an accident—and meaningless besides?" Sheikh Zaid said, gesturing at the starry sky.

"What does it matter to us what the infidels believe? Are the men of the Mutayr to fight because the great powers covet Arabia as they always have?" said Muhammed of Heikal, elegantly tossing the tail of his headcloth over his shoulder, like a woman with a fur piece. A wealthy merchant of the Rualla, he had married one of Zaid's daughters. Although new to the Mutayr, his free-spending ways had given him influence. He knew of the Scorpion only by reputation.

"It will matter. I have been in Afghanistan, where the *Roosees* have rained poison gas on the *moujahadin*. And there is no oil in Afghanistan for the *Roosees* to covet. The land of the *moujahadin* is utterly desolate," the Scorpion replied slyly, his heart beating.

Now they could be turned with the slightest touch, he knew, the way fingertip pressure on a wheel can turn a great ship. In some secret part of him he was shamed at using them. For whose benefit? he wondered. Theirs? The Americans? or his own?

He felt like a hypocrite playing them by Company protocol. "You don't have to teach 'em to hate. They already know that. You just have to aim it in the right direction. Xenophobia— it works every time," Koenig used to say. And now the darkness was coming again, the Scorpion thought. He could sense its relentless approach, like the dark wall of clouds which heralded the monsoon back in Vietnam. Abdul Sa'ad would bring the darkness with no one to stop him, except for his own desperate plan predicated on two pretty shaky legs: the single-shot theory and Bandar's vanity in his marksmanship. And if the eunuch had lied about how they planned to assassinate King Salim, the darkness would swallow them all.

Because Arabia was the flashpoint between America and Russia, he thought. Oil was to the great powers what water was to the Bedu. If Abdul Sa'ad succeeded, there might be another world war. The last. "Assuming you could do it and you knew what was going to happen, would you have assassinated Hitler in 1939?" was the question his philosophy class had debated in college. Back then, he had argued that survival outweighed ethics. The majority of the class had disagreed, he remembered.

"So now we are to prepare for battle on the mere word of a foreigner," Muhammed drawled insultingly.

At this Youssef started up, his *khanjar* already half out of its sheath at this insult to his brother.

"You dare!" Youssef hissed, his eyes like coals in the light from the fire.

The Scorpion put a hand on Youssef's shoulder to restrain him. After a tense second, Youssef squatted back down, his hand still on his *khanjar*.

"It is said, 'Beware of the smile of the infidel,'" snarled Muhammed. He glared defiantly across the glowing embers at the Scorpion.

"It is also said, 'The enemy of my enemy is my friend,'" the Scorpion replied.

"That is so," Sheikh Zaid said.

Muhammed started to reply, but changed his mind as Faisal, trying to ease the tension, clapped his hands twice sharply to call for more coffee. As another thimble cup was again passed around, Faisal moved around the fire to sit next to the Scorpion. Faisal squatted and put his hand on the Scorpion's shoulder, making sure that all saw him do so. A faint wind stirred whispers of sand on the dunes.

"Why have you come back to us now, truly?" Faisal asked.

To find something I lost, the Scorpion thought. He looked into Faisal's eyes, opalescent in the flickering light, and groped for the words.

"There are no accidents in this world," the Scorpion said, holding out his hand as if to catch a falling star. "My coming is no accident, either. Arabia stands poised between greatness and slavery like a spinning globe balanced on the tip of a juggler's finger. My *kismet* has brought me back now, at this dark hour, to do the thing that I was born to do."

"Like Antar of ancient days," Faisal mocked gently, as if to remind the Scorpion of his youthful hero worship.

"Yes, like Antar," Youssef said boyishly. "Why not?"

The Scorpion smiled sadly, remembering his childhood enthusiasm. He wondered if the boy he had been would recognize anything of himself in the icy agent he had become. He doubted it. "No, not like Antar. Like the Scorpion, the oldest of land animals because it has learned best how to survive," he said, looking around the fire at their faces.

"What is it you need of us?" Sheikh Zaid asked.

"A fast *mugathir*, your best, to ride in the King's Camel Race. Allow the Americans to air-drop a radio, a technician to man the radio, and weapons. None need join me. I seek no help from anyone and no harm to the tribe. And let there be no blood feuds to arise out of what I do," the Scorpion replied, ticking the items off on his fingers.

"And we are to do all this, for the Saudi family?" Muhammed sneered and looked pointedly away.

"We risk more by doing nothing. If all we do is sit and talk like women, there will soon be civil war. And in the days after that there will be *Roosees* in the Hasa Desert. Allah has given us this foreknowledge even as he gave us the oil, for his own reasons, not ours. I have come to act, not talk," the Scorpion said.

"So now you are Allah's agent. This borders on blasphemy!" Muhammed growled, holding his hands up to heaven in exasperation.

"All men are Allah's agents, whether they know it or not," the Scorpion retorted.

"Truly," Sheikh Zaid said, clapping his hands on his knees in approval. There were murmurs of *"ya Allah"* from some of the others.

"So—we are to do this thing for the Saudis," Youssef declared, rubbing his hands together like a merchant about to close a lucrative sale.

The Scorpion shook his head. "Neither for the Saudis, nor the Americans, whatever they think. We do this for the Mutayr. The Hasa, its oil and water, belongs to us," the Scorpion said. He stood in a fluid motion and drew his *khanjar* from its sheath. The steel blade reflected the red firelight like a tiny sun.

"I will kill anyone who tries to take it from us," he declared.

A deep-throated cry went up from the assembled tribesmen. Many raised their camel whips and flailed the air. Rifles were fired skyward as everyone rose and shouted. The ululating cries of the women, the trilling to frighten off the *zars* of the night, echoed in the darkness. "Allah!" the men chanted. "God is great!"

As the shouting subsided, Muhammed stood and faced the Scorpion. The corners of his mouth were drawn down as if he had tasted something sour. "To involve ourselves in such intrigues is dangerous—not to mention bad for business. If it is the will of the tribe, I shall not interfere; but neither shall I support such adventurism," he declared. He turned his back on the others and strode away towards his lavish RV van.

"Beware—such a one may betray you," Faisal whispered in the Scorpion's ear.

"It doesn't matter. The enemy already knows of my presence, but I still have a trick or two up my sleeve," the Scorpion whispered back, his lips scarcely moving. His eyes were flames in the fire glow.

Everyone was silent, waiting for the old sheikh to speak. Zaid motioned to Faisal who came over and helped the old man to his feet. How frail he had become, the Scorpion thought sadly. His hands were crooked and brittle as winter twigs. When he was a boy, those same strong hands had lifted him so easily into a saddle.

"Muhammed is entitled to his view. As for myself, I plan to be at the King's Camel Race, as always. Something tells me that it's going to be particularly exciting this year," Sheikh Zaid declared.

As the Scorpion rose, Youssef plucked at his sleeve.

"Come, I have something to show you."

Youssef led him to a cluster of pick-up trucks by the edge of the camp. The trucks were parked in a circle, serving as a makeshift corral. Now he could see the hobbled camels clearly in the pearl-gray light of the stars. As always, they began to roar and snarl whenever men approached.

"What do think of her?" Youssef asked proudly, gesturing at an unusually large honey-colored she-camel, her nostrils flaring as they came up to her.

The Scorpion ran his hands along her flanks and pinched her thighs, taking care not to stand at an angle where she could kick him. She turned her great head towards him and hearing her snarl and gurgle, he just managed to dance aside to avoid being sprayed by slimy green cud.

"May the raiders get you," the Scorpion snapped good-humoredly. He grabbed her head-rope and kicked her sharply in the stomach to gain control of her.

"Good! You must master her spirit right from the start," Youssef said, his eyes sparkling with delight.

"Is she as fast as she looks?"

"Faster."

"How is she called?"

"Basbusa," Youssef grinned.

"But not so sweet, I think," the Scorpion retorted. It was the name of a syrupy-sweet dessert tart.

"Do you still remember how to ride?" Youssef teased, gesturing at a jumble of double-poled saddles off to the side.

"Well enough," the Scorpion smiled. "After all, I don't have to win. I only have to be at the right place at the right time."

"If you don't fall off as you used to," Youssef laughed. The Scorpion could feel Youssef dying to race and felt the challenge rise up inside himself too.

"A race?" he suggested.

"To Wadi Hunnay," Youssef agreed, springing at the pile of saddles. Grabbing one, he ran over to Jiddha, his favorite riding camel, to prepare her for riding.

The Scorpion yanked sharply down on Basbusa's headrope, calling a guttural *"Gehrrr, gehrr"* from deep in his throat. The she-camel dropped to her knees, then swayed backwards. She folded her hind legs beneath her till her hocks were resting comfortably on the cool sand. Then she slid her front knees forward till her chest touched the ground.

Immediately, the Scorpion threw a riding pad over her hump, then fitted the wooden saddle on the pad and began tightening the cinches across her withers and girth. As soon as she was saddled, he pulled her head down, put a foot on her neck and felt himself sailing upwards as she raised her head. He swung himself into the saddle and yanked her head sharply upwards to make her rise. She lifted her hindquarters first, tilting him precariously forward, then with a sudden jerk, she was up.

The Scorpion looked around. Youssef was already well away. His dark form receded in the pale light, the whisper of the galloping camel's strides fading into the sand. The Scorpion called "Hat-at-at" and touching Basbusa's neck with the whip, kicked her into a slow run.

Her stride was very long and at first jerky, as if she were bucking underneath him. He let her get used to his weight, swaying easily to her sudden movement. Then, balancing on the balls of his feet like a gymnast, he struck her smartly with the whip and crooned from deep in his throat, spurring her into a full gallop.

Now she stepped out, lengthening her giant strides and stretching her long neck forward as they chased after Youssef. The dark sands sped by underfoot. The wind pressed against him, sending his headcloth and *bisht* streaming behind him like banners. The only sounds were the camel's breathing and the soft padding of its steps on the firm sand. The desert was flat as a table and stars filled the sky above the horizon, giving him the feeling of racing among the stars.

Ahead was Youssef, rocking eagerly with every stride, his robes and tassels flying, his camel galloping in a high-stepped ground-eating stride, at once clumsy and yet oddly graceful. Youssef glanced back over his shoulder and seeing the Scorpion gaining, he waved gaily, then spurred on his camel with the whip.

Basbusa had a tendency to veer left, the Scorpion noticed. He shortened the right rein to compensate. Also she had a tendency to prance her hindquarters a bit and he made a note to check her udders when he dismounted. He whispered endearment to her and like the finest-bred *mugathirs* she responded even better than to the whip, stretching out her neck and lengthening her stride by extra precious centimeters.

Youssef was only thirty meters ahead. Both riders flew across the pearly sands. The ground was firm and flat and it felt as if they could race like this forever. Far ahead the Scorpion could see faint wavy undulations in the sand, the first intimations of the distant boundaries of the wadi. Youssef's arm was like a piston, flailing his camel with his whip as Basbusa drew closer. Now Youssef was only twenty meters ahead.

Softly cursing Basbusa with mange and a thousand other plagues as though they were endearments, the Scorpion decided to risk it all. With his last curse, he let go of the reins and balancing like a dancer, let her run free, guided only by the pressure of his feet.

She drew up to the other camel's flanks. Now they galloped for what seemed like eons, matching each other stride for stride. Yet because of the extraordinary length of her stride, Basbusa began to inch up until the two camels were even. White slime caked the two camels' mouths and Jiddha began to show signs of fatigue, almost breaking stride as Basbusa surged ahead.

As the Scorpion approached the scrub which marked the beginning of the wadi exhilaration surged through him like electricity. He could feel his skin tingling. It was one of those magic moments which shine like shooting stars across the drab years and as he began to rein in the camel, he felt so overwhelmed for love of this harsh unforgiving land that he wondered why he had ever left.

As Basbusa slowed to a stately walk Youssef came bouncing alongside, grinning from ear to ear.

"Not bad for an old man, *ya*," he said.

"Old and out of shape," the Scorpion replied, catching his breath.

"I meant myself."

"So did I," the Scorpion grinned.

They turned the she-camels around and began to walk them back, letting them cool off. A faint mist of cooling perspiration rose from the camels' hides. For a time, nothing was said.

"Why did you leave us? I never understood that," Youssef asked at last, not looking at the Scorpion in order not to embarrass him.

"I didn't fit any more. Oh, I could look like a Bedu and do everything a Bedu can do. But I wasn't a Bedu."

"We loved you. When you left, my father never said a word of reproach, but I know he mourned as if he had lost a son."

"I know. That only made it worse. The more I cared, the worse I felt I was betraying you."

"Was it better in America?"

"Worse. It is almost the mirror image of Arabia. Here we always had either too little or too much money, so it never seemed to matter. We care about the price of something only when we buy it. There it is considered bad manners to ask someone what he paid for something, but they think of little else.

"And because money is the measure of all things, they define themselves by their work. An American never wants to know who you are, but only what you do for a living. They approach everything as if it were work, even pleasure."

"What of the women?"

"Ah, the women. They have learned how to complain. One wonders what would suffice for them," the Scorpion smiled.

"Why did you stay so long? I thought you would never return."

"They educated me. And then there was the war in Vietnam. That was an education too."

"Was it very bad, the war?"

The Scorpion shook his head. "Worse. It was stupid."

"How could this be? The *Americani* send us experts, miraculous technologies . . . I thought they were so clever."

"They can be very clever at being stupid," the Scorpion replied.

They rode on in silence, each of them lost in his own thoughts. Their dark forms were like shadows against the starry dome of night.

"This thing you do. It will bring much trouble, will it not?" Youssef asked finally.

"Of a certainty. And much trouble if I don't," the Scorpion replied.

"Truly. From the highest mountain to the deepest wadi, trouble is never hard to find."

The Scorpion knew Youssef was thinking of Bandar and Aisha. He nodded.

"This is more than revenge, or helping the *Americani*, my brother. It is a matter of survival."

"I hear you, little Scorpion. But if the lion becomes a jackal in order to survive, has he truly survived?"

Wadi Haradh

"THEY MAY TRY to ambush us in the wadi at Haradh," the Scorpion said, shading his eyes from the windshield glare as he drove west towards the sun. Youssef, hanging on for dear life as the four-wheel-drive pick-up truck bounced across the desert floor, handed him the sunglasses. A plume of yellow dust and sand kicked up by the tires obscured their rear view of Faisal and the others spread out behind them in a roughly organized convoy.

Although they couldn't have used the rear-view mirror in any case. The view was blocked by the majestic figure of Basbusa, kneeling in the truck-bed, facing rearward. Her head, neck and hump towered above the cab as she sat imperturbable and immobile, hobbled and tethered by a head-rope, girth and neck-ropes. There were camels riding in the back of each of the Toyota pick-up trucks behind them.

Ahead, the road stretched flat and endless. The sky was the bleached blue characteristic of the desert. The sun was relentless. Although it was late afternoon, the temperature was still above 120 degrees and the metal skin of the truck was too hot to touch. As always when driving in the desert, despite the absolute flatness of the road the Scorpion had the sensation of forever driving uphill towards a horizon so straight that were it reachable, it could have been used as a carpenter's level.

"What makes you so sure?" Youssef shouted above the roar of wind pouring into the cab through the open windows. His face was powdered white with dust. The air was so hot that the window was like an opening to a blast furnace.

"It's obvious. I've come at them three times now, in Bahrain, Qatar and Riyadh, so they know I'm around. From the condition of the eunuch's body, Abdul Sa'ad has to assume that I know his plans. And with Braithwaite still alive and potentially active, not to mention any other double agents the Russians might have, we have to assume they know who I am and that I'm going to try to interfere with the assassination. Therefore, the element of surprise is gone on both sides," the Scorpion replied, his eyes never ceasing to scan the way ahead in a full 180-degree arc.

"But what makes you so sure about an ambush, specifically at Haradh?"

"Because Abdul Sa'ad and the *Roosees* will want to get me out of the way before we arrive at the Race. An incident there might alert the king and abort the coup. They'll try to minimize the fuss as much as possible by coming at us in the desert. There's only one road from Hofuf to Riyadh, so it has to be along here somewhere."

"But why Haradh?"

"Because of who Abdul Sa'ad and the *Roosees* will have to use for the ambush. Abdul Sa'ad probably won't want to use his own men, or elements of the Royal Army for fear of betrayal or starting a tribal blood feud. As for the *Roosees* they couldn't possibly train and infiltrate KGB or GRU killers into an environment so alien to them, particularly when time is so short. Besides, a *Roosee* would have a hard time sneaking into Arabia and even if he did, he'd stand out like a polar bear in the desert."

"So?"

"So, they'll have to use outsiders who can go relatively unnoticed in this environment, such as Shiites, Yemenis or Palestinians. None of these are well-trained agents or soldiers. The Palestinians come the closest and the PLO has extensive connections to the KGB, so they're the most likely candidates. However, most of their training reflects terrorist and urban hit-and-run, as opposed to true military training, nor are they a desert people, so they'll want some kind of cover for an ambush, like hills or dunes. And the only hills between here and Riyadh—"

"Are at Wadi Haradh!" Youssef exclaimed.

"Just so," the Scorpion grinned.

"Allah be praised. This is most ingenious," Youssef said glancing sideways with approval at the Scorpion like a proud father at a son who has just won a prize.

The Scorpion shrugged. "It's just a skill acquired with practice. The whole art of the soldier is to put yourself in the enemy's place and try to think like him. All the rest is just logistics and training."

"Fascinating, my brother. War is most instructive."

"Oh yes," the Scorpion replied.

"So how will they attack us?"

"Assuming they don't have access to anything heavy, like a tank, or the training on *Americani* equipment, which is the only kind available inside Arabia, they'll probably try to stop us with light stuff they'll have smuggled in from Syria or South Yemen. They'll probably use an MA to make the ambush, then hit us with RPGs, LMGs and maybe a few AK-47s depending on how many of them are out there."

"Surely, you said something just now, my brother, but in the name of Allah, it had no meaning for me," Youssef said, rolling his eyes heavenward in exasperation.

"*Asfa*, my brother. When speaking of such matters, my thoughts slip into the language we used in Vietnam. To make the ambush, they'll have to stop the lead vehicle and then try to destroy the rear vehicle to block our way out in both directions. A moving target is always difficult, so they'll probably try to stop the lead truck with a so-called 'mechanical ambush." Given the Palestinians' experience in guerilla tactics I suspect they'll use either a pressure mine or a remotely detonated electronic mine. Then they'll try to destroy the trucks with rocket-propelled grenades (probably B-40s) or mortars while laying down light machine-gun and small-arms fire from Russian-made RPDs and Kalachnikov 7.62-mm assault rifles."

"Allah forbid! It sounds like a deadly trap," Youssef cried, his brown face turning pale under the layer of dust.

"It can be—in fighting there is always the unknown," the Scorpion said with a nod.

"What would you have done in Vietnam against such an awesome attack?"

"Stayed low and called in a Cobra helicopter. With its

rockets and mini-guns it would have shot the living excrement out of them."

"Mini-guns?"

"Electric 7.62-mm Gatling guns. They can fire a hundred rounds a second."

"Ya Allah," Youssef breathed. "But we don't have such a machine. What are we to do?"

"Oh, we'll just have to be creative," the Scorpion said, a boyish grin creasing his face in a way that made Youssef smile despite his apprehension.

"You say that as if there were little to fear," Youssef remarked. He tied the tail of his headcloth across his nose to help screen out the dust.

"In war there is always much to fear, my brother. But they think they will surprise us, so the surprise will be on them. In battle, this is very useful," the Scorpion said.

"I wish I knew more about war," Youssef said glumly.

"In the twentieth century that is an easy wish to fulfill," the Scorpion replied.

When they were about ten kilometers from Wadi Haradh, the Scorpion motioned the others to follow him as he pulled off the road. After the last truck had pulled up and all were assembled, he went over his plan. Then the weapons were passed around, for the Mutayr were never without weapons. Mostly M-16s, although some still preferred the M-1s and Enfields of older wars. There was no shortage as more arms had been air-dropped in with the American radio technician.

They were now a war party, cartridge belts across their chests. The Scorpion showed them the flare pistol and they spoke with few words, as was appropriate before a raid. Then they unloaded Bashusa from his truck to another.

"God be with you," Sheikh Zaid wheezed, shading his eyes as if from the sun, as Youssef and the Scorpion climbed back into the cab. But it was not the fierce sun that caused him to hold his hands over his eyes, the Scorpion knew.

"And with you," the Scorpion said.

As Youssef drove off in a cloud of yellow dust, the Scorpion broke out his XM-203; a double-barreled weapon with an M-16 rifle mounted above an M-79 grenade launcher.

Just holding it brought it all back for a moment. The dripping jungle, the red dust, the sounds of motor scooters and helicopters, the sharp scents of *nuoc mam* and cordite. Nam.

He shook his head to clear away the memory. At least Macready had been able to supply him, he thought. It was something a control was supposed to do, but still, it couldn't have been easy to coordinate the drop on an undefined desert location on such short notice, he admitted to himself. At least the old wreck was trying; God knows it was going to be murderous at best.

He couldn't shake a feeling of dread. There was something else. Something he couldn't put his finger on. The entry into Abdul Sa'ad's plot had been too straightforward. There was a nasty surprise waiting somewhere. But where?

Had there been anything in his phone conversation with Macready? He had called Doha from a solar-powered radio-phone in the desert. Since the oil boom, there were radio-phones in the remote areas. The conversation was guarded, cryptic. Macready had started by inserting the word "August" denoting the line might be bugged.

"Yes, it is hot, like last August, Mr. Ben Adam."

"Things are warming up all over," the Scorpion replied.

"I know. But you'll be happy to learn that our parent company has agreed to your terms. The full amount has been paid in advance," Macready said, his voice sounding nasal over the distance, as if he had a cold. Or else he was choking on the amount, the Scorpion thought.

Then the Scorpion told him what he wanted. Arms, communications all of it.

"That's impossible," Macready had sputtered.

"But you'll do it," the Scorpion had said and rung off.

At a word from the Scorpion, Youssef swerved off the dirt road and took to the sands, the wheels kicking up showers of sand like garden sprinklers. They would not return to the road until after they had traversed Wadi Haradh.

A sparse line of *rimth* scrub bushes too spindly to sustain even a camel marked the approach to Wadi Haradh. No doubt there was a trickle of ancient subterranean moisture deep beneath the sands. Youssef slowed the truck to a stop behind a rock outcropping. The Scorpion studied the terrain. Beyond this point they could be seen by anyone set up in the wadi.

The floor of the wadi was flat and sandy, its surface broken only by an occasional scrub bush. Probably mined, he thought. Low sandy hills lined either side and an uneven ridge ran along the hill on the left, near the crest. That would be a good place for them to hide, the Scorpion noted. On the right, the hill was rockier, steeper, the top flat. It was too visible for aircraft and it would require experienced troops to keep them in a cross fire and not wind up shooting at each other so they were probably dug in on the left side only. Still, maybe their commander was either very good or very stupid so he had to keep it as a possibility, he decided. In the center of the wadi, near the road, was a large *arfaj* bush near a sandy rise which might serve as concealment, if they were going to use an "L" ambush. The trucks would have to go alongside the right slope, if and when he found the mines.

He touched Youssef's arm. They looked at each other and said nothing. Their faces were shadow and flame in the light of the setting sun, balanced between the two sloping sides of the wadi like a giant red ball in a bowling alley. The Scorpion nodded and then he was gone, slipping noiselessly from the cab of the truck.

All was silence.

The Scorpion scuttled on all fours in sudden starts and

without noise, like a lizard. He remembered Sheikh Zaid's teaching of long ago that a true Bedu can hide in full view behind a rock that wouldn't conceal a *jird*. Like the tiny sand rat, he moved unseen, almost without disturbing a grain of sand. At each pause, his eyes and ears searched for the slightest hint of anything unnatural, his heart pounding desperately.

Something made him glance up. He rolled carefully onto his back. High above he could barely make out the distant silhouette of a falcon sailing effortlessly on a thermal. He scanned the shadows along the slopes searching for an outline or a glint of metal, but there was nothing but the deafening sound of his own pulse and the blink of sweat in his eyes.

This was what it was all about, he thought. All the years and schemes. All for these few minutes when you were tested to the uttermost and the penalty for error was death. He searched desperately for some indication of mines in the dusk light which was turning the sands first to honey and then to a channel of blood between the hills.

They had undoubtedly mined the road and probably a line of mines off the road as well. But there was nothing but millions of choppy little wavelets of sand.

Suppose he was wrong, he wondered suddenly. Suppose there was no ambush and he was just acting out of fear? How would the Mutayr look at him then? Would they still follow him? And then, if Abdul Sa'ad came at him in some other place, surprise would be total. What was it Koenig had taught them? "In combat, you don't get a second chance," Koenig used to say, his eyes narrowed as over a gun sight as he stared them down in the Quonset-hut classroom.

But still he saw nothing. Maybe it was all a mistake, he thought, feverishly wiping the sweat from his face on his sleeve. They had to be here, he thought, a queasy feeling in the pit of his stomach as he took out a curious object from his sleeve; a broken car radio antenna which he opened like a telescope.

He crept forward, flowing imperceptibly from one depression in the ground to the next, his fingers dancing along the surface of the sand like spider legs. He poked the car antenna gently into the sand, using it as a probe for mines.

And then he saw it. A single print of a combat boot perpendicular to the angle of his approach, heading towards the left slope. The Scorpion crouched even lower to the ground, almost certain he hadn't been spotted. In his black *bisht* he was no more than a shadow in the dusk, a time of shadows. Stealthily, inch by inch he probed the warm sands, sweat causing grains of sand to cling to his fingers. He froze, the sweat stinging his eyes. The antenna had hit something.

Carefully he dug a tiny depression until his fingers barely grazed what he had been seeking: a slender tripwire which connected a line of mines, designed to set them all off once it was tripped or any one of them blown. Now he worked quickly.

He drew a coil of wire, fine as spider thread, from his pocket and carefully looped it around the tripwire. He chewed a piece of gum and balled it around the juncture of the two wires, before reburying the wire in the sand. Then he retreated towards the left slope, silent as a desert *zar* and as unseen. As he moved he paid out the wire from the coil, maintaining the slack and at intervals burying it under clumps of sand. When he reached the left slope, he began the slow cautious ascent.

He heard them before he saw them. They were off to the right and above him somewhere. He saw the red glow of a cigarette tip and then someone hissed and the red glow was extinguished, but it had given him the chance to pinpoint them. They were along the ledge below the crest, as he had suspected. He would have to get above them, he thought, already moving up and to the left.

Climbing, he had to make sure of each handhold and step, so that there was no sound. There were several problems to be considered. How many of them were there? Was there an L and where was its blocking leg? Or were they on both slopes to set up a cross fire? His thoughts were interrupted by a dislodged pebble clattering down on to the rocks below. He froze, his pulse pounding in his ear like the sea.

"What's that?" a nearby voice said.

The Scorpion gave a hyena cough once, then again.

Silence.

"It's an animal," another voice said.

"Be still," snapped a third.

The Scorpion waited twenty minutes without moving a muscle, then carefully continued his painstaking ascent.

He might have blown it all at the crest had the sentry not chosen just that moment to relieve himself. The faint ammonia smell rose in the Scorpion's nostrils as the drops pattered a few inches from his face. Instantly the Scorpion dropped the wire coil and struck, heaving himself over the crest in a single fluid motion as he stabbed upwards under the rib cage, twisting the *khanjar* viciously while his left hand choked off the cry that never came. The urine mingled with blood as he let the lifeless body sink down into the sand.

He studied the body for a moment. The sentry had worn a black *bisht* for concealment, but it was an Arab all right. Not a *café-au-lait*-colored Yemeni; either a Palestinian or a Shiite. He couldn't be sure. He had been right about the arms, though. The sentry had carried an AK-47. For the moment the Scorpion left it lying on the ground. He wiped the blood from his hand and the *khanjar* on to the sentry's robe.

He slid closer to the edge. If anyone had heard him or happened to look up as he peered down, he would be trapped with no way down. Had there been a faint clink as he had eased the sentry's body to the ground? He couldn't remember. But he had no choice. He had to see their position.

The Scorpion rolled over to the wadi edge and peered down at the lengthening shadows which covered almost all of the wadi. The sun was almost below the horizon that blazed fire-red as if a war was going on beyond the edge of the earth. Then he spotted the enemy on the ridge below him and his heart sank.

There were at least thirty of them. Far too many for him to kill without catching it himself. Worse, it had grown too dark for him to spot whether they were set up by the *arfaj* down in the wadi. He studied the crest of the opposite hill carefully, scanning it inch by inch. If it was a two-sided ambush that was where they would be, he thought. And if it was a two-sided ambush his plan wouldn't work. Then what? he wondered. Don't think about that, he answered himself. Just deal with what is.

He studied the men below him. They were only twenty meters away. He could hear them clearly, stirring, breathing, the occasional whisper. Someone struck a match to light a cigarette, the flame suddenly bright as a flare and an officer's voice snapped hoarsely for the camel slime to put it out. That was something, at least, the Scorpion thought. They were ordinary soldiers, not professionals.

He saw nothing stirring on the far side. They couldn't be there, he decided. Troops as sloppy as these would have given away their position with some movement by now. The officer had decided to play it safe, relying on the line of mines, the block at the *arfaj* bush and his own entrenched troops, combined with the element of surprise to pull it off. He probably didn't anticipate a well-armed resistance from a few Bedu in trucks and didn't want his fairly green troops shooting at each other.

Allah be with us, because even so thirty is too many, the Scorpion prayed. But he would have to do it, because there was no way around the wadi, he decided, taking a deep breath.

Moving carefully so as not to make the slightest sound, he placed a rock near the edge. Then he propped the sentry's body against the rock with the AK-47 in a firing position, as a decoy. Next to the body, he placed a white phosphorus grenade with a two-minute delay fuse. With luck, they would be firing at the decoy after he had faded into the darkness.

He prepared four fragmentation grenades in position to be rolled down the slope and set up the wire coil still connected to the tripwire below. He anchored a coil of climbing rope to a rock and silently paid it out down the face of the cliff, away from the ledge where the Arabs crouched. Then he laid out the flare pistol and clicked off the safety of the XM-203. When everything was ready, he wiped the sweat from his eyes and took a last look around.

He zeroed the XM-203 on the distant *arfaj* and studied the opposite slope carefully, but he could see nothing. If he was wrong and it was a cross fire setup, then he was sending Youssef and Zaid and the Mutayr to their deaths. Below him he could hear the restless moving of the Arabs strung out along the ledge.

The sky was purple and black and the wadi was filled with shadows. It was the time of the *maghrib* prayer, the time of poorest visibility. As always, the instant before combat was like the instant before you jumped out of a plane. His mind returned to something Sergeant Walker had said during airborne training.

"The thing is—once you've jumped, you're committed. Parachuting down isn't bad, but the moment before you jump is just pure shit!"

The Scorpion took a grenade in each hand and pulled first one pin and then the other. Hoping for maximum confusion, he rolled one down towards the far right position and the other towards the far left. As the grenades pounced down the rocky slope like dislodged pebbles, he heard a voice from below. Then he yanked on the tripwire.

The wadi erupted as the mines detonated one after the other like a string of firecrackers. The Arabs started to pour fire blindly down at the orange flashes before the two grenades exploded among them. Screams of pain and confusion echoed from the ledge and the firing grew even wilder and less directed. An officer screamed orders and pointed towards the crest near the Scorpion, but his voice was ignored in the screams and noise of firing.

Just before ducking behind the crest the Scorpion had seen what he'd been looking for: flashes of muzzle fire coming from near the *arfaj*. And there were no shots from the far side, he thought, his pulse racing. It was an L ambush after all.

A chip of stone flew near his cheek. He'd been spotted!

He rolled on to his back and fired the flare pistol straight up into the sky. Then he scrambled to another position on the crest, shading his eyes to prevent momentary blindness as the flare exploded high above the wadi with a loud pop. Bright white light blazed as the flare floated down, turning the sand to light gray. The Scorpion froze, his eyes closed. Wrapped in his black *bisht* he looked like just another rock on the crest.

Something inside was screaming for him to move, but he forced himself to stay still until the flare went out. Blue-green tracers from several AK-47s began to float towards him like streams of fireflies homing in. They had sent a squad to the crest.

Just then he heard the sound of horns blaring as the Mutayr trucks, their headlights blazing, raced into the wadi near the far slope. But it was too soon, he thought, a horrible feeling in the pit of his stomach. He hadn't neutralized the *arfaj* ambush yet and he was pinned down by the squad at the crest, only thirty meters away judging by their muzzle flashes.

He felt a tug at his sleeve and had to force himself not to move as the bullets splattered on the rocks around him. *Ya Allah*, but that was close! Now the rounds were moving away from him. Shadows danced as the flare dropped below the level of the crest and down towards the floor of the wadi and still he waited, every nerve in his body screaming, as the convoy of Mutayr trucks raced through the heavy fire towards the deadly *arfaj*. He would have to do something no matter what the risk, he decided.

He was about to switch the XM-203 from the grenade to automatic fire position when his ears rang from a deafening explosion nearby. His trap by the body had gone off. White phosphorus smoke poured over the squad which had been moving towards him. He could hear their screams as the burning smoke touched their flesh. As they stumbled and fired in blind confusion, he zeroed again on the *arfaj*. He couldn't afford to miss, he thought, and fired the M-60 grenade. Before the recoil was over, he was reloading; he fired again.

Without waiting to see where the grenades landed, he rolled two more fragmentation grenades down the slope towards the Arabs firing from the ledge. Then he switched to automatic and began firing down along the line of the ledge.

As the Arabs on the ledge began to realize he hadn't been neutralized and started firing back at him, he ducked back behind the crest. In the distance he could see orange muzzle flashes from the *arfaj* aimed at the lead Mutayr truck. Jump! the Scorpion prayed for Youssef. Please jump, he prayed.

The two M-60 grenades exploded around the *arfaj* and he could hear faint screams, like insect chirping, then all was shadow, followed by the almost simultaneous blasts of the grenades down on the ledge.

"To the crest, upwards," screamed the Arab officer and the firing began to intensify around the Scorpion's position. He leaned over and fired another long burst down at the ledge. He saw two shadows crumple before he had to duck back again.

He was just about to make a run for the climbing rope when two Arabs appeared out of the smoke. They were almost on top of him. As they exclaimed in surprise and lowered their muzzles the Scorpion struck. He swung the XM-203 at the legs of the nearest Arab, knocking him off balance just as he fired. The bullets ricocheted on the rock inches from the Scorpion's head. There was no time to aim at the second.

The Scorpion sprang up at him and the two men tumbled and rolled on the ground, grappling blindly for a handhold. The Arab's hands found the Scorpion's throat and began choking him. The Scorpion jammed an elbow into the Arab's ribs, breaking at least one, but the Arab hung grimly on. Meanwhile, he could feel the other man trying to grab his feet, cursing between harsh breaths.

He was choking; his need for air desperate. As spots of light began to dance before the Scorpion's eyes, he managed to kick out, knocking the clutching Arab away for an instant. His fingers felt desperately for his *khanjar* sheath but it wasn't there! The other Arab started to aim at both squirming bodies and the Scorpion gave a desperate heave, rolling them over.

As they rolled, his hand touched the *khanjar*. In an instant he had it in his hand and struck savagely, slicing the Arab's belly open from the pubic area to the sternum. The man's grip relaxed instantly. His scream was terrible as his insides cascaded out in a slippery mass.

A blast sang almost at the Scorpion's ear, a bullet barely missing his head. He rolled on the ground and almost without taking aim, as he had during the long years of practice, he threw the *khanjar* at the second Arab. The flashing blade caught him in the chest and he went down like a log.

Suddenly out of the waning smoke on the crest came a line of shadowy figures firing at him. The remaining Arabs had come to the crest. That meant the Mutayr must have broken through, the Scorpion silently exulted. But what of Youssef?

The firing was coming closer now and he had no weapons left at hand. He rolled on the ground towards the climbing rope and as soon as he found it, grabbed hold and kicked himself over the ledge.

He could feel the skin burning off his palms as he rappelled down the face of the slope in an almost sitting position, left hand holding the rope above him, right hand under his hip. Bounce. He kicked away from the face. The clatter of bullets sounded around him and he could hear shouting above in the darkness. Bounce. The shouting became fainter and the shots wilder, further away. In his black *bisht* among the shadows, he must be almost impossible to see, he thought. Bounce and then he was at the end of the rope and still falling.

He curled himself into a ball, his hands over his head to protect it and tumbled down the incline among the sharp-edged rocks. He took what felt like a hundred blows. It was like being savagely beaten by a gang with clubs. And then he was lying face down, like a shipwrecked sailor on the still-warm sand.

It felt so good not to move. He just wanted to lay there, wherever he was. He somehow managed to roll on his back. The first stars of evening hung over his face, just out of reach like silver grapes above the starving Tantalus. Was it the blind *sufi* at Mazar-e Sharif who told him that tale, or had he heard it at college? he wondered drowsily.

Almost as an afterthought, he realized that he wasn't breathing. The wind had been knocked out of him. His body began to ache unmercifully in a hundred places. He tried to breathe and couldn't. He tried again and again, but still couldn't. Close to panic, he tried desperately, his fingers clawing at the sand and managed a slight breath mingled with a groan. The next breath came easier and soon he was breathing again. He was very tired; almost asleep. One by one, the stars began to come out, blinking on like window lights in a distant city.

Then he heard them, clattering slowly down the slope. What was he about, lolling on the sand as if he were at the beach? he thought, horrified. He had to get going.

He somehow managed to roll over and on to his hands and knees. Sweat poured off his face into the sand. The effort made him dizzy. He heard voices. They were much closer. He had to go on. There was nowhere left to hide.

He began to move on all fours in odd, jerky movements. Like a wounded crab, he scuttled silently into the shadows.

Riyadh

THE WORD OF GOD was heard all over the *souk*, the *muezzin*'s voice echoing from a thousand transistor radios like a tinny chorus of magpies. Cries of vendors and the tinkling bells of the water sellers could be heard amidst shouted wagers on the race and the ear-splitting howls of motorcycles churning up fountains of sand, as teenaged dirt-bikers weaved through the crowds. Bedu tribesmen leading silky saluki hunting dogs or holding their favorite falcons on leather gauntlets mingled with fashionable Arab city dwellers whose closest contact with the desert came from watching reruns of *Bonanza* on television. Thousands of canvas market stalls had sprouted overnight like mushrooms on the sands outside Riyadh where the race was to be held.

Close to half a million onlookers pressed against the barrier of rope strung between empty oil drums along the entire length of the twenty-two-kilometer course. Members of the Saudi National Guard, easily spotted by their red-checked headcloths and the gold crossed swords-and-palm-tree emblem on their headbands, were stationed at twenty-foot intervals to keep the crowd from spilling onto the course.

The greatest crowding was near the starting line, where bettors gathered to see the camels. Over five thousand camels, their riders and attendants were already assembled in the starting area. Another large mass of people had gathered around the royal reviewing stand near the finish line. From afar, it looked like the Costa Brava in summer, the families packed together like sardines under colorful umbrellas unfurled to protect against the relentless sun. Just beyond the TV cameras and vans, green silk pennants flew over the Saudi royal pavilion, densely guarded by Guardsmen carrying loaded M-16s. Veiled princesses, concubines and serving girls mingled freely inside the roped-off women's enclosure, visiting each other's tents.

Only the black-and-white striped tent of Prince Abdul Sa'ad, near the far corner of the royal enclosure, was unvisited. It sat closed and silent, like an abandoned house. A fat eunuch with a curving scimitar stood guard by the tent flap.

At the gate to the royal pavilion the jewelers had set up their stalls. The women were permitted to shop there under the watchful eyes of the Guardsmen, without having to officially leave the enclosure.

"You are robbing me blind! The angel Gabriel is my witness! From Muscat even to Damascus, all know of Abdul and the quality of his gems. But for a princess royal, who can deny anything?" loudly proclaimed a one-eyed jeweler, slapping his hand to his chest as a gesture of sincerity.

He was a short fat man, lavishly dressed in a gold and silver silk robe. His face was round as the man in the moon and radiated good will. He grinned constantly, like a cartoon chipmunk, not unaware that his teeth were his best advertisement. Every one of his teeth was inlaid with gold. Diamonds, rubies and other precious gems twinkled in the sunlight from his gold caps. He wore a platinum patch encrusted with diamonds obver a scarred right eye and rolled his good eye at the sky, that Allah might vouch for the value of his wares.

"You're a rare scoundrel," a veiled elderly woman muttered, a glint of amusement in her dark eyes outlined with *kohl* to hide the wrinkles. "It's not worth twenty thousand, much less fifty."

"Behold the value, mistress and let Allah guide you. Offer what you think is just, no more," the little man said, holding a gold and diamond bracelet so that it caught the sunlight. "Behold!" he declared.

The diamonds were like sunlight, too bright to look at.

"I'll give you thirty thousand and good riddance," the woman snapped and gathered her robe as if to leave.

"Done!" the jeweler cried boisterously and with a flourish, he handed over the bracelet.

The woman pulled an Hermes purse from beneath her robe and took out a wad of thousand-*riyal* notes which needed two hands to hold. She whispered something to the jeweler, then counted out the notes with the speed of a bank teller. The jeweler made another bow and in a twinkling he had whisked the money into his sash and was suddenly gone in the direction of the canvas enclosure used for the men's public lavatory.

The urinal was a trough in the sand. The plump jeweler with the multicolored silk robe made an astonishing contrast to the grim image beside him. He stood next to a desert-lean Bedu with eyes the color of smoke. An ancient musket with an inlaid stock slung across the Bedu's back marked him as one of the riders in the race. The Bedu wore the black robe and face veil of a Saar tribesman.

"Then it's true," the Scorpion whispered to the little jeweler from behind his black face veil.

"The American female is of a certainty in the far fent of Prince Abdul Sa'ad. There are many whisperings among the families. The prince's royal wife is installed at the tent of her sister-in-law, Princess Fatima, second wife of Prince Sultan. They say that she would return to the house of her father, but that Abdul Sa'ad won't let her. Of the other concubines, she cares nothing. But the American female is not unknown and it is becoming a scandal," Abdul replied.

"And what of Prince Abdul Sa'ad?"

"Who can speak of Abdul Sa'ad?" the jeweler said, flipping up his bejeweled eyepatch and looking anxiously over his shoulder to be sure they weren't overheard.

"Abdul Sa'ad is always surrounded by armed guards, especially the evil-eyed one. He of the Mutayr," Abdul said.

"Bandar," breathed the Scorpion.

"He rides today on Bashum, last year's champion. Yes, it is an odd name, isn't it?"

"Truly," the Scorpion replied.

It was odd. It was as if Abdul Sa'ad couldn't resist announcing his intentions by calling his camel by the word that means "sinister," he mused.

"There are many who hesitate to contest against him for fear of what he might do," Abdul added.

"And Abdul Sa'ad?" the Scorpion asked.

"He is with his brother, the king, at the royal tent. There are many whispers. But no one speaks out loud against Abdul Sa'ad. Some say he has become a religious mystic, a *sufi* master, even."

"And Salim?"

"The king, may Allah guard him, loves and trusts his brother. He will listen to nothing against him."

"But that the American female is in the far tent is certain? There can be no mistake on this," the Scorpion insisted.

"So the women say. Trust the wives to know where the she-wolf is. Besides, who posts an armed guard over an empty tent?" shrugged the little man.

"Anything else?"

"Only that you are watched even now," Abdul remarked, glancing towards the tent flap out of the corner of his eye.

"I know. They're all over me like fleas. And they're not bothering to hide, either. Something's come unstuck," the Scorpion said.

"Perhaps it has something to do with the bombing in Qatar last night," Abdul suggested. He looked anxiously around as a tall bearded Arab came up to the trough. He was dressed in western clothes and had the look of a modern Riyadhi.

"What bombing?"

"It's on the radio," Abdul said nervously and glanced significantly at the bearded Arab. He shook himself and turned to leave.

"I have to hurry. I'm thinking of betting ten thousand *riyals* on Bashum, ridden by Prince Abdul Sa'ad's man, Bandar. What do you think?" Abdul said loudly.

"Save your money. I doubt he'll go the distance," the Scorpion said, an odd gleam in his eye.

As he turned to leave, the bearded Riyadhi caught at his sleeve.

"A thousand pardons, *asayid* . . ." the Riyadhi began.

The Scorpion's reaction was instantaneous. He splayed the fingers of his hand and rotated his wrist clockwise, then continued in a circle, gripping the Riyadhi's hand between both hands and forcing him to his knees. The Scorpion winced as he twisted, his sides still aching from last night's fall in the desert fight.

"Who sent you? Macready?" the Scorpion hissed through clenched teeth, and applied pressure on the trapped hand. The Riyadhi groaned in pain.

"*Meester Harrees* . . ." the Riyadhi began in English.

"Where is he?"

"At the tent of the fortuneteller . . ." the Riyadhi began and then blinked in disbelief. The Scorpion was already gone.

The fortuneteller's tent was blue and decorated with gold and silver stars, a crescent moon and signs of the zodiac. A sign advertised visions of the future, promises of great wealth, happiness and cures for arthritis, backache and a variety of liver and stomach ailments. Circumcisions were also available. Another sign, hand-painted on the tent flap, indicated that the tent was closed for prayers and the duration of the race.

Inside, the Scorpion found Harris seated at a wooden folding table, playing a hand of solitaire. He smiled as the Scorpion entered and gestured as extravagantly as an Arab merchant for him to sit down.

"A thousand welcomes, O honored guest," Harris insolently grinned, leaning back. Who else but Harris would wear a silk ascot at his throat in the middle of Arabia? the Scorpion thought. Harris wore a beige tropical jacket over his shoulders as if he'd just finished playing a polo match. The empty sleeves hung like lifeless limbs as Harris dealt the cards.

"Cut the shit, Bob," the Scorpion snapped angrily.

"What's the matter?"

"Are you running an op or a Marx Brothers comedy? You've got amateurs tripping all over me. If you wanted to blow me, it would have been more inconspicuous to use a neon sign. I feel like I'm wearing a bull's eye on my chest," the Scorpion snapped.

"There wasn't time to set it up properly. You know how things can get at this stage," Harris said defensively. He placed a red ten on a black Jack with a little snap of the card to show his annoyance and pretended to concentrate on the game to show he wasn't worried, which meant, of course, that he was.

"If there's a screw-up, I'm surprised you aren't already blaming Macready; everybody's favorite whipping boy," the Scorpion remarked impudently.

"Macready's dead. Car bomb in Doha. Surprised you hadn't heard about it on the radio," Harris said complacently.

So that's what Abdul the jeweler had meant, the Scorpion thought. He remembered the last time he had seen Macready, in the alley behind Hamid's. "Why'd you wait so long?" Macready had asked, still trying to get it right as if it was Saigon again, while insects smashed against the streetlight.

"Is that all you have to say?" the Scorpion asked.

"What did you expect? Taps at Arlington? Macready is history," Harris shrugged.

"What was he up to when he got hit?" the Scorpion asked, a metallic taste in his mouth that might have been regret—or fear.

"Who the hell knows? The incompetent son of a bitch didn't leave any messages behind," Harris snapped irritably and turned up three cards.

He needed a black six and the six of clubs came up as the second card. He surreptitiously switched it with the third card and placed it triumphantly on a seven of hearts, glancing at the Scorpion to see if he had noticed.

"It shouldn't have happened," the Scorpion mused, almost to himself.

"Of course, it shouldn't have happened, We never should have used him in the first place. Of all times to get stuck with a fucked-up has-been," Harris fumed, throwing down the cards in disgust.

"No, I mean there was no reason for it. I was the target. The action had shifted away from Qatar, unless . . ."

"Unless what?" Harris snapped. He reached into his jacket and took out a tiny battery-powered fan. He turned it on and aimed it point blank at his own sweat-slick face. "Christ, doesn't it ever cool off here?" he muttered irritably.

"This *is* the cool time here," the Scorpion remarked. "Wait till late afternoon, then it warms up."

Harris snapped off the fan for a second and looked at him as if the Scorpion was a waiter who had served him soup with a fly in it. "Macready was a pathetic shit and I'm here to see that things go right for a change. I don't give a damn about how hot it gets and I don't need any smart-ass bullshit and most of all I want my questions answered. Now—did Macready get careless or was he terminated before he could get a message to us?" Harris rasped.

"Yes," the Scorpion replied.

"Yes, he got careless, or yes, he was terminated?"

"Yes, it's true what they say about you," the Scorpion shrugged.

"What's that?" Harris hissed, his eyes as bright and murderous as a reptile's.

"Macready wasn't careless. He was famous for his paranoia," the Scorpion said, ignoring Harris' question, knowing it would eat away at Harris later on. The way things were shaping up, that might be the only satisfaction he was going to get out of this assignment.

It felt all wrong, but he didn't know where the problem was. Everything was too straightforward, too convenient. The girl, the assassination attempt and his enemy, Bandar, all here in one place. And the eunuch dead and the ambushes a failure, so Abdul Sa'ad knew he was here and that he knew about the

233

coup, yet did nothing, leaving Bandar and the girl in the open for him to get at them. The path to the target was straight ahead, the gate left open and inviting. It was all there, but where was the mistake? What was it Macready had learned that made it essential to eliminate him, the Scorpion wondered.

"Forget Macready. The whole ball game depends on you being able to stop the hit," Harris snapped.

"Where was Macready hit? How'd it happen?" the Scorpion insisted. There was a key there somewhere. There had to be. He owed Macready that much, remembering George and his Vietnamese girl inviting him over for lemon chicken dinner at their little apartment around the corner from the Caravelle. All of them high on 33-beer and Buddha grass and singing "FTA." Fuck the Army, celebrating because George had managed to postpone getting DEROS'd back to the States so he could stay with—what was her name, anyway?—and in the distance they could hear the soft thumping of Delta Tango rounds fired into the bush, but so far away it could have been the beat of a rock band.

"What difference does it make? Listen—" Harris said, waving his hand as if to brush away a fly.

Suddenly, the Scorpion grabbed Harris by his ascot and lifted him off the ground. "It makes a difference to me. Where was George when the bomb went off, goddamit?" he demanded.

"In his—car—the Corniche—it exploded—a grenade tossed in the window—motorcycle—no ID," Harris managed to gasp.

"Which way was the car headed? North or south?"

"I don't know! South! . . . Jesus," Harris shouted.

The Scorpion shoved Harris back into the chair. Harris winced and rubbed his neck reproachfully. But the Scorpion ignored him, for a moment staring blankly at the tent wall.

"Jeez, if I'd known it was that important . . ." Harris began.

"South . . . back towards the airport. But he had just come

from the airport. He'd just returned from Riyadh. And he left no message, right?" the Scorpion asked, looking at Harris.

Harris nodded slowly. Comprehension dawned in his eyes. The Scorpion was obviously onto something.

"That meant he wasn't about to take a flight out, or he would have signaled. He had to—he was my case officer. He wouldn't have just gone off. Not with the whole damn Indian Ocean fleet, the RDF and the Marines waiting somewhere offshore.

"And it wasn't to send a signal either. He'd have gone either to the embassy or the safe house for that, even if security had been breached," the Scorpion said.

"So why did he leave his post?" Harris asked.

"Because he saw something—or someone," the Scorpion said, his eyes wide as saucers. "Someone on his way to the airport," he breathed.

"Who could it be?" Harris asked, mopping his face with the ascot and rearranging the table, which had been knocked over during their struggle.

"That's the sixty-four-thousand-dollar question, isn't it?"

Harris looked suspiciously at him. "You wouldn't be holding out on me, would you? Not telling me for your own reasons?"

"Of course not. Any more than you'd keep something from me," the Scorpion replied.

The two men smiled at each other.

The Scorpion carefully lowered himself into the chair like someone entering a steaming hot bath. Harris took in his bloodshot eyes and unshaven cheeks.

"You look like you've been through the mill. Are you going to be able to pull it off?" Harris said sympathetically.

"Do I get a choice?"

"Not at these prices."

They shared a quiet chuckle.

"The president asked me to convey his personal regards

and confidence in you. We're all counting on you," Harris said, his voice resonating with manly sincerity.

"Save the half-time speeches, Bob. The only thing the president's counting on is for me to save his political neck. And that's not Number One on my list of Things to Do Today."

"What about the girl?" Harris prompted.

"Which comes first, stopping the coup or the girl?"

"You know the answer to that as well as I do," Harris snapped peevishly and moved the little fan back and forth across his face like a windshield wiper.

He stared at the tiny whirring blades in fascination. A dreamy look came over his face. "You know, it's like living a little piece of history. Like being in Sarajevo in 1914, or Berlin in 1939. There's an appalling amount of misery in store for humanity if you miss," he said in a philosophical tone, as if he were about to brush a blackboard with tweed-covered elbows.

"Thanks Bob. That's just what I needed right now. More pressure," the Scorpion remarked wryly.

Harris leaned forward with a worried look. If Harris let that much worry show through, then the Scorpion knew he himself probably had the life expectancy of a rare butterfly at a convention of lepidopterists.

"Don't miss," Harris said earnestly.

"How bad is it? Can you tell me?" the Scorpion asked, glancing around the tent as if to search out any bugs.

Harris leaned forward to whisper. "We have independent confirmation from both the Israeli Mossad and the Egyptian Moukhabarat of a PLO strike at Sea Island, which would shut off the oil. The Russian fleet is stationed off the Straits of Hormuz and there have been a number of bow-scraping incidents between them and our Indian Ocean fleet. The RDF and the 82nd Airborne have been committed and are en route to Masira Island. The Russians have the Caucasus Red Army Group poised at Yerevan. And the Cuban military advisors and Palestinians have suddenly disappeared from the streets of Aden. Just how bad do you want it? I'll tell you, friend, anyone who bought oil futures is going to make a killing," Harris said, then bit his lip as if he had said too much.

"We're not friends, Bob. We just share the same lifeboat," the Scorpion said quietly.

Harris' face flushed. He looked at the Scorpion as if that was a remark he was storing away for repayment. Then he smiled bravely, like a heroine in a soap opera. He still needed the Scorpion. "How are you going to get away when all the action starts?" Harris asked.

"Why Bob, I didn't know you cared?"

"I don't. This is business. The embassy can't be involved in any way," Harris said, gathering up the cards.

"Good. For a second I thought I was going to have to listen to some of your less credible inventions."

"Well," Harris said, looking at his watch as if he had somewhere to go. Then he smiled to show how patient he was.

"I'll try to fade in with the Mutayr in the desert. I'll contact you," the Scorpion said.

"Anything else?" Harris asked, rising briskly to his feet.

"Yeah. It feels wrong. It's too straightforward. There's a nasty surprise waiting somewhere, but I don't know what," the Scorpion admitted.

"It's just your devious mind. Abdul Sa'ad's nastier than he is clever. All you have to do is make sure you hit the right target," Harris said, aiming his index finger like a gun at the Scorpion.

The Scorpion stood up and pulled his veil back across his face. "The next time you point something at someone, Bob, I suggest you make it more threatening than a finger," he remarked. The two men faced each other, hatred naked in their eyes.

"If you miss the assassin, don't bother to come home, Scorpion," Harris said hoarsely.

"There's no going home for any of us, Bob. Haven't you learned that yet?" the Scorpion replied and headed for the tent flap.

"Forget about Macready. It can't be that important," Harris called after him.

The Scorpion stepped outside and blinked in the bright sunlight. So now it was all up to him, he thought.

A single shot with an ancient musket, which was all that the security-conscious Royal Guardsmen allowed any contestant to carry. And he had the CM rocket pistol taped to the small of his back for the rescue attempt for Kelly. One on one. Kill or be killed. Things reduced for a single moment to utter simplicity.

Except he couldn't forget about Macready and how fishy it all smelled. Because it was obvious who Macready must have seen, that caused timid George to make a U-turn and start barreling down the Corniche towards the airport. The one member of the opposition George could have personally recognized. And all because he, the Scorpion, had made a fundamental mistake.

Braithwaite was back in the game.

The Race

THE AIR SHIMMERED in the heat, so that the thousands of camels gathered near the starting line looked as if they were wading in water to their knees. The noise of the rumbling camels, the riders and attendants shouting instructions, and the screaming crowds made ordinary conversation impossible. Youssef, tightening the last cinch on Basbusa, had to shout to be heard by the Scorpion standing beside him.

"Can you see him?" Youssef shouted.

The Scorpion shook his head. Together they walked around the camel, checking each tie and rope for tightness. With the Scorpion holding the camel's head still, Youssef unslung a water skin and poured water into her nostrils to calm and refresh her. The Scorpion had to yank hard on the head-rope to control her. The smell of so many camels excited her.

An announcement came over the loudspeakers telling the riders to mount. The babble of voices rose in anticipation. The camels grumbled and roared as riders began to mount. One camel nearby rose up and began bucking wildly, tore away from its handlers and began running desperately out on to the course. Riderless, she raced across the level plain to the raucous cheers of the onlookers.

Youssef plucked at the Scorpion's sleeve and looked towards the stands. The Scorpion followed Youssef's glance, searching among the riders. He understood without words that Youssef had been signaled by his brother Faisal, who had been stationed with binoculars on top of a Toyota truck cab, parked behind the crowd.

At first the Scorpion missed him, then a tingle of electricity coursed through his body as he recognized Bandar, wearing the red-checked *kaffiyeh* and uniform of a Royal Army captain. Bandar swung himself into the saddle atop a magnificent brown camel, which the Scorpion assumed was the famous Bashum. Even after all these years, the Scorpion recognized him instantly. In memory, the features and gestures had blurred. But seeing his enemy in the flesh, there was no mistaking him.

Like the Scorpion, Bandar also wore an ancient musket slung across his back. Except that the Scorpion was willing to bet that the guts of the musket weren't ancient at all, and that like the Scorpion's musket, it was loaded and ready to fire.

Ever since the eunuch had confirmed that Bandar would be the assassin, the Scorpion had operated on the hunch that it would happen just that way. A planted bomb under the royal reviewing stand would have been found beforehand by one of the king's own security people. A car bomb was too uncertain. Besides, the Royal Guardsmen were all Bedu, excellent shots and likely to be able to shoot a driver before he came close enough. And even if he did and the bomb exploded, it was too messy. It might miss King Salim and it might get Prince Abdul Sa'ad.

The possibility of a number of Saudi soldiers suddenly turning their automatic weapons on the king had to be dismissed, not because it was impossible, but because in the Byzantine atmosphere of the royal court, with intrigue and counterplot as a daily occurrence, there was little likelihood of Abdul Sa'ad training a group of soldiers to kill the king, not one of whom would betray the plot.

That left the single assassin with a high-powered rifle approach. The classic method and most difficult to stop. Again, the approach and the getaway were the key problems. The added factor was Bandar himself. Both his skill as a marksman, and his vanity in that skill, had to be taken into account. And so, the assassination method had suggested itself to the Scorpion with breathtaking simplicity.

As Bandar raced past the royal reviewing stand at the finish line, he would unsling his presumably decorative—but actually deadly—musket and fire at the king before any of the guards could react. The getaway would be equally simple. Bandar would just sweep past on his camel and continue racing to a getaway vehicle, army helicopter, or whatever Abdul Sa'ad had arranged, before anyone could mount a pursuit.

The Scorpion's own plan to stop the assassination was equally simple. He had to wait till the attempt was already under way, so that it would be too late to put some alternative backup plan into effect. He would have to shoot Bandar at precisely the right instant. Too late and the king would be dead. Too soon and he himself would surely be shot down by the king's security forces mistaking him for an assassin and Abdul Sa'ad might yet go to a back-up method. So he would have to shoot Bandar just before Bandar himself was to fire.

The only difficulty he faced was the same one Bandar faced, the trickiness of an accurate shot while riding a camel at full gallop.

Youssef slipped under the camel's belly and stood next to the Scorpion.

"*Ya*, beloved; beware the Ruallai with the thin moustache. Muhammed of Heikul was seen speaking to him," Youssef whispered, indicating a rider with the kind of pencil-thin moustache popular in 1930s high comedies and wearing the black-and-white robe of a Rualla noble.

The Scorpion nodded. "Be sure that our father Zaid and the others leave as soon as the race starts. There may be much shooting and many may die," he said.

"Of a certainty. We will all meet at the encampment south of Hofuf, *Inshallah*," Youssef replied. He kept patting the camel's side. His hands were like birds, never still. His eyes were soft and he avoided looking at the Scorpion.

"What is it?" the Scorpion asked softly.

"Last night . . . driving the Toyooti in the wadi . . ." Youssef began, hesitating. "It was . . . I was . . ."

"I know. It is the same for all," the Scorpion said and swung himself up into the saddle. He felt constricted by the special mesh fabric wrapped tightly around his chest and he wondered for the hundredth time whether it was worth it. All around, riders were moving towards the starting line. With a tap of the whip and crooning "Grrr" from deep in his throat, he made Basbusa rise in slow jerky stages, like a mechanical creature.

"Go with God," cried Youssef and turned to leave.

"And upon thee, the blessings of God," the Scorpion murmured, almost to himself.

Basbusa began pulling to the left and the Scorpion shortened the rein, wheeling her in a circle and then stopping her. He pulled her head close and whispered curses like endearments into her ear, breathing the sharp camel smell of her. The air was white with dust as thousands of camels began to rise and gather in clusters near the starting line. There was no order, no course boundaries and, once the race started, no rules. There was only an approximation of a starting line. The finish line was the line of sight from King Salim some fourteen miles away.

As he reined Basbusa in close to the hindquarters of several other camels already crowding the starting area the Scorpion turned to glance over at Bandar. The camels around them skipped skittishly, growled and tried to bite each other. Just then Bandar looked towards him and their eyes met. It was as if a bolt of lightning crackled between them. They knew each other utterly in that instant and that only one of them would survive the race.

The Scorpion could see a curse come to Bandar's lips. He smiled coldly in response, but his stomach felt like a volcano about to erupt. Bandar sneered, then turned and kicked Bashum into a lead starting position. Out of the corner of his eye, the Scorpion noticed the moustached Ruallai edge into position behind him. His back prickled, his spine tensed so tightly for an inevitable bullet that he had to force himself to relax.

What other surprises did Abdul Sa'ad have in store for him besides the Ruallai, he wondered.

The Scorpion fastened on a face veil and was not surprised to see Bandar, like most of the riders, follow suit.

The air was misty with fine white dust kicked up by thousands of camels. Pressing forward on every side were contestants from almost every tribe on the peninsula: the white-and-black-clad Rualla from Wadi Sirhan, the dark-garbed Anayzah from the great Nafud desert, from the Najd, the Harb and the Shammar, and the Rashidis, ancient enemies of the House of Saud, and the dog-eyed Hutaym who look no man in the eye, the Huwaytat who roam the Red Sea coast near Aqaba and bow to no man, the Utaybah out of the mountains of the Jabal Tuwaiq, who measure their words as if they were pieces of gold, and from the Hejaz, the Bali, Juhaynah and the tribes of the holy places, the Al Jahadilah and the Quraysh, tribe of the Prophet himself, who wear the green silk of the Sharif, the soft men of the Ghamid and the Rijal al ma Munjaha, from the green hills of Asir, and the hard tribesmen of the Empty Quarter, the Qahtan, Yam, al Rashid, the Al Murrah, they of the great soft-footed camels who can cross the endless sands of the Rub al Khali, and from the Hasa and the Gulf, where the oil comes from, the Mutayr, the Awazim, the Bani Khalid and the Bani Hajir, and those of the lesser tribes. It was a vast panoply of riders out of a distant age and at the sight of them the women, veiled and kept to the back, began to trill the eerie cries to frighten off the evil *zars* of the desert and a guard unfurled the pennant of Saud bearing a sword and the words of the *shahadah*, "There is no God but God and Muhammed is his prophet." It was a sight to stir the heart, one few westerners had ever seen, the Scorpion thought, and he felt his own pulse quicken.

At the sounding of the starting gun, thousands of camels surged forward over the yellow plains kicking up sprays of sand as they galloped on. A roar exploded from half a million throats as the riders swept forward in a vast wave, as if a great tribal raid or *jihad* had been launched.

With a cry of *hatatatat* and a slash of the whip, the Scorpion urged the camel forward. Basbusa gathered herself together, then seemed to leap into a furious gallop. Basbusa's stride was very jerky and the Scorpion had to hang on desperately, leaning far forward over her outstretched neck to guide her into a smoother pace. Excited riders around him jostled against her flanks, then pulled away as space began to open up between the camels. Basbusa tried to veer left, but the Scorpion guided her into a gap between two fierce Huwaytat riders, furiously whipping their light-colored *theluls* on. Now, he was comfortably situated in the middle of the pack. As Basbusa settled into a smooth motion which, with her long stride, enabled her to start gaining on the other camels, the Scorpion was able to look around for Bandar.

A chill passed through him. He couldn't locate Bandar. He should have been ahead and off to the left and fairly easy to spot in his army uniform, but he was nowhere in sight. The Scorpion twisted left and right, but he saw only other riders and in the far distance, screaming crowds, partially obscured by the fine white dust which filled the air as the camels pounded across the sands. To the right and behind him, he spotted the moustached Ruallai trying to cut obliquely behind another rider and angle towards him. But where was Bandar?

The Scorpion pulled back on the reins and Basbusa obediently began to slow down. With whoops of delight, the two Huwaytat riders surged past him. Others followed. The Scorpion half stood, balancing only on the balls of his feet and Basbusa bobbed beneath him, desperately scanning the course. Bandar had somehow disappeared.

Then he glanced back over his shoulder and spotted the veiled Bandar far behind him. Incredibly, it appeared that he was just mounting up. He must have dismounted for some reason just before the starting gun. But why? What was he up to, the Scorpion wondered.

But there was no time to think about it. Bashum, Bandar's magnificent brown camel, was already galloping in that high-prancing almost mincing gait characteristic of the best racing camels and gaining rapidly on the early stragglers. Bandar was leaning forward, riding well, his red-checked headcloth fluttering behind him in the breeze. He was moving off towards the left sideline near the crowds. If he stayed close to the sidelines, it would give him easy shooting distance to the king, perhaps twenty yards at most. Even a mediocre Bedu marksman could hardly miss at that range—and Bandar was a world-class shot, the Scorpion mused grimly.

All around him as far as the eye could see, thousands of

camels pounded ahead, the drumming of their feet on the hard-packed sand making the earth tremble with an oddly muffled sound, like rain.

He gave Basbusa a little more slack, allowing her to stretch her neck out and add an inch or two to her stride; letting her step up the pace but still saving her, because it was a long race and he didn't know how much effort he'd need from her. He felt her rocking under him, planting her feet just so, as if she knew exactly what she had to do. She started to overtake a small grouping of soft-soled *Nafud* camels ridden by Anayzah tribesmen in their blue-black *bishts*. She was galloping easily with plenty of reserve left, when he noticed Bandar sweeping ahead along the sideline.

Bandar's head was down and he was flailing Bashum with his whip. The big brown camel was beautiful as he struck out with those long legs that seemed to go on forever, moving as if the other camels were standing still and holding so level and smooth that it gave the Scorpion a hollow feeling just watching him. Bashum looked as if he were prancing on parade with enough left to do it all day and yet he was passing camels one after another.

The crowd was delirious, calling "Bashum, Bashum" and the Scorpion suddenly felt his insides turn to water. He was in a race and if he didn't do something in a hurry, Bandar would be too far ahead to head off.

He started to angle Basbusa towards the sideline for a run at Bashum, who was already a good twenty meters ahead. As he raised his whip to urge Basbusa on, he felt it jerked out of his hand. As he whirled towards the right, some instinct caused him to duck, saving his life as a bullet whizzed by his ear.

The moustached Ruallai had come up behind him to within a yard and had used his own whip to yank the Scorpion's away. He was aiming a pistol, the barrel covered by the bulbous snout of a silencer, at the Scorpion's head.

The Scorpion had barely an instant left. Only luck had

saved him. There was only one thing he could do. Any distance between them would be fatal, he thought. He swerved Basbusa into the path of the Ruallai's she-camel.

As the two camels collided, the Scorpion heard the popping of another shot. He couldn't look. The impact had jarred his balance and he clung to the pommel for all he was worth. He heard a loud grunt somewhere ahead of him and was vaguely aware that a rider had gone down. An inhuman screaming gave him the sickening realization that the downed rider was being trampled by the on-rushing camels, even as he himself desperately struggled not to fall off Basbusa. The collision had broken her stride and she was bucking badly to stay up. The other she-camel had stumbled, and in so doing had saved his life by spoiling the Ruallai's aim. The Ruallai had been forced to hang on with his whip in order to stay up.

That gave the Scorpion what he knew would be the only chance he would ever have. As the Ruallai drew abreast on his bucking she-camel and started to level the pistol, the Scorpion pulled his *khanjar* from his sheath and flung the blade across his body, as though throwing a frisbee. The blade flashed for an instant in the sun like a strobe, before burying itself in the Ruallai's neck. The gun wavered as the Ruallai's eyes turned red and empty and then it fell from the trembling hand. A bright red arc of blood spurted from the Ruallai's neck even before he went down. As he slumped off the camel, his head began to flop to one side. The neck muscles on that side had been severed.

The Scorpion's sleeve was splattered with the Ruallai's blood; so close had they come. With a savage yank on the rein, he pulled Basbusa into a steadier gait and away from the now-riderless she-camel, who was running aimlessly across the line of oncoming riders, dragging the dead Ruallai behind her, his foot caught in a stirrup.

The Scorpion raised himself as high as he could and urgently scanned ahead for Bandar. He groaned inwardly when he spotted Bandar flying along the sideline; a good hundred meters ahead and gaining.

They had already passed the television platform at the halfway mark and the gap between him and Bandar was widening. Worse, he had lost his whip. He had to do something, or the king was certain to die. And Kelly too, a small voice whispered inside him.

Holding the reins in his teeth to keep Basbusa heading straight, the Scorpion tore at the fringed leather cartridge belt around his waist. Freeing it, he grabbed the reins with his left hand and veered Basbusa towards the sideline, cutting across the path of an onrushing Harb rider, his eyes wide with fear.

The Scorpion slashed at Basbusa's flanks as hard as he could with the cartridge belt. Hitting her again and again, as he shouted "Al an, now, my beauty, my she-bitch," into the camel's ear and urged her into a flat-out gallop.

It was like dropping off a cliff, so sudden was Basbusa's acceleration. She crossed just in front of the Harb's camel, her tail in its face, as she shot obliquely towards the sideline, then at a touch from the Scorpion, galloped after Bandar who was flying well ahead. She was moving very fast, overtaking one camel after another.

The roar of the nearby crowd, almost near enough to touch, was in his ear as they thundered after Bandar, who had overtaken the leaders and had broken into the clear with no one in front of him. He was still a good eighty meters ahead and moving strongly, holding the pace with only a mile to go. Basbusa was bleeding where the Scorpion had whipped her and her mouth foamed green with slime. Her breath was beginning to labor, but the Scorpion sensed that she still had those reserves he had saved for her.

"Al an, now," he called again to her and she thundered ahead, almost wild, her ears flat against her head. He was only sixty meters behind now, but his way was blocked by two *Najd* camels running neck-and-neck. They were too close together to slip between and he would lose too much ground if he tried to go around them. Worse, the finish line was fast approaching, perhaps only a quarter-mile away.

He saw Bandar reach behind him and unsling his musket. The onlookers would no doubt assume that it was to fire a victory volley, but the Scorpion knew that there were only seconds left. But he couldn't shoot through the two riders blocking him. And it was still too far a shot.

There was only one chance left. It was a long shot at best and he would have barely a millisecond to aim from such a position. It would require going flat out with Bandar, plus incredible riding skill and balance. In the instant in time when he realized this he expressed none of it with words, only saying, "Inside and up," to himself. That and the knowledge that ready or not, this was his moment and it would never come again.

He slashed once, viciously, at Basbusa with the cartridge belt, then flung it away as he steered her next to the sideline rope, almost running over a guard as he jostled against the near camel, barely slipping through on the inside. The noise of the crowd was like a windstorm as he dropped the reins and let Basbusa run wild and free.

The camel extended her neck almost parallel to the ground and thundered forward, inching ahead of the two riders beside him. He could see Bandar clearly now. He was only forty meters ahead and approaching the finish line. He was just starting to swing the musket into the firing position against his shoulder. There were shrieks and gasps from the crowd, but it was all happening too quickly for anyone to react. Others screamed wildly as they saw the Scorpion suddenly stand almost fully erect atop the charging Basbusa and snap his own musket into firing position.

He had the sensation of falling even as he stood, but he knew it didn't matter because there was only that millisecond and he couldn't hear the crowd, or feel the camel pounding beneath him, or see anything beyond the sight at the end of his gun barrel moving towards Bandar. And then it was like looking down a dark tunnel at a distant shape silhouetted against the light, as the sight on the front of the ancient barrel came to rest lightly as a butterfly on Bandar's back and the Scorpion discovered that he had squeezed the trigger before he had realized it.

For what seemed like minutes, but must have been a second or two at most, Bandar aimed directly at the king as he swept by the finish line, then he seemed to throw his rifle forward, as if he had been violently shoved from behind. As the Scorpion threw his own musket away and slid back down to a squatting position, Bandar started to tilt sideways. Reaching forward alongside Basbusa's neck to grab back the rein, the Scorpion watched Bandar topple to the ground, his arms flung wide as if to catch at something. As Bandar hit the ground, Basbusa's giant foot came slamming down on his face, crushing it. But Bandar was beyond screaming.

The Scorpion spotted a gap in the rope barrier just past the reviewing stand and swerved Basbusa into it, barely missing Royal Guards who dived out of the way at the last second. The Scorpion bent low as Basbusa raced through the royal compound, a few wild shots ringing out behind him.

But it had all happened too quickly for them to react, he told himself, as he headed for Abdul Sa'ad's tent and Kelly. He struggled with the holster at the small of his back as he slalomed between the tents. Women screamed and figures raced back and forth without registering on him. Ahead, he could see only the black-and-white tent. In front of it the eunuch stood brandishing the sword in shaking hands.

The Scorpion managed to free the pistol just as Basbusa came pounding up to the tent. As he started to aim, the eunuch shrieked and dropped the sword. He fled behind a nearby tent, screaming.

The Scorpion knew he had only seconds before half of Arabia was on him. He leaped from the camel and yanked at the tent flap, but it was fastened shut. As he picked up the eunuch's sword, he heard screaming and gunshots and the sound of a helicopter from the direction of the royal reviewing stand.

Something had gone wrong. Very wrong. But he had no time to find out what had happened. He had to get Kelly now. It was the only chance either of them would ever have. With a single sword-slash, he cut an opening in the side and stepped into the cool dark interior of the tent.

The tent was completely empty except for a single female figure veiled from head to foot and seated on a chair in the center. She was so perfectly still that she had to be either bound and gagged or asleep, he thought. He refused to even think of the possibility that she might be dead.

As he ran to free her, he heard odd sounds from outside, muffled by the tent fabric. Something very strange had happened, but all he could think about now was Kelly. He placed his hand on her shoulder and ripped the veil from her face.

He staggered back in shock, unable to believe his eyes. Because it wasn't Kelly, but a department-store mannikin tied the chair. Its face was white as marble, the painted eyes at once doll-like and sinister.

He barely had time to react or even realize what a fool he had been when the sound of a gun being cocked caused him to whirl around.

Standing only a few feet away was Bandar, his good eye glittering like dark ice. He was very much alive and he had an AK-47 pointed straight at the Scorpion's chest. As did a dozen more of Abdul Sa'ad's soldiers stationed all around the tent.

The Ruins of Dariyyah

"ALL THAT B-B-BRAVERY w-wasted. How s-silly, dear b-boy," Braithwaite said, fondly patting the Scorpion's knee.

They were in a silver-gray Mercedes limousine racing down an untrafficked single-lane road. The Scorpion's hands and feet were tightly tied with nylon flex. He sat in the middle of the back seat, wedged between Braithwaite on one side and an unsmiling Shiite on the other. The Shiite kept a Walther automatic jammed into the Scorpion's ribs. Facing the Scorpion on one of the jump seats was Bandar, lovingly caressing an AK-47 pointed at the Scorpion's chest.

The Scorpion would have recognized Bandar anywhere, even after all these years. Bandar's bad eye was white as a statue's; it had no iris, no center. His moustache was ragged and he needed a shave. He would always need a shave. His lower lip had a hungry droop to it, as if he had swallowed something dark and squashy. He looked at the Scorpion with a kind of triumphant hatred. If a spider had a face, it would have an expression like Bandar's as it prepared to devour a fly.

The others in the limo weren't that pretty either. One of Abdul Sa'ad's soldiers, a man with an ugly harelip, sat next to the driver, who glanced with frank curiosity at the Scorpion in the rear-view mirror. After all, it is always interesting to observe the face of a man about to die.

Braithwaite, on the other hand, was positively beaming. He seemed a lot younger. Then the Scorpion realized that Braithwaite had dyed his hair jet black. It made him look like one of those aging Lotharios at singles bars trying to charm sweet young things with hints of convertibles and condominiums and trips to places with palm trees on the brochures.

The Scorpion glanced out of the window. The sun was high

251

and there were no shadows cast by the distant Jabal Tuwaiq. The yellow desert was empty and still. A telephone line ran alongside the road. The line drooped in long valleys between the widely separated metal telephone poles. He watched the wire rising and falling like the sea as they rode along.

"So it was a snatch, not a hit," the Scorpion said, the metallic taste of failure in his throat somehow more bitter than the knowledge that he was about to die. They just wanted to do it where it would be more convenient.

"Q-q-quite. The assassination was a r-r-red herring all along," Braithwaite cheerfully agreed.

"Oh Ralph, what you did for love," the Scorpion sighed. Braithwaite smiled.

"Is this Amair?" the Scorpion asked, glancing sideways at the sullen-faced Shiite with the Walther.

"All in g-g-good t-time, you rogue," Braithwaite smiled, batting his eyelashes like an ingénue.

"Just out of curiosity, who did I kill?" the Scorpion asked.

"No one important. Just one of Abdul Sa'ad's men who had no idea what he was volunteering for," Braithwaite replied, airily gesturing as if to brush aside a cobweb.

"We switched at the start of the race. That's why we were off so late. The prince said you would not suspect and he was right. Where is your sting now, O Scorpion?" Bandar mocked in a harsh guttural voice. His smile revealed brown and broken teeth, like stained and tilted gravestones in an old church cemetery.

"You're still the same charmer you always were, Bandar," the Scorpion observed mildly.

Bandar's face tightened like a fist. He slapped the Scorpion viciously across the lips.

The Scorpion licked at a trickle of blood out of the corner of his mouth. "Knowing it was Bandar, I was bound to believe he would be used for an assassination," he continued conversationally.

"The assassination attempt was the p-p-perfect cover for

Abdul Sa'ad to b-b-bring in a helicopter to spirit His Majesty away—presumably to s-safety. He actually m-m-managed to incorporate you into his p-p-plan. You were q-q-quite useful, d-dear b-b-boy," Braithwaite smiled.

"Ingenious," the Scorpion admitted. It was. Everyone had underestimated Abdul Sa'ad.

"Oh, the R-R-Russians will have their h-hands full t-t-trying to run Abdul Sa'ad," Braithwaite said cheerfully, as if reading the Scorpion's mind.

Hearing him say that made the Scorpion's heart sink with certainty. Braithwaite would never have mentioned the Russians unless they planned to kill him. "So the Russians are finally moving south, after all these centuries," he mused aloud.

"Not q-q-quite yet, dear b-boy. But the revolt is on. The Shiites are rioting in Q-Qatif. The Yemenis are moving into the Tihamah and pushing towards Mecca, and the PLO are b-blowing up the oil facilities at Ras Tanura and Sea Island."

"No more filthy Yankee dogs," Bandar growled.

"Only Russians dogs now," the Scorpion shrugged as best he could and was rewarded with a flicker of something in Bandar's one good eye.

"Oh, surely you knew the R-Russians were in on it, d-dear b-b-boy. We always assumed that," Braithwaite said. He seemed years younger. His eyes were positively sparkling. And then the Scorpion realized what it was. Too late, he thought bitterly. He had understood everything too late.

"So you're back in the game at last, Ralph," the Scorpion said.

"You all wrote me off. A h-has-been. I'm only taking my d-due, dear boy," Braithwaite said. It reminded the Scorpion of an old saying of Sheikh Zaid's: "Take what you want," said Allah, "take it and pay for it."

"You lied to me Ralph," the Scorpion said softly.

"You are naive, dear boy. I'm a s-s-spy. Lying is my b-b-business," Braithwaite snorted.

They drove to the ancient ruins of Dariyyah, lying desolate and abandoned in the desert. They left the limo and marched him through the rubble of the empty city, the roofless ruins of the ancient mud brick fortress rising in jagged spires to the perfect blue sky. The town had been abandoned long ago. No one knew why. But there were whispers that it was inhabited by *afreet* and *zars* and other evil spirits. They stood the Scorpion next to the lip of an old dry well as two of Bandar's men struggled to move the massive stone covering the mouth of the well. The Scorpion's mind was racing. He remembered Sheikh Zaid teaching him how a Scorpion will sting itself rather than be taken alive. He thought of how most of the wells in this part of the Najd were about twenty feet deep and sand often seeped in when the wells went dry. Most of all, he was counting on Bandar's vanity and skill.

"Where is the king?" the Scorpion asked.

"Q-quite nearby," Braithwaite said, unable to resist a glance at the old fortress. "Prince Abdul Sa'ad is 'persuading' Salim to abdicate in f-favor of Abdul Sa'ad." A faint cry, thin and distant like a bird trill, came from the direction of an ancient tower. Bandar smiled.

"Shouldn't take long now," Braithwaite remarked, squinting at the Scorpion in the bright sunlight.

Bandar stood near the lip of the well and called down. *Kelly*, the Scorpion thought, his heart leaping.

"Do you want up—be for me—no more escape—or stay under dark—think more?" Bandar called down in clumsy English.

"Leave me alone," a defiant voice echoed from the depths of the well. Good girl, the Scorpion thought.

"Not alone! I send friend—keep company on you!" Bandar growled.

The Scorpion's heart pounded. He stood alone on the lip of the well, his hands still bound behind him. He looked around at the silhouettes of the ruins against the blue sky, blue and unblemished from horizon to horizon. At that moment, he never had wanted to live so badly.

Bandar had backed away about twenty feet and cocked the AK-47. The sound of the bolt slamming home had a feel of terrible finality.

"Because you are a Mutayri, I give you a choice to be a man. Do you want it in the head or the heart?" Bandar called, sighting at the Scorpion.

The others stood there, watching.

"Heart—and I bet you can't do it with a single shot, you slimy offspring of a Hutaymi camel," the Scorpion shouted, his mouth dry as the desert.

Bandar's face was terrible to see in that last moment. The Scorpion's last conscious memory was the sound of a single shot and the impact of a terrible blow in his chest, sending him flying backwards into the well.

The Well of Death

THE SCORPION WAS AWAKENED by the most hideous sound he had ever heard: the scraping of his coffin lid as it closed over him. He opened his eyes and saw only blackness. He tried to fight the panic bubbling up inside him. But the thought of being trapped forever in the dark was overwhelming. A groan escaped his lips.

"Oh dear God, it's alive!" a frightened female voice cried out in the darkness and he suddenly remembered everything. The scraping sound was the heavy stone that sealed the old well being rolled back into place. He was trapped, like a fly in a bottle.

"Please, if you're alive, say something," the frightened female voice said. She was very near. He could feel her breath on his cheek.

"Hello, Kelly," the Scorpion said.

"Oh God," she groaned and began to cry. He could feel her tears dripping on to his lips like raindrops. He licked his lips. They tasted salty.

There was a hysterical note somewhere in her crying, like a piano with a bad key, and he knew that she was very close to the edge. He stretched his neck up and grazed her cheek with his lips. It felt as soft as bird's down.

"So soft," she murmured and then it hit her. He heard the rustle of her clothes as she sat up sharply in the pitch darkness, the hysterical note giving a stridency to her voice.

"But you're dead. They shot you," she said.

"The bullet hit a transmitter over my heart wrapped in a special bullet-proof plastic mesh fabric. Bandar is a world-class shot and I was counting on his accuracy, only I thought he would try a shot at the race, not later on."

"The race! They mean to kidnap the king!" she exclaimed.

"It's already happened," he said.

"And you must be the American agent they were talking about—the Scorpion," she said.

"I'm here to get you out," he said.

"Fine job you're doing of it," she snorted and it seemed so funny that they both couldn't help laughing, the sounds of laughter echoing in the well.

"I've had better days," the Scorpion admitted, and that set them both off again. They laughed till their sides hurt and as the echoes died down, somehow the darkness seemed a bit friendlier.

"What are we to do?" she asked at last, a pensive note in her voice. It was an interesting voice, smooth as cream, with a catch in it, and he felt he was truly hearing it for the first time, without the fear. But it had such sadness in it and he sensed how terrible it had been for her.

"I'm taking you home," he said softly.

"Oh sure. I've tried to escape but they keep catching me," she began bitterly.

"This time we finally have a couple of advantages."

"Like?"

"For one thing, they think I'm dead."

"Might as well be. Trapped in here," she muttered glumly.

"Don't ever say that! Ever! Life is everything, death is nothing," he snapped, his voice like a whiplash. He had to jolt her out of it. And it was time to see what she was made of, he thought.

"I'm sorry . . . I . . . well, you're stubborn. I'll give you that," she admitted.

"Stubbornness is a survival characteristic. One of the two key characteristics," he said, remembering the gospel as Koenig used to expound it in that Quonset hut hidden in the green Virginian countryside.

"What's the other?"

"Intelligence."

"When do we get to the intelligent part?" she asked, forcing him to smile again.

"We're already there. Help is probably already on the way. I'll be sure once I check my transmitter."

"Well, what are you waiting for?" she asked.

"You—to untie my hands," he said.

"I'll do better than that. I'll cut you loose," she said brightly.

"You have a knife!" he exclaimed.

"Sort of. It's an old stone thing I found in the sands down here. It's sharp enough," she said, showing him a flint chisel, its edges chipped and serrated, perhaps left behind by some ancient workman, aeons ago.

"It's perfect," he said.

"Before they threw you in here, I was thinking of using it on myself," she added softly, then caught herself. "I don't know why I told you that," she said.

"I think it's the darkness. It's like a confessional. In here, appearances can't get in the way of our true selves. There's no image to pierce or hide behind," he said.

"I'm not that brave. I've always used my looks. Maybe there's no substance to me at all. Maybe my appearance is me."

"No one's that brave. And if all you were was a pretty female, they'd have turned you into a house pet by now," he replied.

"And you, Mister—whatever your name is . . ."

"Nick. Call me Nick. You're one of the only people in the world to know it," he said, his voice thickening as if he were catching cold.

"And you, Nick. What's your secret?"

"Untie me first," he said.

"I'm afraid of you," she said, her voice small and little-girlish.

"Look where we both are, Kelly. What do you have to lose?"

"Well, that's the damn truth," she admitted and began groping in the dark, feeling for his hands, still bound behind him. He felt a tugging as she sawed at the knots and then his hands were free. He unwrapped the cords from his wrists and rubbed them hard. His hands tingled painfully and he was sore in a dozen places from the shot and the fall. He tried to stretch and winced at the pain. His back felt as if it had been used for karate practice.

"What is it?" she asked.

"Just thinking about how attractive almost any other line of work looks right now," he said, listening to his vertebrae cracking like walnuts as he stretched. Thank Allah for the sand. It had cushioned his fall. Now it felt smooth and cool as he felt his way around the well in the darkness.

The mound of sand sloped down on all sides from the center and the well had a diameter of about six feet. The walls were rough sandstone. If only he had a light, he thought.

"I wish we had some light," he said.

"We do. I have a lamp. Abdul Sa'ad's orders. I put it out when I heard them opening the stone," she said, flicking on a gold and diamond Dunhill lighter and lighting the spout of an old oil lamp. Her face was gold and shadowed in the flame-light, like a face on a renaissance church panel. She was even more beautiful than her pictures had suggested and it was all he could do to keep himself from grabbing her. Having come so close to dying, the life force surged inside him and at that moment, he had never wanted a woman so badly. He felt himself coming so sharply erect it was almost painful. But she had been so badly used by others, he told himself bitterly. She was fragile and wounded and the last thing she needed was another man just grabbing at her.

She held the lamp up to see him better.

"You have an interesting face. Not a pretty face but one can see something in it. I can see why there have been whispers about you," she murmured almost to herself.

"In the desert a whisper is only the sound of the wind on the sands," he said.

"No it's more than that. You're a kind of legend. Some of the soldiers said you were a demon. Others said you were an assassin. What will they say now if you return from the dead? . . . that the Scorpion is a kind of god."

"Ignorant people always try to make good men into mediocre gods," he said impatiently. He could smell the closeness of her. There was a clean sweetness about it, like the desert at dawn.

"What else have you got?" he asked, clenching his fists to keep from taking her in his arms.

"I don't know. There's an old stick in here. It looks like it might have been part of an ancient spear," she said.

"What else?"

"That's all there is . . . except for me," she said. She was very close. They were almost touching. The tips of her breasts grazed the bulletproof fabric wrapped around his chest.

"The transmitter!" he shouted suddenly, bringing them

259

both out of a trance. They hurriedly unwound the dense plastic mesh from around his chest.

He brought the lamp close to check the transmitter. Even protected by the bulletproof plastic, the bullet had still managed to smash the metallic casing. The transmitter had saved his life, but it was useless now.

"No help," she said, crestfallen.

"Not necessarily," he said.

"I don't follow."

"If you were tracking somebody and all of a sudden the transmission stopped, where would you look for him?" he said grinning.

"The last place the signal came from," she said brightly.

"It's a bit of a stretch, but I think even those room-temperature-IQ geniuses in the CIA can figure out that much."

"But can they find you from that?" she asked dubiously.

"The signal from this is designed to be picked up by a receiver in an SR-71 flying too high to be seen or heard and bounced back to a RAVEN on the ground. I think our side knows exactly where we are," he said confidently. It sounded good, he thought. With a little luck, it might even be true.

But he'd already had a lot of luck. Too much, he thought. In battle two mistakes are not permitted, Sheikh Zaid used to say. But they'd need every bit of luck, because unless an overflight had picked up his last signal as the bullet smashed the transmitter, they'd had it. Because even if he could somehow get them out of the well, he couldn't take on all of Abdul Sa'ad's men single-handed. They'd need an army of Scorpions to do that, he thought.

"How does it feel to come back from death?" she asked, her voice sounding odd in the shadowy light as she fingered the smashed transmitter. For a moment, the odd note confused him and then he recognized it. She was beginning to hope again. The life force was surging inside of her too. His pulse began to throb in his temple like a drumbeat.

"It feels like I've been blind all my life and suddenly opened my eyes on a magnificent sunrise," he whispered. She came up to him and rested her silky head on his shoulder.

"It's like electricity," she whispered, her fingers dancing lightly down his chest. Every place she touched tingled with a feeling that had no name. He had almost forgotten how special it could be.

He felt himself being drawn to her like an iron filing to a magnet and then he couldn't stop himself. His arms wrapped around her. He could feel her body trembling against him and their lips found each other. They were so soft and salty, because she was silently crying and then they were grabbing desperately at each other like survivors from a shipwreck. Their mouths sought each other out, tongues exploring and they shared the sensation of floating in the shadows of space.

"Oh God, I want you. Make me feel. For the first time in so long, make me alive," she cried, her hands groping at his clothes, tugging him free as they sank down to the soft cool sand.

He felt the quickening gathering inside him as he explored her naked body in the flickering light. He pressed his mouth against the soft mounds of her breasts, grazing her erect nipples with his lips, then down to the dimple of her navel and on down to the soft skin of her belly while his hands caressed her silky thighs and the moistness between them.

"Tell me your secret, now," she whispered, pulling him to her, guiding him to her center and wrapping her long legs around his hips.

"You're my secret," he gasped, feeling the old, familiar yet almost forgotten excitement as he entered her.

"Don't hurt me," she cried and then her words were no longer words as they began the ancient rhythm. Their shadows moved and intertwined in the light of the flame like fingers . . . from the dawn of time.

He must have slept . . . for a few minutes, because when he awoke, cradled in her arms, he thought he was with Tuyet and the child that last night on the sampan. He remembered how the sentries had refused to let her into the embassy compound to catch the last choppers evacuating the city at the last minute. He had left the embassy and had raced through the city streets, the pounding of the heavy guns drawing nearer as the North Vietnamese prepared to enter the city. The sound of Bing Crosby singing "White Christmas" came from a hundred radios along the way. It was supposed to be the evacuation signal and it became a kind of theme as he ran and he knew he would never be able to hear it again without remembering Saigon and that endless day. It was MACV's last foul-up because they'd had to shut down Tan Son Nhut airport and there weren't enough choppers to ferry out anyone who wasn't American.

They made their escape by sampan that night, with the city full of North Vietnamese regulars and the water red with the reflections of flames along the shores of the Saigon river. Then the VC gunboat opened fire and Tuyet grunted with surprise as a white-hot round passed through her and the baby.

"Does it hurt?" he had asked.

"*Titi*," which was pidgin for "a little" she had replied, and then they were in the water because the gunboat had rammed them . . . and he was flung out into the burning river.

"You're so quiet . . ." Kelly said, her voice tender.

"I must have fallen asleep," he said.

"Are we ever going to get out of here?" she asked, her voice little-girlish again.

"We have to. World war may erupt if we don't," he said.

"How did you get into this line of work?" she asked.

"I went back to the States. Dropped out of Harvard. Got drafted and sent to Vietnam."

"That seems so long ago. I was just a schoolgirl," she said.

"Oh yes. Vietnam is ancient history. Hardly worth talking about," he said, his tone offhanded.

She stroked his hair with her hand, as if he were a feverish child.

"I don't believe you," she said finally.

"I haven't thought about it in a long time," he lied.

"What was it like? Really?" she asked.

"What? Nam? If you survived, it was a kind of Lost and Found Department of the Soul."

"What did you lose?"

"My innocence. It was common enough in those days," he shrugged.

"What did you find?"

"My profession. I found I had a talent for this kind of thing," he said, feeling the sweat break out all over his body, remembering the Ashau Valley. He remembered how the dewdrops clung like strings of pearls to the concertina wire along the perimeter that morning and how the mist boiled up from the stream to the treetops, wisps of fog tangled in the branches like spider webs. He remembered how still the fields were, the only sound the faint tinkle of a tin can against the wire. And then how they found his buddy Cool's body. The VC had left him slumped over his M-60; blood still spilling out of the place where his head used to be.

That night, Nick volunteered for a LRP patrol. Carrying nothing but a combat knife, a bicycle chain covered with black tape and a Colt .45 he stayed out for eight days and nights straight. When he finally came back to the laager, the VC had fled the area, amidst whispers of a hundred headless bodies strewn across jungle trails.

The legend of the Scorpion had been born.

"Did you work for the CIA?" Kelly asked.

"At first. But working for 'the Company,' as it's called, required a bit more spinal flexibility than this particular vertebrate is capable of. So I became a freelancer."

"You sound so matter of fact about it."

"Sorry. Like I said, Vietnam is ancient history."

"Is it? Is it truly?" she demanded.

"No," he said.

He rested his head on her breast. He heard the pounding of her heart in his ear.

"So you're a kind of modern-day knight errant," she jeered gently.

"That's making it a lot more romantic than it is," he said. He felt her stiffen, then will herself to relax.

"What is it?" he asked.

"Did you mean what you said . . . just before we made love?"

He thought for a moment. "Yes."

"Because I feel I should tell you. I mean it seems silly now, but . . ." she hesitated and he wondered if she was thinking of another man. "It' s just that being together now, so close to death . . . it didn't seem to matter so much," she said lamely, a catch in her voice.

"Everything matters," he said, wondering what had gone wrong.

"What happened just now was magic," she said, placatingly.

"That's good," he said.

"I just want you to know that whatever happens, what happened between us mattered. It mattered a lot."

"This isn't the Girl Scouts, Kelly. You don't have to play by somebody else's rules. Why don't you just say what you mean?" he said, certain she was thinking of someone else. He wondered why Harris never told him there was another man in her life. It wasn't like Harris to have missed something that crucial. It wasn't like him at all.

"Suppose there was someone else; someone far away," she began.

"Right now far away sounds like a good place to be," he said.

Ascent

"HOW ARE WE EVER GOING to get out of here?" Kelly asked, her throaty voice echoing in the hollow silence.

"There's only one way out of a well," the Scorpion replied, looking upwards as he marched around the sides of the well. He held the lamp high above his head, examining the rock walls in the dancing light of the flame with the careful attention of an archaeologist in an ancient tomb.

"How are you going to get up there? By flying? Not to mention that it takes at least two men to move the rock sealing the opening," she said, unable to conceal her disbelief.

"We're going to climb out," he said, scrutinizing every detail of the rock. He stopped and held the lamp as high as he could so that the light from the flame was cast high up the side of the well. He studied the rough face, the cracks and crevices in the worn rock on one side for several minutes, calculating distances. Even fractions of an inch might make all the difference, he thought.

"I hate to mention this, but I skipped boot camp this year. The highest thing I've climbed since the fourth grade is a bar stool," she said.

"It's never too late to start," he grinned and tore a long strip off his headcloth. He wrapped the cloth around the handle of the stone-age chisel and tied it tightly. He squatted down and after a moment's hesitation, began chipping at the rock at a spot about two feet above the sand. At the first blow, tiny chips flew and a small white dimple appeared in the stone. The handle twisted in his hand on the next blow and he tightened his grip. He stabbed again and a large chip flew past, barely missing his leg.

The Scorpion stood up, inserted his toe in the depression and stood for a second, balanced on the toe like a clumsy ballerina. Then he came down on the other leg. He grunted with satisfaction. The sandstone cracked fairly easily. That was crucial. Otherwise, the attempt was impossible. As it was, it would take every last drop of strength and skill he possessed to even come close.

He turned and studied the mound of sand. Without a word, he moved to the center of the mound, got down on his knees and began to shovel handfuls of sand at the base of the rock face under the depression he had just made. All the while, Kelly watched him with the kind of pained, yet polite expression reserved for madmen.

"I could use some help," the Scorpion said, glancing over at her.

"I can see that," she said carefully.

"I want to pile the sand over there to cushion that area in case I fall," he explained. Without waiting to see her response, he went back to work. He shoveled mound after mound with his bare hands towards the rocky face. After a moment's hesitation, he felt her working beside him.

When a small mound had been built on that side, they collapsed against the far wall to rest.

"You're really serious," she said, when she finally caught her breath.

The Scorpion wiped his sweating brow against his forearm, gritty with sand. Then he caught her by her shoulder and held her tightly.

"Listen to me. Twenty-four hours from now, you'll be sitting in an air-conditioned lounge somewhere and this will all seem like a bad dream," he whispered intently.

"Please don't lie to me. I don't want to live on false hopes. Before you came I'd resigned myself to death. Don't tease me," she whispered, her lips buried against his hard-muscled shoulder.

"I'm not lying. I've climbed out of worse places than this," he said, remembering the tunnels near Dai Loc, and thought that it was true. "Besides, the only dying that's going to happen will be done by Abdul Sa'ad and Bandar," he said quietly.

She shuddered. It was utterly clear that he meant it.

She straightened up and wiped the tears from her eyes. She brushed the sand out of her hand with her fingers and the gesture touched him more than anything she had said.

"What can I do to help?" she asked, her voice calm and resolute.

"Can you braid?"

"I haven't done that since I was a little girl. Why?"

"Because we'll need a rope. You said you weren't the world's greatest lady climber, so you'll need a little help," the Scorpion said, undoing his headcloth and *bisht*. Using the chisel to start a cut, he tore it all into long strips. He hefted the bundle of strips thoughtfully.

"Won't be enough," he sighed.

"What about that bulletproof plastic you wore around your chest?" she asked.

"Too short. And there's no way of cutting it or tying it to anything else."

"There's my dress," she said. She took off the dress and a silk slip until she was down to just her panties and bra, gleaming white against the creamy skin of her firm, slim body. Her legs were long and fine, her rump nicely rounded. Her breasts were small, pert and uptilted and he had to clench his fists to keep from reaching out for them.

Clad only in panties and bra, she began to attack the dress. It was soon in strips.

"Too bad about the dress," he said, obviously delighted to see her undressed.

"It's all right. I never liked this dress anyway," she smiled back and began to braid the cloth strips into a rope.

The Scorpion nodded and looked away. If he kept looking at her, they'd never get out. He grabbed a handful of strips and soon they were both intently braiding.

They worked quickly, yet methodically. Their lives would depend on the strength of their knots. Soon they had a rope about twenty feet long.

"Is it enough, do you think?" she asked.

"It'll have to be. We don't have any more cloth," he said and began checking everything he would need. The rope, chisel, lighter, lamp, the wooden stave about five feet long that had once been part of a spear or shepherd's staff, and some hand-sized rocks.

The Scorpion stood up, clad only in his underwear, the remains of his white *thaub* tied around his waist, like a short skirt. In the flickering light from the lighter, he looked like an ancient Greek warrior ready for battle. His rock-hard muscles were finely etched and his skin was slick with sweat. Kelly could see the muscles rippling under his skin as he prepared his gear. He was so much of a man he seemed more than a man. His sheer male beauty made her tremble. If ever a man was made who could do the impossible, it was this dark stranger, she thought, a spark of hope stirring.

He showed her how he wanted her to use the lamp, holding it so the light would hit the rock face above him where he would have to make his next move. She nodded, then looked up into the darkness. It seemed so high up. It was insurmountable, she thought, her heart sinking. She held the flame so she could see his face. His eyes were gray as flint and she could see the flame reflected in them.

"How will you do it?" she asked, her voice barely a whisper.

"There's only one way to do anything. One step at a time."

"But why did you pick that side? More handholds or something?"

"Not really. It's pretty uniform all the way around. But there's a little ledge near the top on that side. It was probably used to rest earthenware jars. We'll need it to get you up."

"If you can get me up, you mean," she said.

"No. When I get you up."

They smiled into each other's eyes.

"Anything else I should know?" she asked.

"Yes. Stand away from that side. A falling human body can do a lot of damage if it lands on top of you."

"You have such a delightful way of putting things."

"It's part of my charm," he smiled.

They looked into each other's eyes as if saying goodbye. The Scorpion gave her the wooden spear to hold. Then he moved boldly up to the rock wall.

For a moment he contemplated the rock, planning the sequence of moves. He tried to keep up his spirits, but the wall looked utterly formidable, as high up as he could see.

"One of the basic laws of the universe is that everything looks a hell of a lot easier than it really is," Alex used to say back in Bangkok. And Allah knows the Pathet Lao had shown Alex the hard way to die, the Scorpion thought, trying to shake the memory. Negative thinking can defeat you before you ever start, he knew. Instead, he forced his mind to imagine himself successfully moving upward, one step at a time. That was what he wanted to keep in his mind. He took a deep breath to relax every muscle and clear his head. Then he began.

Using the flint chisel and one of the rocks as a mallet, he chipped pairs of indentations shoulder-width apart every two feet, starting at knee level and going upwards until he was stretching his arms as high as he could reach. The rock cut and split easily and large chips of sandstone flew by as he worked. Once he started climbing the rock face, he would be able to use only one hand to cut, but for the first eight feet or so he might as well make it easy on himself, he thought.

The Scorpion stepped away from the rock and wiped his sweaty face on his forearm, gritty with sand and dust. He now had four pairs of hand and footholds carved into the rock. He dropped the rock he had used for a mallet and carefully rewrapped the rags around his right hand. He wrapped the braided rope around his waist and tied the end. Then he clenched the chisel in his teeth.

The easy part was over.

He took a deep breath, exhaled and stepped up to the wall. Inserting his toe in the lowest notch and grabbing the highest notch on the left side, he pulled himself up. He placed his left toes in the lowest left notch and clung to the wall like a fly. His toes, inserted into the two bottom notches, supported most of his weight as he pulled himself towards the wall with the fingertips of his left hand.

Already he could feel gravity trying to pull him backwards and he pressed his fingertips against the unyielding rock to hold on. His fingers began to ache almost at once. It was going to be murderous, he thought, then pushed the thought away.

He took the chisel from between his teeth and holding on with his left hand, used his right to stab at the rock an arm's length above his left hand. Once a sufficient notch had been cut, he repeated the process on the right side, carving a hand-hold parallel and about a foot away from the new left-hand notch. Then he gripped the chisel in his jaws again and inserting first his left hand and right foot into the higher notches, pulled himself up again. With both hands and feet secured to the rock face, he caught his breath for a second.

It was, he knew, the exact opposite of a normal rock climb. The professional method was to work out a path up the rock face, then climb from notch to notch maintaining a smooth ongoing rhythm, sustaining upward movement with the momentum of the climb. Ideally, the rock climber should never actually stop at any point, hanging by his fingers, where fatigue and gravity begin to take their deadly toll.

But the standard approach was impossible for the Scorpion for several reasons. The first was that he was facing an absolutely vertical surface. The sheer 90-degree face made it impossible to climb all the way up, non-stop. The second difficulty was that because of hundreds of years of erosion, water and sand particles scouring the rock, there were few if any natural crevices. The rock was steep and smooth for its entire height. Every notch would have to be hand-cut. The final and greatest difficulty was the lack of pitons. He had no way of hammering in anything to support his weight, so that he could rest and use both hands to hammer in the next upward hold.

No, this would be a slow, methodical, crab-like approach, an agonizing step-by-step process whereby he would cling by the fingers of one hand while he hammered out notches with the other. As each new pair of notches was hammered out, he would grip the chisel between his teeth like a movie pirate, then use both hands and feet to inch up to the next higher set of notches and then begin all over again.

It was the kind of slow grinding climb designed to take the heart out of anyone, he thought, trying to blink the sweat out of his eyes. Better not to think, he told himself. There were a lot of things he had better not do. Like looking up or down. Up was bad because the sight of how far he still had to go could destroy his will to go on. Down was bad because the fear of falling could set in.

The best was just to concentrate on the next step. You don't have to climb all the way, he told himself, just the next step. You can swim an ocean, one stroke at a time. No, you can't. That's not progress, it's megalomania, he contradicted himself. Don't think about it. Don't think about anything except the next step. Lots of pain in fingers. Cramping badly and it's much too soon. Don't panic, he argued back. It's only one step. Now bend the right knee sideways. Keep it close to the rock, otherwise leaning out puts too much weight on the fingers. Feel for the next notch with the toes of the right foot. Don't try to look down. You couldn't see it anyway. Can't find it. Where is it? It has to be there. Move the toes left and right. Find it fast! Fingers giving way. *Ya Allah!* Can't hold it. Have to. Hurry!

"It's there. Just to your left," Kelly's voice called out.

Desperately, his toes scratched at the lip of the notch to the left. He found the notch and with his last strength, jammed his toes into the notch, let his toes take his weight as he pushed up, grabbed the higher handhold with his right hand, stuck his left foot into the foothold and once more, he clung by all fours to the rock.

His left hand was slippery with sweat. He started to wipe it on what was left of the *thaub* around his waist, but it felt sticky. He glanced at his hand and instantly regretted it. His left hand was curled into a claw and slick with blood. His fingers were raw and bleeding.

The Scorpion started to straighten his fingers, then changed his mind. Leave it alone, he told himself. The hand is more useful as a claw. He grabbed at the notch with his left hand and began to chop away with his right. He pulled himself up like a crippled monkey, one link at a time.

His fingers were hurting now. His bare chest heaved for breath as he crushed it against the rough stone. Don't think about the pain, he told himself. It's just pain, that's all. Just minor abrasions, so don't feel sorry for yourself. A nurse in any hospital emergency room would laugh at them and put you at the end of the line. And what about Nam and all the guys who lost a lot more than fingers? Remember the black plastic body bags stretched out on the ground in Danang? A long line of them waiting to be picked up like so much garbage. What would any of them give to be still clinging to life, even by raw fingertips? Just hang on.

How far had he come? No. Wrong question. How far to go? he began to wonder, knowing he shouldn't think about it, shouldn't look up. Keep focused on the light, on the next step, he told himself. Forget the girl. Forget the CIA. Forget Arabia and the war. There's only the rock and the next step. His universe had shrunk to a few feet of rock and darkness. There was no longer up or down, no past or future. Only the rock and the pain, he thought, pulling himself painfully up to the next set of hand and footholds.

"You're almost there!" Kelly's voice sang out from below. There was excitement in it. "You're doing wonderfully," she called and the Scorpion didn't know whether to laugh or cry at her warm encouragement.

Only about five feet to go, he told himself, gathering his reserves for a last push. Wearily, he reached up and began stabbing at the rock again. The instant he struck the blow he knew it had gone wrong. The clang of the flint against the rock sounded different and then the awful snap and whirring as the broken blade flew straight at his eyes, spinning like a propeller.

Instinctively, he jerked his head back and even as he turned he knew it was wrong. He tried to duck his head back into the rock, but it was too late. He could feel his balance going and there was nothing he could do. His hands were peeled off the rock by the momentum and before he could even think to react he was falling, briefly aware of the rush of air and somewhere Kelly's scream and in that last second, his body took over, pulling his knees into a tuck position because it would be fatal to land on his head. He felt his feet hit the ground with a thud that jarred every bone as his body collapsed like a puppet whose strings have been cut.

When he came to, Kelly was holding his head cradled in her lap. She had moistened a cloth with her saliva and was using it as a washcloth on his face. Feeling him stir, she bent over and kissed him passionately, their lips almost bruising each other, her long blond hair folding around their faces like a tent.

"I thought you would be killed," she whispered, her eyes shiny in the dancing flamelight.

"So did I," he said.

"You were wonderful," she said and tried to smile, but it didn't come off. She stared blankly into the darkness.

The Scorpion didn't say anything.

"It's not your fault. You were going so well. It's just lousy luck."

He didn't say anything.

She held his hands in her own and looking at the battered fingers her eyes began to fill with tears.

"Poor hands. Poor poor hands," she said. She lifted his hands to her mouth and kissed them tenderly. He winced and she quickly put them down.

"My hands are all right. Don't worry about my hands. I'm not a concert violinist," he snapped.

"You never let anyone get close, do you?" Kelly said. There was a tremble in her voice.

"I can't afford to. There's no time."

"Then you can't afford not to," she retorted.

He smiled, but it changed to a grimace of pain as he tried to get up. She pulled him back to the warm comfort of her lap.

"How long have I been out?" he asked.

"Just a few seconds."

He tried to struggle up but she held him back.

"Easy. Rest first. You're exhausted. Just relax for a minute," she soothed.

"I can't."

"Why not? There's lots of time."

"No. If I don't get up now I'm not sure I ever will. Every bit of me doesn't want to move, so I know I should. Besides, there is no time. King Salim's being tortured right now. If he gives in and abdicates, we'll be too late. Abdul Sa'ad will have won," he said and rolled over on to his hands and knees. Groaning in pain like a wounded animal, he crawled on all fours back to the wall.

Using the wall for support, he somehow pulled himself slowly and awkwardly erect, like a creature who had never walked before.

"Where's the chisel?" he demanded.

274

"Here," she said and sifting through the sand, grabbed at the black stone shard.

"But it's broken," she said, handing it to him.

He examined the blade in the shadowy light. The blade had snapped in two almost in the middle, leaving a jagged edge. The Scorpion fingered the broken edge thoughtfully. It was razor sharp.

"Might even be better," he rasped. He studied it in the lamplight.

"It's odd, isn't it? The fate of nations in the Atomic Age hanging on a stone-age implement," he said.

She looked into his eyes and was jolted by what she saw. His eyes were underlined with dark circles. They looked old as the rock itself.

"You look awful," she said quietly. He shook his head.

"If the warranty hadn't expired, I'd trade this body in for a new model," he said.

He wrapped the soiled and torn rags around his hand again. Then he rewrapped the cloth around the broken chisel, put it between his teeth, and turned to face the wall once more. It seemed more forbidding, even hostile this time, the dark shadows gathering like demons in the faint flickering light. The Scorpion took a breath and suddenly he was scrambling back up.

"Go with God," Kelly murmured softly. She wasn't sure if he heard her.

The Scorpion moved quickly, agilely, from notch to notch, like a great awkward monkey. He cursed each time his fingers took the weight, but never stopped moving upwards. Groaning and climbing and not stopping as if he knew that if he stopped he might never start again. By the time a minute had gone by he had managed to climb back to where he had fallen from. He paused at last to catch his breath, clinging to the wall by all fours like a spider to a shaky web.

Now the battle for the last few feet began in earnest, inching his way up in near darkness while clinging to the rock only with his bruised fingers and toes. The air was stale and lifeless. He wondered if they were running short of oxygen or was it just his imagination running rampant. "Cowardice is the inability to control your imagination," Koenig once said. Don't think, he told himself. Move! His strength was going fast.

He could feel his fingers slipping in the darkness. He had no strength to stop it any more. The scraping sound of fingernails on stone and tiny pebbles told him he was losing it. The Scorpion screamed in frustration and struck again with the stone blade, but this time he missed the rock wall entirely. He balanced for a desperate instant on the toes of his right foot, flailing at the air while his numbed and bewildered brain tried to understand what was happening.

As he began to fall again, an electrifying thought flashed through his mind. He had reached the ledge! Thrusting out both arms in the darkness, he dug his battered fingers into the ledge and with a final desperate effort, heaved himself up so that he was balancing on his palms. He kicked his right leg over the ledge and threw his body into the niche.

He lay for what seemed like hours, panting like a horse ridden almost to death. It had been a near thing, he knew. His head throbbed unmercifully and white and blue spots sailed across the darkness before his eyes. He tried to focus his mind, but couldn't. His breath wheezed like a bellows, his chest heaved and it was all he could to just to breathe. But he had done it! He exulted. Done what? some cynical part of his mind retorted. You're still trapped in the well like a fly in a bottle. The heavy stone sealing the opening to the well was a five-hundred-pound cork. At that moment, his desperate little stratagem to get the two of them out seemed hopelessly pathetic.

"Hey, Nick? Are you all right?" Kelly called, her voice faint and echoing in the darkness. It caught him by surprise and jolted him upright. He had to get her up, he thought.

And then, somehow, he would kill Bandar. By the living Allah he would.

"I'm fine. Now's your chance to show boot camp what it missed," he called down, his voice barely a hoarse whisper.

"You mean you made it?" Her voice was incredulous.

"Did you ever doubt it?" he called back.

"Not for a minute!" came an exuberant girlish voice from the darkness below.

The Scorpion wedged himself into the niche, his back against one side, his feet against the other. His battered fingers explored the rock, trying to get a feel of the space he occupied. He was seated in a den about three feet across scooped out of the rock. There was barely enough space to sit up without cracking his head and it couldn't have been more than a foot and a half deep. Getting the two of them in there would be like shoe-horning a size ten foot into a size four shoe, but it would have to do. The cramped space worked to his advantage in one regard; it made it easier to brace himself tightly. And he'd need every edge possible if he was to get her up.

He called down for her to catch the rope and used it to bring up the wooden stave. She would have to carry the lamp up. They couldn't risk dropping it. At last he was ready to bring her up.

Tightly braced, he placed one end of the braided rope so that it was pressed by the bottom of his foot against the opposite side of the niche. Then he ran the rope from his right hand across his back to his left hand. He dropped the rope from his left hand.

"Got it!" she called up.

His thirst was terrible. His mouth had a foul taste. He licked the sweat off his forearm. His tongue felt swollen, and as raspy as a cat's. He had to swallow his own spittle to try to talk.

"All right. Loop it around you under your arms. Make sure to use a knot that doesn't slip. Use a bowline or a square knot or something," he called down.

"I knew being a Brownie would come in handy some day. I finally get to tie a square knot," she shouted.

Her voice echoed dully in the leaden air, bouncing between the sides of the well like a tennis ball gone flat. He felt tugging at the other end of the rope; at first faint, then stronger, as if a fish were taking the line. It seemed to take a long time until she called up that she was ready.

The Scorpion flinched as he grabbed the rope. He was literally holding her life in his hands, he told himself. He couldn't let go. No, he wouldn't let go, he vowed. He would obliterate any thought of letting go, remembering Sheikh Zaid's ancient prayer from the Holy Koran: "I seek refuge in the Lord of men from the mischief of the slinking prompter who whispers in the hearts of men."

"Hang on, Kelly," he shouted down and pulled, taking her weight in his hands and across his back. The strain was unbelievable and he could barely manage the weight. He pulled with his left arm and shoulder and pushed with his right. Then he stamped his feet against the few precious inches of slack he had gained. He slid his hands back to their original position and pulled again, twisting his shoulders as well to gain a few more inches.

The rope left a trail of fire across his shoulders and back. The strain on his spine felt like one of his vertebrae was about to snap at any second. "I seek refuge from the slinking prompter who whispers in the hearts of men," he repeated to himself over and over.

Suddenly, the line went slack.

"Hey, I'm taking a breather," Kelly called, her voice much closer. She must have found a foothold, he thought excitedly, gaining all the slack he could.

He looked down and was rewarded by the sight of the lamp flame barely six feet below him. His heart leaped up. Almost there, he thought.

"I just thought I'd let you know. I'm planning to go on a diet," Kelly called up impishly.

"Good timing," the Scorpion managed to choke. Then he was laughing, trying to control it so he wouldn't let her slip. She'd done it, he admitted to himself. She'd reached through to him.

The last few feet came quickly. The rope grew shorter and shorter and suddenly she was there, grabbing hold of his arm with both her hands. He heaved with every last bit of his remaining strength and she was up, slumped across him, both of them panting as if they would never get enough air.

Later, after they had caught their breath, she whispered, her lips almost touching his ear.

"I was teasing before, but you really are what every woman dreams about whether they admit it or not: a knight in shining armor. Someone to lean on when . . . you know."

"Like Antar and the maiden Abla," the Scorpion breathed.

"Who?"

"It's just an old story; something from long ago," he murmured.

Kelly bit her lip hesitantly. Then she brought it out. "I lied when I said I never doubted you for a second."

"So did I," he replied.

For a long time that might have been seconds or minutes or hours, they lay together in silent exhaustion. Finally, he became conscious of her weight heavy on him. She lay face down, her head on his shoulder, her breasts flattened against his chest, her body molded tightly into his. He felt his manhood begin to stir, feeling her pelvis pressed against him.

"How tired are you?" she teased.

"Too tired," he grunted and half-struggled to ease part of her weight off him. The clock was still ticking, he thought.

"Well, now that we're here, what do we do? It takes at least two men to move that big rock," Kelly said.

"That's where the broken spear comes in," the Scorpion said.

While Kelly held the lamp the Scorpion used the chisel to cut a small notch in the end of the wooden shaft. Then he wrapped cloth around the butt end of the chisel and jammed it into the notch, tying it to the staff with a piece of the cloth rope. He soon had a functional spear about five feet long.

The Scorpion wiped his sweating brow on his forearm and longed for a cool drink. If they didn't get water soon they would begin to die.

Kelly looked at him anxiously. Her lips were dry and cracked. Her eyes were huge and luminous. They seemed to dominate her face. It reminded him of the faces of starving children back in Asia. He looked away, not wanting her to know what he was thinking.

"Cramped up here," he muttered.

"Yeah, now I know how a sardine feels," she sighed, wedging her body against the hard rock to give him a few extra millimeters of space.

He showed her how he wanted her to hold the lamp so that the light shone dimly on the opposite side of the well at the junction of the top stone and the lip.

"I'm going to chip away at the far side. When the underpinning rock is gone, the stone will tilt or fall that way and we'll be able to get out."

"What makes you so sure it won't fall this way, on top of us?" she asked.

"Because they haven't repealed the laws of physics yet."

"With my luck, they're probably working on it right now," she wisecracked.

"Don't worry. The only time you can get politicians to agree on anything, they're probably making a mistake," he grinned and hefting the spear in his right hand for a second, thrust it hard at the opposite lip of the well. The clink of flint hitting true was followed by a big chunk of rock splitting away from under the massive top-stone sealing them in.

"Wow! You hit that like you mean to kill someone," Kelly remarked.

"I do," the Scorpion replied, tight-lipped.

He braced himself against the niche, holding on to the

bare stone with his left hand as he jabbed savagely at the far rock edge. As each blow landed, the reverberations passed down the wooden shaft to his battered hand, causing him to wince at every blow. But he was only inches away from freedom, he thought, stabbing relentlessly at the far wall, his face almost demonic in its intensity.

Suddenly Kelly's voice broke through his concentration.

"What was that?" she asked.

"I didn't hear anything," he said, stopped.

They listened intently. There was nothing but the sounds of their own labored breathing.

"That!" she cried, fear rippling through her voice.

A sound like distant thunder filtered through the silence.

"What do you think . . ." she began.

"Shh . . ." he hissed.

The thunder came again. Then the rumbling was much closer. The ground trembled. Pebbles trickled down in the blackness. The ledge began to sway and shake. The Scorpion and Kelly embraced desperately as the rumbling engulfed them.

"Is it an earthquake?" she screamed, her voice barely audible above the ear-splitting roar of sound. Even as she cried out, the realization of what was happening hit him square between the eyes like a bullet.

"No, bombs! Our side is attacking!" he shouted.

Suddenly they were blinded by brilliant sunlight flooding the well. An ear-shattering explosion seemed to tear the earth open. The giant slab which had sealed the well stood upright for one impossible instant. Kelly screamed.

The Scorpion had a split-second view of blue sky before it was blotted out by the slab's massive black shape hurtling down upon them.

The Citadel

THE SKY HAD NEVER seemed so blue, so bright. He stared up at it in wonder. Then he remembered that he was alive.

It had been a near thing. He was running through his nine lives very quickly, the Scorpion admitted to himself. The giant boulder had just missed them, tucked securely in their niche, as it crashed down into the well. All around he heard the sounds of battle, the explosions and shouts and the air thick as rain with the rattle of small-arms fire. He had to get to Abdul Sa'ad at all costs or King Salim was history, he knew. He grabbed the crude spear and prepared to spring over the side. The noise was deafening.

He shouted at Kelly to stay in the niche.

"Where are you going?" she cried.

"I have work to do," he snapped.

"I'm coming too," she said, starting to get up. He shoved her back down.

"Don't be stupid! This is the safest place. It'd take a direct hit from above to get you. Just keep your head down, and you'll be OK," he said, crouching on the ledge, his head just below the lip of the well.

"What about you?"

"I'll be back for you."

"Will you? Will you, really?" she cried.

"Yes," he said, looking into her incredible violet eyes for an instant before vaulting over the edge.

Almost immediately he found himself being fired upon. White-hot fragments of metal whizzed all around him as he crawled like a scurrying insect on the burning ground. He couldn't get a fix on the source. It seemed to be coming from everywhere all at once. He crawled blindly without direction.

Suddenly a shape loomed up off to the side barely ten feet

away. It was one of Abdul Sa'ad's soldiers rising up and aiming his AK-47 directly at the Scorpion's head. In desperation, the Scorpion flung the spear with all his might.

The soldier stared with stunned disbelief at the wooden spear shaft protruding from his belly. He seemed too shocked to do anything but stand there, as if unable to believe that he had been killed by a spear in this day and age. The Scorpion leaped forward, kicking at the soldier's thigh and grabbing for the AK-47. As the soldier fell abruptly backward, the spear standing straight up like a flagpole, the Scorpion had already grabbed the Kalachnikov away. He fired a round into the soldier's head to make sure the gun worked. The bullet shattered the skull like a smashed melon.

Ricochets whined all around the Scorpion's feet, the fire coming from the direction of the old fortress. He dived behind the body, burying his face in the blood-moistened sand. He could hear the thunks as bullets slammed into the body. If he didn't get to King Salim soon, everything was lost, but he was pinned down with nothing between him and the fortress but flat open space and rubble.

In the distance he could see a line of slowly advancing Saudi National Guard tanks and APCs, white puffs of smoke billowing from their guns. And beyond was a ragged army of tribesmen on foot and in pick-up trucks, firing wildly as they advanced under the billowing green banner of the House of Saud strung from radio antennae. And his heart leaped up as among them he saw the white Toyota trucks of the Mutayr as they charged screaming their battle cry, "Allah Akhbar!" "God is Great!" at the top of their lungs. It had worked! he thought triumphantly. They had found him by the transmitter and the tribesmen and National Guard had rallied around the king.

As the tanks approached Abdul Sa'ad's forward positions, the lines erupted in white smoke. He saw a National Guard tank hit a mine and explode in a fireball spitting metal fragments and black smoke. Three army tanks lurched out of the citadel behind him like prehistoric beasts, their cannons pointed like ugly snouts. They lumbered forward, firing straight at the attackers. Fire erupted on all sides and the attacking line began to waver. The Scorpion could see the tribesmen being mown down like wheat and still he could do nothing.

Short savage firefights reached a crescendo at a dozen points. It was hard to determine what was happening, like a chess game with a confused board. Suddenly, the thought struck him that in this battle as in chess, the winner would be determined not by how many of the enemy you removed, but by who captured the king.

Salim! he thought, a sinking feeling in the pit of his stomach. He had to find Salim! There was no time left.

The Scorpion fired from behind the corpse at the fortress, then rolled sideways from the body and suddenly began an insane zig-zagging sprint towards an ancient rubble pile near the fortress wall.

One of the tanks swerved towards him and began firing its machine gun at him. The steel treads ground towards him, cutting him off from the fortress. The bullets stitched a jagged line in the sand, racing relentlessly towards the Scorpion. He was running wildly, as if his lungs would burst. The bullets drilled into the sand with tiny explosions of white dust almost at his feet. His spine tensed for the inevitable bullet in his back. Just then, a royal Saudi jet fighter loomed behind him firing at the tank. He dived behind the rubble pile.

There was a massive explosion close by. The Scorpion buried his face in the sand as a clatter of red hot metal rained all around him. He heard screams and looked up. Thick oily black smoke poured from the burning tank. He saw two crewmen, their clothes on fire, leap from the turret and run blindly towards the minefield before collapsing in blackened heaps.

The jet fighter banked in the distance, then tore back for another pass, its cannons blazing. The fighter's needle nose seemed to be pointed right at the Scorpion. It came in very fast and so low he could see the pilot's face. The fighter's bullets tore through the ancient mud-brick fortress wall behind him. A large section of wall, virtually puréed by the slugs, collapsed in a heap of dust. Even before the fighter had passed over, the Scorpion was already up and running at the newly created gap in the fortress wall. Leaping over the shattered brick remnants of the ancient wall, he was through the gap and into the courtyard before Abdul Sa'ad's men even realized he was there.

The courtyard was a mass of confusion, like an ant-hill kicked open. Soldiers ran about aimlessly, firing wildly into the air or at each other for no apparent reason. All along the sides of the courtyard ran a long colonnade. At the far side was the inner citadel of the fortress. That was where he had to go, the Scorpion thought. But his way was blocked by the panicked soldiers. He cocked the rifle and aimed.

A knot of khaki-clad soldiers along the parapet turned their weapons down on the courtyard, then froze at the sight of the Scorpion who was methodically mowing down a scurrying crowd of soldiers with a long burst from the AK-47. Their mouths dropped open in horror. They had thought him dead. Prince Abdul Sa'ad had told them the Scorpion had been destroyed, but clearly he was too powerful a demon. He had risen from the dead!

Few doubted that he was a demon, standing there naked except for a tattered white rag around his waist, his hair matted and unruly, his eyes demon-red and wild. His sun-bronzed body was magnificent, every muscle clearly etched as if carved out of solid stone. He seemed oblivious of the firing around him, as if the legend was true, that bullets fired at him turned to drops of water.

One soldier, fear rattling in his throat, made an incomprehensible sound and suddenly took to his heels. An officer screamed at them to fire and when they hesitated, he grabbed a gun and aimed it at the Scorpion. With a kind of sixth sense, the Scorpion glanced up just at that moment and in a single sweeping movement fired almost without aiming. The officer toppled from the parapet, a bloody scoop of flesh where one of his eyes had been. Screaming in terror the soldiers threw down their weapons and fled through the gate, where they were cut down by the cross fire from the approaching tribesmen.

Bandar came rushing from a corner turret, his good eye darting left and right as he sought the Scorpion. Without bothering to check whether his own men were in the way or not, he lobbed a hand grenade down into the courtyard. He fired into the explosion, spraying bullets all around the courtyard, but when the smoke cleared, the Scorpion had gone, vanished into thin air. With a terrible scowl Bandar turned on the poor corporal who had dared tell him the Scorpion was alive and shot him between the eyes. It was impossible! He himself had shot the vile spawn of camel slime in the heart!

But Scorpion or no Scorpion, Abdul Sa'ad was doomed, Bandar decided. No one was supposed to have found them until the king had abdicated and the succession was clear. By what demon's trick had they been discovered? Treason or worse, he thought darkly. But one thing was certain. Abdul Sa'ad could not be the *Mahdi*, the Chosen of Allah, after all. The *Mahdi* would never have failed so badly, Bandar thought. But he, Bandar, still lived and there were debts due him. The image of the American woman came to him, her white breasts heaving in fear, her loins moist with desire. It was *kismet*, he swore to himself. With a wolfish howl, Bandar whirled and ran for the fortress gate closest to the old well.

Even as Bandar broke for the gate, the Scorpion emerged from behind a crumbling column, his face half-concealed in the shadow of the colonnade. For a split second he might have had a shot at Bandar, but he was almost out of ammunition. He would find Bandar with Abdul Sa'ad, he told himself. There would be time to settle old scores.

Suddenly, he felt his spine prickle, somehow aware of someone behind him. The corner of his eye caught the gleam of a *khanjar* blade. The Scorpion whirled and fired almost point blank into a bearded Shiite soldier's face, opening a bleeding red hole where the nose used to be. The dying Shiite slashed savagely with the *khanjar* as he fell forward. The Scorpion fired again, but there was only the hollow click of the hammer on the firing pin. He had fired his last round! The blade sliced into the Scorpion's arm even as he tried to sidestep. He swung the rifle with both arms, smashing the butt into the back of the Shiite's head, cracking the skull like an eggshell.

The Scorpion retrieved the dead Shiite's *khanjar* and his M-16 rifle. It had a full clip. Two more Shiites ducked under the portico, their guns blazing. The Scorpion shot them where they stood.

He charged across the colonnade, jumping over the bodies of the dead Shiites and through the arched doorway into the ancient citadel which stood at the heart of the fortress. He raced for the stone stairs leading to the old tower, where he had heard Salim's scream coming from, just before Bandar had tried to execute him at the well.

The narrow steps were steep and barely a foot wide. There was no banister and only a dim light filtered through the dusty air which seemed as ancient as the fortress itself, as if it had been here since the beginning of time.

The Scorpion paused before ascending. His left arm had been cut near the bicep. It was bleeding steadily, but there was no time left to bind it. His luck still held, he thought, at least the muscle hadn't been sliced through.

He glanced around the citadel corridor, but it was empty. A long line of colonnaded arches made of mud brick stood lonely sentinel over the dust of centuries. The sounds of battle outside were muted, as if he were under water. He peered cautiously upward. There were about a hundred stairs, made of stone worn smooth as glass and concave in the centers from centuries of long-ago foot traffic. At the top of the stairs the outline of a square opening could be dimly seen; the stairway was a death trap, but there was no help for it, he decided. It was the only way up.

He began to climb the stairs carefully, as if walking on eggs. He kept the M-16 aimed up at the opening on top. As he glided upwards silently as a ghost, the roar of explosions outside began to grow louder. He was about halfway up when he heard the clicking sounds of something bouncing down the steps.

Two hand grenades!

There was no escape! He couldn't duck or sidestep or outrun them. There was only one chance. The Scorpion leaped upwards to meet them; only a second or two left. He caught one in his bare right hand and hurled it up towards the opening at the top of the stair as he swept the second grenade sideways with his foot. Balance gone, he fell back against the fortress wall. He was tumbling back down the stairs when both grenades went off at once.

The grenade he had kicked exploded in mid-air well below him, the stairs partially shielding him from the razor-sharp fragments. His ears rang from the concussion and he couldn't hear the screams from above.

The Scorpion clawed at the stone stairs to arrest his fall and scrambled crazily upward on all fours, pouring automatic fire into the opening.

He shot up through the opening like an exploding champagne cork, firing in mid-air in a wild blind arc. The bullets stitched across the middle of a wide-eyed Bedu officer holding a Colt. 45 and staring in terror at the three bleeding carcasses collapsed around the stair opening where the second grenade had blown. The Bedu tried to raise the pistol, but it clattered to the stone floor even before the Scorpion emptied the last M-16 rounds into him.

The Scorpion dropped the M-16 and grabbing the Colt, leaped at the wooden ladder in the corner leading to the top of the turret. As he grabbed the bottom rung, a dark face peered down at him from a narrow opening at the top of the ladder. The Scorpion fired and the man's rifle fell with a clatter down to the turret floor. The dead Arab slumped across the narrow opening. The bullet had hit him in the forehead, making it look as if he had three eyes.

The Scorpion pulled himself up the ladder. He paused at the top for a second. What if he was too late? In a single movement, he yanked the dead Arab down and dodged sideways. As the body hurtled down, the Scorpion sprang up on to the roof of the turret, his heart pounding.

The three men froze like figures in an improbable tableau.

Prince Abdul Sa'ad stood in the center of the turret, a scimitar held high above his head. His face was dark with rage. The long curved blade glittering like ice in the brilliant sunlight. At his feet knelt the half-naked figure of the king, his torn white *thaub* hanging from his waist like a skirt. His hands were bound behind him, the fingertips red and bleeding from where his fingernails had been ripped away. It was an execution, the Scorpion realized. Another second and he would have been too late.

The prince seemed to be standing in space, the small platform surrounded by the immense blue sky. Far below, from the crenellated parapet around the rim of the tower, the battle could be seen raging among the ruins, jagged as a lava field. The ancient tower swayed with the explosions like a tree in a summer storm.

Abdul Sa'ad's eyes glittered murderously as a snake's.

"Who dares . . ." Abdul Sa'ad hissed and the Scorpion realized that he was utterly insane.

"You know who I am, O Prince of the Destroying Flame," the Scorpion replied, his eyes narrowed to slits against the blinding sky glare.

"You are too late, O Scorpion who was dead and now is spewed up from Hell. Thy sting cannot harm the *Mahdi*, the

Chosen of Allah. Now all the nations shall see his sword out-stretched in glory, shining like the Night of the *Qadr*," in-toned Abdul Sa'ad, his eyes fixed upward.

"No, by the Dawn and the Ten Nights. Your armies are scattered like the evil tribes of Aad and Thamoud," the Scorpion said.

"Too late," howled Abdul Sa'ad beginning to slash down with the scimitar at his brother's bared neck.

The Colt bucked in the Scorpion's hand as he fired. The bullet caught Abdul Sa'ad in the temple. The sword clattered on the hot stone slate. Abdul Sa'ad collapsed over the kneeling king. As King Salim straightened up, Abdul Sa'ad rolled face down on the roof.

With a slash of the *khanjar*, the Scorpion freed the king's hands. Together, they shakily rose to their feet. Salim looked sadly down at Abdul Sa'ad's body. He sighed as only an Arab can sigh, from the very depths of his soul.

"He was my half-brother, you understand. A son of our father, the great King Abd al Aziz himself. He had much promise once. Too much perhaps. But unused talent is like uneaten food; after a time it begins to fester and rot. It will poison a man's soul, O Scorpion.

"It is hard. To be betrayed by a brother and saved by a stranger is hard," Salim said wearily. He leaned heavily on the Scorpion's shoulder. Then he forced himself to straighten up. He walked on shaky legs to the parapet.

"I must show myself. It will hearten my soldiers," he said, and waved down at his soldiers still cleaning up the last pockets of resistance. Then he turned back, an oddly playful look in his eye. "What took you so long? I was beginning to worry."

"So was I, Your Majesty. So was I."

The king gestured awkwardly at the Scorpion's wounded arm as if he wished to bless it somehow.

"Your arm. It's bleeding badly."

"I know. There'll be time for it now," the Scorpion replied, cradling his blood-slick arm. Then something in his expression changed, causing King Salim to touch his shoulder with concern.

"What is it?" Salim asked.

"I was wrong. There is no time. Bandar must have gone back for the girl," the Scorpion replied, a sickening feeling in the pit of his stomach.

The Sands of Dahna

THE HOT WIND blew steadily into their faces as they pushed deeper into the heart of the desert. Youssef drove the Land Rover hard, its four-wheel drive ploughing across the flat sandy plain.

Youssef's face was battle-weary and grim. Climbing into the Land-Rover, the Scorpion had said the forbidden word at long last.

"It's time to settle all accounts—and for Aisha," he had said. Youssef had nodded. Nothing is forgotten. He followed the tire tracks of Bandar's stolen Jeep as fixedly as a bloodhound. It wasn't hard. The parallel lines were the only tracks on the virgin sand. From time immemorial, travelers had avoided the uncharted wastes of Dahna. Perhaps that was why Bandar had fled in this direction. Youssef glanced over at his brother. The Scorpion lounged beside him, cradling an M-16 against his shoulder like a baby.

It was late afternoon; still enough time, the Scorpion thought. The desert air had the opalescent sheen it acquires just before the long shadows and colors of dusk begin to emerge. The elongated shadow of the Land-Rover raced far ahead of them towards the distant rolling dunes of the Dahna. They had to catch Bandar before it grew too dark. Some of the dunes in the Dahna were over a hundred meters high. There were countless places for Bandar to hide among the steep hills of sand which could move ten or fifteen feet in a day.

The desert air was blistering on his skin. He could smell the odor of the desert. It was an odor that had no odor—only heat, like water that has no taste yet is unmistakable. Youssef and he both leaned forward and scanned the empty horizon ahead like a pair of hunting falcons. Behind the Land-Rover was an endless plume of dust churned up by the wheels. Ahead, he could see only the twin tire tracks leading onward across the honey-colored plain and the distant shapes of the dunes on the horizon.

He tried to put the girl out of his mind. He didn't want to think about how he had come back to the well, knowing he would find it empty, yet still getting that hollow kicked-in-the-stomach feeling when he found her gone.

It wasn't hard to track Bandar's movements. A trail of bodies, including some he had simply driven over, led them into the desert. There was still fighting and mopping up to do and Harris tried to fill him in over the radio. The Saudi National Guard had rallied to the king and loyal elements of the Royal Saudi Army had halted the Yemeni drive towards Mecca at Taif. There was a report that the Cuban, Huevas, had been killed outside Taif. Fighting had broken out at Qamr Bay on the Yemeni-Omani border. PLO commandos had blown up the oil facilities at Sea Island and Ras Tanura, but were now trapped by Saudi National Guard troops supported by U.S. Marine helicopters and naval air support. Fighting was reported at Basra in Iraq. Iran had mobilized forces on both its Soviet and Iraqi borders and had vowed to destroy the U.S. fleet and close the Straits of Hormuz. Apart from some bow-scraping incidents and a few dog-fights in the Straits, the U.S. and Soviet fleets stalked each other but hadn't gone to DEFCON Red yet.

Harris wanted a report on the ground situation, but the Scorpion left the receiver dangling and Harris talking to the air. A Rualla tribesman picked up the receiver and listened to the incomprehensible English sounds.

The Scorpion had grabbed clothes and an M-16 from a dead Mutayri and he and Youssef had driven off.

Why had she left the well, he wondered. Was it fear? Or was it getting too hot there? Or panic—after all she'd never before been in the sheer chaos and horror that is battle. Or maybe something else. Or maybe Bandar.

But Bandar had found her. Bandar, whose very touch made her shudder like the slithering caress of a snake. And now they were racing for the darkness. It was *kismet*, the Scorpion knew. Either he or Bandar would die before the evening star rose over the dunes.

The Land-Rover began to buck as the plain broke up into wavelets. The wheels sprayed plumes on either side as they drove straight through hillocks of sand. Behind them the sun began to droop towards the horizon, a blood-red tinge beginning to smear across the sky.

Youssef nudged his shoulder and pointed dead ahead. "Allah is good. Look there!"

Then the Scorpion saw it: the tiny shape flickering in the windshield glass, the man and woman like toy figures in the distance.

"Faster. We have to get them before they reach the dunes," the Scorpion shouted and was rewarded with a surge as Youssef floored the accelerator.

The Land-Rover began to skid and fishtail as they bounced roughly across the humps of sand. The Scorpion had to grip the M-16 tightly with one battered hand and hang on with the other, but they were closer. They could see the two figures clearly now. The slender image of the woman, her golden hair streaming in the wind and the man in his black *bisht* fighting the wheel, glowed in the reddish dusk light as if outlined in neon.

The Scorpion leaned dangerously out of the open window. Hanging on to the side and rocketing swayingly over the uneven ground, he raised the M-16 and fired short sharp bursts at the Jeep. He had to stop it, even at the risk of hitting Kelly. Ahead he saw Bandar raise a rifle, turn and fire a single shot back at them.

The bullet ricocheted off the door mirror with a metallic whine, leaving a deep scar in the twisted chrome. It was an incredible shot, firing backwards while driving over uneven terrain. Bandar's skill had to be taken into account, the Scorpion realized, even as he leaned out and fired again, emptying the clip. Whether any of the bullets hit the Jeep he couldn't tell. They seemed to have no effect.

They were beginning to close up, the skidding Jeep barely a hundred meters ahead. But the light had turned fiery red, as if the horizon was burning. There was little time left.

Then, on his third clip, the Scorpion got lucky. He clearly heard the metallic whunk as the bullet slammed into the Jeep's gas tank. The air filled with the strong scent of gas as the Jeep's tank began to leak as though a tap had been turned on. Suddenly the Scorpion was thrown sideways as Youssef swerved to avoid Bandar's aim. The slug tore through the windshield, creating an instant spider web, and embedded itself in the Land-Rover's roof, passing cleanly between Youssef's and the Scorpion's head.

They could hear the Jeep sputtering ahead. Youssef pumped the brakes like a demon and swerved the Land-Rover broadside, across the sands. He and the Scorpion dived for cover behind it as it skidded to a stop. Even before it had stopped they were already firing across the hood at the stalled Jeep.

With a savage growl, Bandar hurled Kelly out of the Jeep and leaped after her, using her as a shield between him and the Land-Rover. He grabbed her by the throat and kept the muzzle of the AK-47 jammed into the underside of her jaw.

"Scorpion! Throw down your rifle or by the Prophet's beard I'll blow her head off!" Bandar shouted.

His voice had an ugly edge to it that caused the hairs on the back of the Scorpion's neck to rise. He and Youssef looked at each other. Then they looked back at Bandar standing behind the girl. Her eyes were blank and mute as a rabbit's. She was utterly terror-stricken.

"Scorpion! I'll kill her! I mean it!" Bandar howled, a fleck of froth at the corner of his mouth giving him the appearance of a mad dog. The Scorpion had no doubt whatever that he meant it.

"Shoot her and you'll be dead before she hits the ground," he called back.

"Throw down your gun and she lives. This is your last chance," Bandar screamed.

"No, Bandar. If I throw down my gun, we're all dead. Either way the woman dies. She means nothing to me. All I want is a clear shot at you."

"You have murdered her! Let it be on your head!" Bandar howled in a frenzy. His finger tightened on the trigger.

"Wait!" Youssef called.

Bandar hesitated. If he fired, he was doomed. His last card had been trumped. He had only malevolence left.

"Settle this the way it began . . . with *khanjars*. The woman is the prize for the victor," Youssef said.

An utter silence settled like dust over the desert. The wind died and the sand ceased its timeless whisper. Only the ragged animal breathing of the woman could be heard anywhere.

"So be it!" Bandar announced contemptuously. He flung the woman aside and tossed the AK-47 back into the Jeep. The *khanjar* glittered in his hand as he waited. A trembling Kelly crawled behind the wing, her eyes wide as saucers, an unreadable look in them.

"Do this for me. If he should win, shoot him," the Scorpion muttered to Youssef out of the side of his mouth.

"As Allah is my judge," Youssef swore.

The Scorpion stood and dropped his gun. He pulled the *khanjar* from his belt sheath and stepped out from behind the Land-Rover.

Bandar and the Scorpion stood facing each other about ten

feet apart. The sand was warm and red as blood. The setting sun had turned them all into figures of fire and shadow. The Scorpion's heart pounded. It was for this moment that he had been born. His *kismet* had brought him to this desolate arena as surely as if he had been guided along a track. Now all the remembered insults and humiliations came back. Rage bubbled under icy control within him, the optimal killing attitude. They both went into a crouching stance, knives held before them, circling in a deadly rite as ancient as time itself, never taking their eyes off the opponent's dagger. The blades were razor sharp. They glittered like rubies in the scarlet dusklight.

Bandar suddenly dropped his shoulder and stabbed forward, the blade tip coming within an inch of the Scorpion's belly, but the Scorpion didn't flinch. He had judged it a feint.

They circled in the sand, feinting and dodging to test each other's reflexes. The Scorpion flicked his *khanjar* at Bandar's wrist. Bandar's blade circled under the Scorpion's and stabbed at the Scorpion's heart. The Scorpion twisted aside at the last second. Allah, he thought. Bandar was quick as a cat. Bandar's bad eye glowed red as a bloodstone.

The Scorpion moved. He feinted at Bandar's arm, then circled under Bandar's parry and thrust forward. Bandar's *khanjar* slashed back at the Scorpion's, blade ringing dully against blade and then they were apart, circling again. This time a new wariness had come into Bandar's good eye.

Bandar stepped back two paces, whirled and as he turned back towards the Scorpion, there was a shadow of something dark in his other hand. The Scorpion heard a muffled scream from Kelly's direction even as he reacted with a back-to-front crescent kick. His foot caught Bandar's automatic as the trigger jerked and sent the gun spinning into the shadows as it fired. The loud report shattered the stillness like crystal.

With a wild howl, Bandar came at the Scorpion, slashing savagely and methodically. The Scorpion backed away, parrying the blows, blade to blade, counterslashing back. Suddenly, Bandar feinted left and struck right. The Scorpion twisted away from the thrust and kicked out, his foot catching Bandar's shoulder and knocking him sideways. But his own footing slipped and he went down.

Bandar was on him like a bull on a matador, stabbing in a frenzy. The Scorpion saw the blade coming at his groin as if in slow motion. He grabbed a handful of sand with his left hand and flung it into Bandar's face as he rolled just out of reach. Bandar howled like a blinded Cyclops and slashed wildly at the Scorpion.

Now, the Scorpion told himself as he scrambled to his feet. Now!

He stepped inside the circle of Bandar's frenzy, using a forearm to block against Bandar's forearm and side-kicking at the inside of Bandar's knee. As Bandar began to go down, he thrust desperately up at the Scorpion's rib cage. The Scorpion chopped at Bandar's wrist with the hard edge of his left hand as he simultaneously made a wrist-twisting slash with the *khanjar*, disemboweling Bandar with a single wrenching cut.

Bandar's scream was not human. His insides spilled out on to the sand like tangled snakes. He slithered on the ground like a dying worm, slashing at the Scorpion's feet in his final frenzy. The Scorpion danced out of the way and with a single savage slice, cut the forearm muscle of Bandar's knife hand to the bone.

He watched Bandar writhing in agony on the ground, screaming unintelligible sounds. Suddenly, an M-16 opened fire. Bandar arched his back like a bow and was still. His good eye stared open and empty at the evening star rising over the dunes of Dahna.

"Now it's over. Aisha is paid for," Youssef said, standing over Bandar, the M-16 dangling from his hand.

Kelly came wordlessly up to the Scorpion and they stumbled back towards the Land-Rover, their arms around each other. Before they got into the Land-Rover she put her blistered lips to his ear and whispered:

"I have to know. Would you have let him kill me?"

The Scorpion caressed her long blond hair with his torn fingers and kissed her lips with great tenderness. His eyes were sparks of fire in the last red rays of the sun.

"No," he said.

It was the first lie of their relationship.

Bub al Bahrain

THE MIDNIGHT SILENCE of the dark narrow street was broken by the barking of a small dog. It belonged to the owner of the *dar*, who kept it in the tiny courtyard shaded by eucalyptus trees that he shared with the *Inglizi*. The yellowish mongrel stood in the center of the courtyard barking at the shadows. A dark figure came out of the shadows and the dog flattened his ears and charged, yipping wildly. A sudden movement and the dog lay motionless in the shadows. The figure stumbled hurriedly across the moonlit courtyard and knocked at Braithwaite's back door. The door was flung open and a rectangle of light splashed almost, but not quite, to the feet of the small carcass.

"Amair! C-c-come in, d-dear boy," Braithwaite stuttered.

The young Shiite slipped in, glancing nervously behind him as Braithwaite carefully closed and locked the door. He turned and tenderly taking the Shiite's hand led him to the divan. The Shiite leaned his expensive lizard-skin attaché case against the divan. It looked out of place next to the threadbare upholstery.

"I fear for you," Braithwaite said.

"You should," the Arab burst out petulantly. "Your Scorpion has ruined us."

His sweat-slick face reflected the lamplight like a discolored mirror. At the sound of his voice, the cobra stirred evilly in its basket, flicking its forked tongue repeatedly in their direction. At the sight of him, Amair shivered like a trapped animal. It reminded him of how much he had dreaded coming here. But Nuruddin had insisted.

"I hate that crazy old *cuni*. Him and that filthy snake of his! Every time he touches me, it makes my flesh crawl," he had protested.

"Remember Qatif," Nuruddin had replied, his eyes narrowed. In 1979, a group of religious zealots led by a fanatic who proclaimed himself to be the long-awaited *Mahdi* had invaded the Sacred Mosque in Mecca. When they heard the news, the suppressed Shiite minority had rioted for days in the city of Qatif. The rioters had been ruthlessly suppressed by the Royal Saudi Army. Although none of Amair's family had been hurt, his mother's family had come from Qatif and he had taken it personally.

"Why not just leave him? Let the old *cuni* take his chances," he had objected, a spoiled whine in his voice. When he had first become involved with Nuruddin, they had told him he was a hero. But when he heard the sounds of battle as they fled Dariyyah and their Mercedes had been buzzed by a Royal Army helicopter, he could scarcely breathe. And when he saw the bodies near Riyadh airport after the fighting there, he had gagged and barely had time to stick his head out of the window to be sick. They hadn't told him it was going to be like this.

"If either the Scorpion or al-Amir, his police *ashab*, gets to Braithwaite, they'll get to you and through you to me," Nuruddin had said.

"Better to kill the old fool," Amair had truculently insisted, not realizing the implication of what he was saying.

"In time," soothed Nuruddin, an odd gleam in his eye that made Amair tremble. "In the meantime, you must get the old man to Europe. Once there, you can abandon him as you like. It is all arranged. The *Roosees* will protect you."

But how to convince Braithwaite to leave, Amair wondered, glancing at the old man. The *Americani* was supposed to have died. It was Nuruddin's fault. Now they were all marked men.

"Al-Amir is after me. And after him, the Scorpion. They will kill us," Amair cried.

"I'll t-t-talk to him, *habibi*. I still have some c-c-clout, you know," Braithwaite said. In the corner, the snake began to coil, as though to strike.

"It's too late for that. We have to run—to Europe. It's all arranged," Amair insisted. Why was the old man being so stubborn?

"I c-couldn't let you, not with martial law and all," Braithwaite insisted. He hugged the younger man to his bony chest, holding him tightly.

"Help me!" pleaded Amair, tears starting out of the corners of his eyes. When all else failed, tears had always worked for him.

"Oh my d-d-dear, my dear," Braithwaite murmured, and kissed Amair full on the lips. Amair suffered it. He'd do anything to get the old *cuni* to move. Sheikh al-Khatifa's police might come barging in at any minute.

"I have been given false passports, money, instructions, everything," Amair gasped, pulling out of the embrace. He placed the attaché case on the coffee table.

"Where did you get this? Nuruddin?" Braithwaite inquired, throwing a sudden suspicious glance at Amair. How deep in was Amair, he wondered. He began to realize that it might be too late to save the boy.

Amair nodded. He was to go over everything with Braithwaite. The papers and the money would convince the old man, Nuruddin had insisted, handing over the locked case. And they must do it when alone and in a place safe from prying eyes. To have such papers was proof of their treason, he had reminded the Shiite. The prescribed penalty for such an offense was one hundred lashes, followed by beheading. The very thought of it made Amair queasy.

"Show me," Braithwaite commanded. Amair took the key from his pocket and turned it in the lock.

The sudden explosion shattered the silent night. The street was illuminated by a brilliant orange fireball that made the old stone houses glow red as though dusk had returned.

In a white Mercedes parked far down the street, Nuruddin leaned forward and tapped his driver on the shoulder. As the Mercedes passed the shattered ruin of Braithwaite's building, Nuruddin nodded with satisfaction. What was left of the side of the building was a wall of flames. There could be no survivors.

Now at least two loose ends were taken care of, he thought. As the car sped through the silent streets of Manama back towards the old walled gate of the city, the Bab al Bahrain, and then on towards the Airport Road, Nuruddin nervously fingered his prayer beads and tried to decide what to do. He had to get away from Bahrain, but where? Salim's forces had put down all resistance and the American presence in the Gulf was stronger than ever. How would Moscow react now that the Molotov Plan was a complete shambles?

Ya Allah, but it was all because of that Scorpion and Prince Abdul Sa'ad's incompetence. Who would have believed it? The man was a demon. Four times they had set traps for him and four times he had escaped. He had blown the plot and sent the survivors scurrying in the darkness like rats, their nest destroyed.

But at least he, Nuruddin, had tied up the last two loose ends which could link the Arabian fiasco to the Russians.

Moscow hated loose ends.

Well, at least his immediate plans were set. He had to catch the Concorde flight to Paris, then on to Geneva with the help of sympathetic French communist intellectuals. Once in Switzerland—well, the Swiss knew how to treat someone with a large numbered bank account. Then he could safely gauge Moscow's mood.

The Mercedes began to slow. Annoyed, Nuruddin began

to lean forward to tap his driver. Didn't the fool understand he had a plane to catch? Then he saw the flashing yellow lights of the police road block at the Bab al Bahrain.

Nuruddin frowned. Was it possible that al-Amir had reacted so quickly? He began to sweat. Then he relaxed. It was a standard police roadblock. Since the fighting in Arabia, Bahrain had been under martial law. There were roadblocks at all major intersections, he reminded himself.

He leaned back and reached for his well-upholstered wallet. Allah be praised, Bahrain was still a civilized place, where *baksheesh* could buy any official. With a familiar sigh, he began calculating how much he would need to bribe his way through the roadblock.

The two figures watched the white Mercedes approach the roadblock from the darkness of a parked sedan. One of the figures lit a cigarette. It glowed in the darkness like a firefly. They watched the Mercedes stop and said nothing.

A Bahraini police sergeant glanced in the direction of the parked car and spotted the cigarette glow. He motioned to his men as they approached the Mercedes, submachine guns at the ready.

The sergeant motioned for the windows to be rolled down, then demanded their papers.

The two figures in the sedan watched the nervously smiling brown face in the back seat of the Mercedes lean forward to hand over an identity card together with what was obviously a thick wad of *riyals*.

Suddenly, Nuruddin's smile froze as the submachine guns swung into position. The sound of automatic fire shattered the night as the three policemen sprayed the interior of the Mercedes for a full thirty seconds, turning the car into a bleeding metal sieve. Then the police jumped into a patrol car and sped away. Other policemen quickly dismantled the roadblock and drove away in another car. It was over in seconds.

An unreal silence returned to the intersection blocked by the unmoving Mercedes.

The two figures in the sedan glanced at each other.

"Good job, lieutenant. I'm sure *asayid* al-Amir will be pleased at your efficiency," the Scorpion said.

"I'll tell him of your approval. And will you be leaving Bahrain shortly?" the young Bahraini police lieutenant asked, raising his eyebrow to indicate that this was al-Amir's polite way of telling the Scorpion to get out.

The Scorpion nodded and said, "I have only to go back to the hotel and collect the woman, who has suffered much in all this."

The Bahraini raised his hands as if in surrender.

"Everything is understood. Go with Allah and unto you peace. This," he said with a nod to indicate the unmoving Mercedes, "is the last of them, isn't it?"

"It's all over now," the Scorpion said and started to leave the car. Then he turned back to the Bahraini for a moment.

"Just out of curiosity. How will you explain all this to the public?" gesturing at the Mercedes.

"We'll blame it on foreign agents. After all, it's foreigners who cause all the trouble in the Middle East anyway," the Bahraini shrugged.

From the moment he entered the Gulf Hotel lobby, the Scorpion knew something had gone wrong. For one thing, there were too many Arabs in western suits with nothing to do at that hour of the morning in the lobby. An Arab who had "cop" painted indelibly all over him was taking an exaggerated interest in his copy of yesterday's *Al Bilad*.

He could feel eyes on his back as he entered the elevator. He pressed the button for the floor above his and took out the big Colt automatic, standing to the side of the door in case they were waiting to cut him down as soon as the door slid open, as they'd done to Fleming in Vienna. If it weren't for Kelly, waiting for him in the room, he'd be heading for the exit now, he thought.

The elevator slowed and he checked the mirror before leaping out, gun first. The hotel corridor was silent and empty. He crept quietly to the emergency exit and down the stairs to his floor. The corridor near his room was also empty, but he sensed it was being watched. He glanced up at the lighting fixtures as if they were looking back at him.

When he came to the door to his room, he found proof that it wasn't his imagination lying on the carpet next to the door: a tiny sliver of transparent, almost invisible plastic which he had wedged between the door and the jamb.

The Scorpion cocked the automatic. His palms began to sweat. According to standard procedure, he was standing in the red zone and should get out. If the door was rigged to an explosive, they could mail him home. But Kelly might still be there, he told himself. There was no going back.

With infinite care he turned the key in the lock. He held his breath. Nothing. He flung the door open and somersaulted into the center of the room, coming up in a crouch, his gun ready, but it was pointless.

"That was quite an entrance, Scorpion, but I think you're outgunned," al-Amir said, glancing around the room at the half-dozen of his men, their automatic weapons trained on the Scorpion.

"Where's the girl, Jassim?" the Scorpion asked.

"Gone. No—we had nothing to do with it," the Bahraini Chief of Police added hurriedly, seeing the iciness come into the Scorpion's gray eyes. "It was your own people. Company business. And I fear she seemed quite willing, *habibi*."

The Scorpion shook his head. It made no sense. "What about all this? A welcoming committee?"

Al-Amir bit his lip and absentmindedly rubbed the scar on his cheek. He was obviously troubled.

"It's your own people. CIA. They want you terminated, Scorpion. This is your firing squad."

"I don't get it."

Al-Amir shrugged and said, "Neither do I. If it were up to me you'd get a medal. You *Americani* are very difficult to understand."

The Scorpion aimed the Colt at al-Amir's head. "I'll take you with me, Jassim," he said.

Al-Amir raised his hands in mock surrender. "No need, Scorpion. I'm letting you go. A matter of sentiment. My lord, Sheikh al-Khatifa, is related through his maternal grandmother to your adopted father, Sheikh Zaid. Also, he wants to stay in King Salim's good graces and Salim owes you a life. But I must ask you to leave Bahrain at once. Things have been very noisy since you came to Manama, Scorpion," he said, leaning back on the sofa.

The Scorpion nodded and put away the gun. He sat on the sofa next to al-Amir and poured himself a drink of iced mineral water. His heart was pounding and there was a roaring in his head as if he were holding seashells to his ears.

"I wouldn't go back to the States if I were you," he heard al-Amir say.

The Scorpion shook his head.

"I'll report you dead. With both the CIA and the KGB wanting to terminate you, it's your only chance," al-Amir added.

"What will you do for a body?" the Scorpion asked.

"The driver of the Mercedes will do nicely for the CIA. The guns made quite a mess of him. I'm having his body brought here now."

The Scorpion stared into space. He raised the glass to his lips, but didn't drink.

The pattern was rearranging in his head. None of it made any sense and then all at once, it all made perfect sense. He drank the mineral water as if it were hemlock.

He had made the worst mistake an agent can make. He had completely misunderstood the nature of his mission.

One day a scorpion stood on the bank of a river. He wanted to cross it, but scorpions can't swim. So he went up to a frog and proposed that the frog carry him across. But the frog was afraid.

"You might sting me and I'll die," said the frog.

"Nonsense. If I sting you and you die, then I'm bound to drown too," the scorpion replied.

So the frog agreed and he began to swim across the river with the scorpion on his back. When they were halfway across, the scorpion stung the frog. With his last gasp, just before he sank, the frog asked the scorpion:

"But why? Now you'll die too. It doesn't make any sense."

"I can't help it. I'm a scorpion. It's in my nature to sting," said the scorpion.

—An Arab story, circa eighth
century A.D.

Part Four

Watergate

"DON'T TURN ON the light!"

Harris' hand hesitated by the switch. He had just come in. The apartment was dark except for the lights of the city reflected on the glass balcony door. Was that how the intruder had come in, he wondered. He carefully began to reach for his shoulder holster with his free hand.

"Another inch and I'll blow it away," the voice snapped sharply. It was at once chilling and yet oddly familiar.

"Who are you? What do you want?" Harris whispered nervously. His throat was dry.

"Use your left hand. Take out your gun and toss it on the carpet," the voice ordered.

Harris did as he was told. He tried to locate the voice. It seemed to be coming from somewhere in the living room.

A blow to the stomach doubled him over, knocking the wind out of him, followed by a savage kick in the mouth which sent him spinning to the floor. By the time he regained his senses, his hands had been tied behind him. He didn't have to check to know that the knots were tight and professional. Although it wasn't cold, he began to tremble.

He had recognized the voice.

"Is that you, Nick?" Harris asked in a shaky voice.

"Nick disappeared a long time ago," the voice said.

"The Scorpion," Harris managed to whisper.

"He's dead, haven't you heard?"

"How did you get into my apartment?"

"Come on, Bob. I thought security at the Watergate was a pretty clichéd topic," the voice said.

"You wouldn't do anything crazy . . . I mean, you're too

smart for that," Harris squeaked unable to conceal the quaver in his voice.

"A scorpion only knows how to do one thing, Bob. It knows how to sting," the Scorpion replied.

"Listen—I can explain—" Harris began.

"I know. You're good at that."

The Scorpion was seated in an armchair. He motioned Harris to the couch opposite him. Like Harris, the Scorpion wore a dinner jacket and black tie. Lounging across from each other like that against the backdrop of the city lights, they could have been posing for a whisky ad. For a moment they sat silently in the dark apartment, Harris watching the Scorpion, the Scorpion glancing away at the city lights.

From this side of the Watergate complex the floodlit dome of the Capitol Building sparkled white and clear, as if sculpted in snow. Below, he could see the lights of moving traffic reflected in the Potomac. In the distance the marble spire of the Washington Monument pointed at the sky like a rocket. It was the kind of view real-estate agents spend a lot of time talking about in order to avoid mentioning the price.

"Nice view," the Scorpion commented, gesturing at the lights. The movement of his hand set the ice cubes in his drink tinkling. His other hand held Harris's Smith and Wesson.38.

"Are . . . are you going to kill me?" Harris asked.

"Sheikh Zaid once taught me that it is easier to kill a man than to trust him."

"Trust was never a part of our relationship," Harris snapped. Suddenly, what had happened earlier at the embassy began to make some sense.

"No, we're not in the trusting business, are we?" the Scorpion admitted.

"I've been promoted. I'm deputy director now, Scorpion. You can't do business without me—" Harris began. He leaned back and crossed his legs, trying to look relaxed. But with his hands tied behind him, he simply looked uncomfortable.

"How was the party at the French Embassy tonight?" the Scorpion asked, knowing Harris would understand and hate him for it.

"Where's Kelly?" Harris demanded. His handsome all-American face suddenly looked very ugly. It made the Scorpion think of the picture of Dorian Gray.

"What's the matter, Bob? Lose your girl?" the Scorpion mildly observed.

"You son-of-a-bitch!" Harris exploded. He tried to struggle to his feet. The Scorpion's icy eyes narrowed. Harris subsided at once.

Harris swallowed hard and said, "How did you know? I didn't see you at the party."

The Scorpion grinned as widely as a Cheshire cat. He pulled out something dark and furry and tossed it onto the coffee table. It lay there like a dead animal.

"It never ceases to amaze me how unobservant people are. A bit of silly putty in the nostrils, some furry foliage"—gesturing at the phony beard—"a few chest decorations and you could fool your own mother," the Scorpion said, watching comprehension light in Harris's eyes as he remembered the bearded bore at the party complaining in atrocious English about the disastrous impact of U.S. interest rates on the franc.

"What made her run away? One minute she was fine and then all at once she turned white as a ghost and bolted," Harris asked.

"In a way, she did see a ghost at the banquet. She saw you speak to Gerard," the Scorpion said.

"Don't worry about Gerard, He's a dead man," Harris said.

"He's not the only one," the Scorpion replied.

Harris looked away. He seemed to be glancing around his apartment. It was furnished in white and chrome in the kind of expensive yet sterile luxury which says nothing about the owner except that he has money. When Harris turned back, there was a queasy look in his eyes, as if he had swallowed something that didn't agree with him.

"How did you do it?" Harris wanted to know. Despite everything, he couldn't suppress a note of professional curiosity.

The Scorpion shrugged and said, "Given the French connection, I knew Gerard had to be working for either the Sûreté or the SDECE . . ."

"SDECE," Harris said.

"Yes, they go in for subcontracting the pushers and pimps. At that point, it was just a matter of putting out the word and offering the right amount."

Harris nodded. He tried to force a smile. It looked like the smile on a politician's face as he's being grilled by reporters on his unreported taxes.

"You were jealous, weren't you, Scorpion? You did it to hurt her," Harris whispered.

"Not her, you."

The sound of a police siren hee-hawing through traffic grew louder, then faded into the night. Other tragedies, the Scorpion thought. He glanced at the gleaming white monuments to dead presidents: Washington, Jefferson, Lincoln; islands of light in a sea of darkness, like civilization itself, he mused. He thought about Kelly and sipped his drink.

Harris leaned forward. He looked longingly at the Scorpion's drink and licked his lips. The Scorpion held it out and let him sip at it like a thirsty child.

"I couldn't stand the idea of that greasy pig Abdul Sa'ad all over her. It kept getting in the way," Harris said. His face was pained, as if something had broken inside and he was trying to hold it together.

"You really take the cake, Bob. Blaming Kelly for what was your fault, not hers," the Scorpion sniffed.

"I can't help it," Harris confessed.

"Neither could she."

For a long moment neither man spoke. They sat in their dinner jackets waiting for the conversation to resume, like two retired club members who never liked each other but who are the last survivors of the old crowd and have no one else left to talk to.

"How did you figure it out?" Harris asked quietly.

In some way, the shared knowledge that they had used each other and that each of them had used Kelly made it possible to talk.

"Oh, I'm pretty shrewd. When I get hit in the head by a two-by-four I'm bound to take notice. Like someone with your description seen leaving Bahrain with Kelly. Another thing: ever since the well I knew there was another man in Kelly's life. You were my control, you should've briefed me about it, but you didn't. That was a very odd omission. Seeing you tell Gerard to fuck off at the party was only the final nail in the coffin. I should have caught on long before," the Scorpion said.

"How?" Harris asked, his eyebrows raised in a quizzical manner that made the Scorpion think of an intelligent chipmunk.

"All the things I should have spotted in the first place, but was too blind and stupid to see," the Scorpion admitted.

"You were programmed. But never mind, we all are," Harris responded.

"First, it was an outside operation right from the beginning. The President and the DCI in Langley never knew about it, that's why you didn't want me to go near the CIA stations in Arabia.

"The Molotov Plan was your idea, Bob. You knew Arabia was about to explode before it happened, so you had to have a mole in the Kremlin who either knew about it or set it up himself. You could have let the Russians know the game was up before it happened through a hundred different channels, but you didn't.

"Because you wanted it to happen, didn't you?" the Scorpion insisted.

Harris nodded. "That's quite a fairy tale you're concocting. Go on."

"But, because the director wasn't involved, you needed

313

someone to put his finger in the dike and make sure that the Russians wouldn't actually pull it off. Me!" the Scorpion said, pointing at himself.

"You," Harris agreed.

"And you had to be sure to run me yourself, so you could control the situation. So you chose Macready, knowing he would fuck it up and you'd be able to come in yourself," the Scorpion continued.

"Poor George," Harris said blandly, wearing an expression of mock sympathy that a politician might use at an opponent's funeral.

"Poor George nothing! He did all right. He did so all right it almost came unstuck for you. He redeemed himself, Harris. Admit it," the Scorpion insisted.

Harris shrugged. "You really are a rank sentimentalist, Scorpion. Forget Macready. Everyone else did. Just get on with the story."

"The problem was how to hook me in. So you set up the perfect bait and I fell for it hook, line and sinker. The knight in shining armor charging off to rescue the fair maiden from the nasty dragon. Given my nature and what happened in Saigon, it was perfect. You must have consulted with a brilliant psychologist or something," the Scorpion said, an edge of bitterness in his voice.

"Three psychiatrists actually," Harris remarked drily.

The Scorpion nodded. "The next step was to arrange for the kidnapping. That's where I should have figured it out because there were French footprints all over it and I never bothered to check it out. The snatch took place in Paris. Back in Peshawar you told me the data came from the rue des Saussaies, the Sûreté and the SDECE, all French intelligence agencies. And you set it up with the oldest trick in the book. Recruiting an amateur like Kelly for what she thought was one organization, in this case, the Mossad, and actually running her for another, namely your own little op within the CIA," the Scorpion finished.

Harris sat like a sphinx, not giving anything away. "What

makes you think she thought she was working for the Israelis?" he asked drily.

"In a minute. First let's talk about why you chose Kelly. The bit about the Israelis comes out of that. You needed a beautiful blond because of Abdul Sa'ad's slimy little fantasies. Someone you could place in the right place at the right time. Then, because of who Kelly was, Max Ormont's daughter. Ormont's family came from France originally. I should have spotted it sooner. The name 'Ormont' translated from French into Yiddish is 'Goldberg!'

"Max achieved the American dream. He married a beautiful wealthy *shicksa* and made millions in oil. But he didn't want his WASP friends, not to mention his Arab business partners, to know he was born Jewish. And here was Kelly, rebelling against her father and going to France and maybe Israel to try to find her roots.

"It must have been like taking candy from a baby to recruit her for the Israelis. Did you share your little Zionist dreams with her? Run off to a kibbutz and make the desert bloom?" the Scorpion sneered.

"Go on, finish it," Harris growled.

His eyes glittered with anticipation. He wanted to hear it told, the Scorpion realized, like an actor anxious for a critic's review.

"That's all of it. You used the little fish Kelly to catch a bigger fish, me. And me to catch Abdul Sa'ad. And Abdul Sa'ad's fall to catch Braithwaite and then Nuruddin and the Russians, who thought it was their op all along and never knew that you were the one who knocked over the first domino and set them all toppling. It was brilliant, Bob, a four-star performance. And the only thing left to ask is 'Why?'

"Why did you do it, Bob? Or should I ask, how much?" the Scorpion finished.

Harris straightened up. An odd gleam of pride came into his eyes, like a teacher watching his best pupil win a prize.

315

He raised his eyebrow in acknowledgement, as if it were a checkered flag.

"Six million dollars, Scorpion. That's a little better than civil service pay," Harris said, a winning smile breaking across his face.

"You maniac! You risked World War Three for a lousy profit," the Scorpion said, contempt almost choking him.

Harris was indomitable. He grinned with the guilty charm of a small boy with his hand in the cookie jar.

"You have to admit, six million isn't exactly a *lousy* profit," he said.

The Scorpion raised his glass in a silent toast to Harris. He had a certain con man's style. No wonder Kelly fell for his line, he mused. The thought of her sobered him again.

"That was my final mistake, Bob. Not spotting it when you made that slip about somebody making a fortune in oil futures. That was how you did it, didn't you?" Harris nodded amiably.

"Once the crisis hit the media, oil futures went sky-high," he admitted.

"Who staked you? Who put down the cash to buy up six million bucks' worth of futures?"

Harris leaned forward, his eyes twinkling with impish evil. "Can't you guess?" he whispered.

The Scorpion sat stunned, scarcely able to believe what his mind was telling him was the obvious truth.

"Max Ormont," he breathed.

Harris grinned. "The great Max Ormont! Pillar of Society, millionaire, congressman, statesman, friend of presidents, power in the party caucus. He sold his own daughter into slavery to keep her quiet and to make a killing in the market," he agreed.

The Scorpion picked up his drink and sipped. It had gone flat. So had everything else somehow.

"His own daughter," he repeated, shaking his head. With a weary sigh, he aimed the gun at Harris. "Is that why you tried to terminate me in Bahrain? To keep me quiet and make a killing in the market?" he asked quietly.

316

"Don't get all 'holier-than-thou' on me Scorpion. You made a million dollars on this business too," Harris snapped.

"But not as much as you, Bob. I obviously still have a lot to learn," the Scorpion said. He cocked the gun to a hairtrigger and moved the muzzle forward until it touched Harris' sweat-slicked forehead.

"Wait, Scorpion. I did it to save your life and usefulness," Harris stammered.

"Go on, Bob. Show your hole card. I've paid a hell of a lot to see it," the Scorpion said.

Sweat beaded on Harris's forehead. The Scorpion watched a drop of sweat trickle down to the tip of his nose and hang there, tempting gravity. Harris took a deep breath and began.

"First of all, the Molotov Plan was always a Russian idea. For centuries it's what they've really wanted. We just deflected it our way because it gave us the chance to remove hardliners like Fyedorenko from power. That's avoiding nuclear war, not causing it.

"You're damn right we have a mole in the Kremlin. And thanks to the Molotov op he's moved to the very top. Do you understand? The Politburo itself! You're an intelligence professional. You tell me what a coup like that is worth?

"As for terminating you, that was Ormont's idea. He had the Russian connection and the only motive to keep you silent. You were a danger to him, not to me. On the contrary, you got me a big promotion. In fact, you were my insurance policy against Ormont, so I deflected that one too.

"But I had to let everyone think you were dead. The president wanted to give you a medal, for Chrissakes. Blow you and the whole op wide open. And if the media had caught wind of the Molotov Plan it would have been a political disaster. We would have performed the almost impossible feat of snatching defeat from the jaws of victory," Harris said hurriedly.

"Go on," the Scorpion said. He watched the drop hanging

from Harris's nose, glimmering in the reflected lights like a seed pearl. He wondered when it would fall.

If Harris fell, he would take the government with him, the Scorpion thought. Like Humpty Dumpty, not all the king's horses and all the king's men would put it together again. Not that he gave a damn about the president. One politician was little better than another. But he cared deeply about America. His father had taught him that much. He'd had so little time with that oil redneck who had left him with little beyond the memory of a tweedy embrace and the smell of pipe tobacco. But Tim Curry had left the Scorpion with that love for what America wanted to be, if not for what it was.

"Besides, if they thought you were alive, every KGB agent in the world would be on your trail right now. You're good, Scorpion. But nobody's that good. Sooner or later they'd corner you. Bad for you, bad for us.

"This way, you've been marked KIA. All records to be archived, purged and forgotten. You're as safe as I can make you, until the KGB picks up your trail again. Bahrain was the old 'possum' ploy. Al-Amir was supposed to let you go," Harris finished.

The Scorpion pressed the muzzle against Harris' forehead as if he wanted to push it into his brain.

"Was it for Kelly? Is that why you did it? Or didn't do it, if I'm supposed to believe you?" the Scorpion demanded harshly.

"Neither," Harris whispered. He closed his eyes. "I did it because you were too good an asset to lose," he smiled lamely.

The Scorpion watched the drop finally fall from Harris' nose. After a second, he stepped away and released the hammer on the .38. He stood for a moment, silhouetted against the skylight. The hell of it was that everything Harris said made sense.

"I have a little business to take care of and then I'm going to see her again," he said, not looking at Harris.

Harris exhaled loudly like a diver coming up for air. "Am

I to assume that an off-year election to fill Ormont's soon-to-be-vacated congressional seat is anticipated?" he asked innocently.

The Scorpion said nothing.

"He won't be missed. Not by anyone. Especially Kelly," Harris added.

"You never had her, you know. It was all bullshit. You're not the kibbutz type," the Scorpion said, turning to face Harris.

"Do you know where she's going?" Harris asked.

"I can make a pretty educated guess."

"It won't work, you two," Harris insisted.

"I know," the Scorpion said.

"Then why? Why dig it all up?"

The Scorpion shrugged, then turned, a boyish smile dimpling his right cheek. "I'm sentimental," he said.

Harris grunted and shifted uncomfortably on the couch. His hands ached fiercely from the knots and he knew it would take hours to undo them and get help, which was precisely the head start the Scorpion wanted. His mouth hurt viciously from the kick. He explored a loose tooth with his tongue and wondered if it could be saved. He looked up at the Scorpion.

"You know what your problem is, Scorpion? You're a romantic!" Harris declared triumphantly.

"And you're not, Bob. That's *your* weakness."

Dallas

DALLAS (UPI)—Congressman Max Ormont (R-Tex) plunged to his death from the balcony of his high-rise penthouse early this morning. Paramedics from Dallas Memorial pronounced him dead at the scene at 11:53 p.m.

319

The multimillionaire oilman-turned-politician had returned to Dallas for a political fundraiser before leaving on a fact-finding trip to the Soviet Union, police officials said. Preliminary indications are that the congressman may have been drinking. However, determination of the cause of death is pending the coroner's report.

"There appears to be no evidence of foul play, but our investigation is continuing," said Daryl Dobson, chief of homicide.

There were no witnesses to the incident.

The congressman is survived by a daughter. She could not be reached for comment.

Ein Gev

THE RESTAURANT WAS on a tiny spit of land sandwiched between the sheer ridge of the Golan and the lake. Two wooden fishing boats belonging to the kibbutz were turned upside-down on the rocky beach bordering the terrace. During the day fishermen from the kibbutz fished for the small bony St. Peter's fish which made the restaurant famous.

Men had always fished these waters. Even in prehistoric times, fishemen had harvested here, leaving nothing behind but the name they gave to the lake. They called it Kinneret, because its shape reminded them of a harp. The name was kept by the Hebrews who documented it in their records, which became the Bible, until the Romans came and gave it the name of the soft rolling hills to the west. They called it "the Sea of Galilee" and so it stayed for two thousand years, until the Jews returned to reclaim the land and rename the lake once more. Kinneret again, still harp-shaped, still mysterious.

It was the dusk hour. The restaurant was closed. A couple sat on the deserted terrace and looked out over the lake, turned to molten gold by the last rays of the sun. Across the lake they could clearly see the rounded outlines of the hills of Galilee against the red sky. The Sabbath stillness was complete, except for the lapping of the waves against the low terrace wall, a few feet from their table. At such a moment, it was easy to imagine Jesus walking along this shore, followed at a distance by the shy fishermen of the village struggling to understand what he meant by talking about love in a world which seemed to have no place for it.

This is where she thinks she belongs, the Scorpion thought, looking across at Kelly. She was slim and tan and healthy-looking in a frayed white shirt and khaki shorts. This is her world now, as alien to her as Arabia; but she believes in it and maybe that makes it her world, he thought.

"Call me Chava," she had told him when he found her at Kibbutz Shaar Ha-Golan, in the Jordan Valley where Wadi Yarmuk divides the three territories, Jordan, Israel and the occupied Golan. After dinner in the kibbutz dining hall, they had driven the three or four miles to the restaurant at Ein Gev.

"I wanted to show you this," she said, gesturing at the lake. "I like to come here on *erev shabbat* when it's quiet like this. It's a special place."

"I can see why they called it a Land of Milk and Honey, coming out of the desert," he said.

The mention of the desert brought back the memory of Arabia. The shadow of it flickered in her wonderful violet eyes and she looked away for a second. The Scorpion cursed himself for being an idiot.

"I'm sorry about your father," he said, keeping his voice carefully neutral.

"Don't be. Nobody else is," she shrugged, her face a mask against pain.

"I suspect you'll be inheriting quite a lot," he said.

"It's a lot," she agreed gravely.

"You could go anywhere. Do anything," he said.

"I am doing something," she said, her chin set defiantly. She sat up straight and looked directly at him, wearing her independence like a flag.

"I know," he said.

A bullfrog croaked down by the water's edge. Across the lake he could see the lights of the resort town of Tiberias shining on the water. Under Prince Judah, the rabbis of Israel had written the Mishna and determined the final form of the Old Testament there. Nearby twinkled the lights of Kfar Nahum, the biblical Capernaum, where Jesus used to preach. There was no escaping the past in a place like this, he thought.

She leaned across and kissed him on the mouth, her hand at the back of his neck, and for a moment they were lovers in the truest sense. Then he thought of Harris and the shadows of the past fell between them like a guillotine blade.

"You know why I had to leave Bahrain with Robert, don't you? I thought he was my case officer," she said, looking down for a moment. "And I had to find out where we stood with each other," she said in that throaty voice which still tugged at his heart like a string.

"But I never thought he was . . . when I saw Gerard and him talking at the party and realized they were in it together—" she began, her eyes shining.

"Back in Paris you thought that one of the men you met— Gerard, or Jean-Paul, or Randy—was a contact from Israeli intelligence, didn't you?"

She nodded.

"They were contacts, all right. Small-time informers working for the French SDECE. It was Harris who was pulling the strings," he said.

"Some Mata Hari. I was pretty naive, wasn't I?" she asked softly.

"Yes," he said and held her close. She vibrated in his arms like a tuning fork. He held her until she was still, knowing it was a moment he would remember until he died. She pulled away and looked directly into his eyes as if peering into the back of his brain. No one had ever looked at him like that, he thought.

"You're the most special man I've ever known," she said and he knew it was her way of saying goodbye.

"Don't underestimate yourself, either. There'll be lots of nights when trying not to think about you will be the hardest thing I'll ever have to do," he said.

She cupped his chin in her hand and smiled fondly. "My knight in shining armor," she said, her eyes brimming again. "But it wouldn't work. Somehow, I can't picture you in a kibbutz cow barn, shoveling manure. That's not how the story goes. The knight's supposed to kiss his lady-fair goodbye and ride off to his next adventure. So, where's your next adventure?" she said bravely.

"I have some unfinished business in Afghanistan," he said, wishing it didn't sound so much like Indiana Jones.

"You see," she said brightly, her mouth twisting as if she was about to cry.

He reached towards her and then hesitated. He let his hand drop on to the table and lay there like something dead. "I could try. Who knows? Maybe I'd like kibbutz life?" he ventured awkwardly.

She put her hand to his cheek. "Dear Nick. You know that's not you. There are a hundred reasons. You're not Jewish—and that matters here. But mostly you'd resent it because that's not who you are. And I'd resent it because I'm a romantic too and I love who you are."

They looked helplessly at each other.

"You're right," he said.

A yellowish full moon rose over the brooding shadow of the Golan Heights and shone down on the lake like a beacon, its light shattered into millions of fragments.

"Beware the Russians. Robert told me you're Number One on their list," she said, concern etched on her face.

"I won't forget the Russians," the Scorpion said in a quiet voice.

She shook her head and looked out over the water, shining white as fields of snow in the moonlight. She listened to the lapping of the waves and the croaking of the frogs and tried to think of a way to say goodbye. Smile, Kelly. Let him remember you smiling, she told herself and turned to face him. The terrace was deserted.

The Scorpion had gone.

MOSCOW

FYEDORENKO SAT UNMOVING as a statue in the Penal Chair. His famous stone-face stood him in good stead, giving nothing away even now, as Suvarov's searing invective poured over him like molten metal.

Every face was turned towards him, their hatred naked and plain to see at long last. He had seen it before and understood it well. They were like a pack of wolves tearing one of their own to pieces as soon as he went down. Always before, he had led the attack.

This time they were attacking him.

Two six-foot blond Neanderthals stood at his sides. As soon as this little farce had been played out, they would take him out to the courtyard and bundle him into a limousine. It would be a short ride, he knew. It wasn't far from the Kremlin to the Black Wall in Lubyanka Prison.

Now Andreyev, head of the KGB, joined the attack. His voice cracked like a whiplash as he denounced Fyedorenko as "a mad dog Enemy of the People." That wasn't his crime, of course, Fyedorenko knew. He was guilty of the only crime in the world for capitalist or communist alike: failure.

Fyedorenko's glance fell on Svetlov, the newest member of the Politburo. It was his reward for betraying Fyedorenko to Suvarov and Andreyev. Svetlov's bulging frog eyes blinked repeatedly as he stared in sneering triumph at Fyedorenko. Yes, I engineered your downfall and I'm glad of it, his eyes said.

But his triumph would be short-lived, Fyedorenko thought grimly. At least he had made sure of that.

After the Molotov Plan had fallen apart, he had launched a complete top-secret security check on everyone involved. The only way the Scorpion could have been positioned to interfere was if there had been a leak. His agents reported that there had been meetings between Svetlov and the capitalist, Ormont. Then there was the rumor surfaced by the KGB that the Scorpion wasn't dead and that he was the one who had terminated Ormont in Dallas. But up until last night, he still hadn't known what hold Ormont had had on Svetlov. Then he got a midnight call from Novorossisk.

One of his agents found Svetlov's great-aunt still alive. Under torture, the old woman had revealed that Svetlov's mother was a Jewess and that Svetlov's twin brother hadn't been killed by the British as Svetlov had claimed all these years. The Jews had smuggled the infant to France, where the family name "Goldberg" was translated to Ormont.

But by then, it was too late. Svetlov had made his move. Fyedorenko barely had time to pass a hand-scribbled note to his housekeeper with instructions to get it to Kishinev. Although the foreign minister was his enemy and was now staring at him with barely concealed delight, Fyedorenko knew

Kishinev would know how to use the information against Svetlov.

As for himself, it didn't matter. The Molotov Plan was too big a fiasco to paper over by pointing the finger at Svetlov.

Suddenly, it was over. Calling him a "*sukin sin*" for the last time, Suvarov motioned for the guards to take him away.

Fyedorenko stood and faced his accusers.

"What I did, I did for the good of the Party," he said.

His words were met by stony silence. He remembered his father reading something from the Bible when he was a child. Something about wheat sown on stony ground. Strange, he hadn't thought of that in so many years.

As they led him from the room he heard Svetlov's voice cut through the silence. It was for his benefit, too. Svetlov wanted him to hear it, Fyedorenko thought.

"And now, comrades, the next item of business is to order a worldwide effort to terminate the enemy agent known as 'the Scorpion,'" Svetlov said.

EPILOGUE

The old man was dying at last. Frankly, Captain Mayakovsky was surprised he had lasted so long. But these Pathan tribesmen were tough. They had been torturing the old buzzard for six hours straight and he hadn't told them a thing about the Scorpion.

Mayakovsky walked to the doorway of the army hut and glanced outside. The landscape here in the Khyber Pass was the most desolate anyone could imagine. Bare rock gullies and mountains, one after another like waves of the sea, with nothing green growing for as far as the eye could see. It looked like the debris left over after the world had been made. In every gully there were a thousand places for the *moujahadeen* to hide, every one of them a crack shot. The children here had rifles in their hands before they could walk.

His eyes roamed the barren scene, the air shimmering like water in the baking heat. It was the most God-forsaken fly-bitten ass-end spot on earth, he thought. He longed for the green parks of Moscow and the taste of ice-cold *kvas*.

They were wasting their time. He had told those GRU idiots that. All of the tribes in these parts were Pathans. They never talked. The GRU officer had looked blankly at Mayakovsky as if he didn't understand Russian.

"Orders are orders," the officer had pedantically remarked.

Mayakovsky shrugged. Orders were orders, but the sooner he got out of this God-forsaken shit-hole the better.

With a sigh, he turned back and motioned to his men. Once again they took the red-hot iron from the coals and held it to the old man's feet, the skin long since burnt to a blackened crisp.

The old man's thin scream pierced the silent hut. His breathing was labored. He was going, Mayakovsky thought.

He leaned down to the old man's ear. A fly buzzed his cheek as he did so and he irritably brushed it away.

"Tell me where the Scorpion is and I'll make the pain go away," Mayakovsky whisperedd seductively.

The old man's eyes were half-closed. Mayakovsky wasn't sure he even heard him.

But the old man had heard. His pain would soon be over, he knew. Soon Allah would gather him into his bosom and he would drink the cool waters of the Fount of Selsabil. What a fool this Russian was, he thought. As if anyone could reveal the Scorpion's whereabouts. The Scorpion was as the desert wind.

The old man smiled.

Who can capture the wind?

By the year 2000, 2 out of 3 Americans could be illiterate.

It's true.

Today, 75 million adults... about one American in three, can't read adequately. And by the year 2000, U.S. News & World Report envisions an America with a literacy rate of only 30%.

Before that America comes to be, you can stop it... by joining the fight against illiteracy today.

Call the Coalition for Literacy at toll-free **1-800-228-8813** and volunteer.

Volunteer Against Illiteracy. The only degree you need is a degree of caring.

Ad Council Coalition for Literacy

Warner Books is proud to be an active supporter of the Coalition for Literacy.